THE COMINTERN
IN MEXICO

THE COMINTERN
IN MEXICO

By Donald L. Herman

INTRODUCTION BY

ROBERT J. ALEXANDER

PUBLIC AFFAIRS PRESS, WASHINGTON, D. C.

TO MY PARENTS,

JOHN AND ROSE HERMAN

INTRODUCTION

The twentieth century's "Age of Revolution" began in Mexico. The Mexican Revolution started in 1910, before those of China, Russia, the colonial world, or other Latin American countries. In the eyes of many Mexicans their country's great upheaval still continues.

As Donald Herman points out in this volume, the existence of a revolutionary situation was one of several factors which, a priori, one might think created favorable soil for the growth of the Communist movement in Mexico. Others noted by Prof. Herman include the long tradition of anti-Yankeeism in the republic (which legitimatized the Communists' emphasis on "anti-Imperialism"), the wide prevalence of violence in Mexican history (which did not make early Communist emphasis on the need for revolution seem particularly unacceptable), the miserable social and economic conditions of the great majority of the population, and the long-standing anti-clericalism which has existed since Mexico received its independence (which was compatible with early Communist opposition to religion.)

Yet the fact is, as Herman makes amply clear, that the Communists have never been very successful in Mexico. Although for a very short period in the late 1920's the Communist Party had a leading role in the national peasant movement, and during the Cardenas administration it had some friends in high places in the government and some power in the organized labor movement, it never played a major role in national politics. By the end of the period with which this book is concerned (that of the existence of the Communist International, 1919-1943), the party had been reduced to the very small proportions and insignificant influence which has marked it since that time.

The present volume gives a worthwhile survey of the kind of issues which the Communists raised over the years in which the Comintern existed. They pictured themselves as the principal spokesmen for the country's working class, the only advocates of a "real" agrarian reform, the most stalwart defenders of the national interest against grasping Yankee imperialism. Most of all, they pictured themselves as being the group destined to assume leadership of the Mexican Revolution when it passed from its "petty bourgeois" to its "proletarian" phase.

However, looking at the Mexican Communists from the outside, one cannot help but have the feeling that they engaged in a great deal of self-delusion. The fact is that they never controlled the national labor movement; that with the possible exception of a couple years in the late 1920's they had no significant influence on the agrarian reform process; their attitude had little to do with the relations between Mexico and its powerful northern neighbor.

Finally, as Herman points out, the great majority of Mexican workers and peasants supported the Mexican Revolution as it evolved during the years covered by this book. They supported the Revolution in terms of what it was, or what they conceived it to be—a nationalist effort to free Mexico from foreign economic and political control; a movement to reverse the concentration of land in the hands of the few which had for centuries characterized the country; an attempt to give the workers adequate organizations through which to defend themselves and participate in determining the conditions under which they would be employed; an effort to establish the kind of political democracy and individual freedom such as Mexico had never experienced. Few if any Mexican workers or peasants supported the Revolution merely as a "first stage" towards the achievement of a Marxist-Leninist-Stalinist Utopia.

I suppose that neither Herman nor I had any way of knowing whether the leaders of the Communist International, and of the Soviet party which dominated the Comintern, ever sat down to have a serious discussion of the reasons why their Mexican affiliate failed for such a long period of time, in spite of apparently having such propitious circumstances in which to work and having, from the Communist leaders' point of view at least, such strong arguments with which to convert the Mexican workers and peasants to support of the Partido Communista de Mexico. However, had they done so with any real degree of objectivity, Professor Herman might have given them a few cues to explain the disappointing performance of their Mexican comrades.

This book amply demonstrates that the Comintern itself, including the constant twisting and turning of its "line," was one of the major handicaps under which the Mexican Communist Party labored. The Third International's dispatch of leading agents to Mexico in the very early days of the Comintern's history to try to develop a maneuver against the United States on behalf of the Soviet Union, with little regard to Mexican circumstances, was the first example of this. The insistence of other Comintern agents that the Mexican Communists attempt to organize an insurrection against the government of their country in 1929, in conformity with the "line" of the Third Period, was a second instance, which brought virtually unmitigated disaster to the Mexican comrades. The change in line precipitated by the Nazi-Soviet Pact in August 1939 was a third case, undercutting the gains which the Mexican Communists had made in the previous few years. The involvement of leading figures in the Mexican party in GPU attempts to murder Leon Trotsky brought the Mexican C.P. further great loss of prestige and influence.

Similarly, the insistence of the Comintern on changing leadership of the Mexican Communist Party at will on several occasions, did much to reduce the credibility of the Partido Comunista de Mexico as an indigenous force in national politics. Prof. Herman notes such actions during 1929 and again in 1940, when accredited agents of the Third International removed all or part of the party leadership without bothering to ascertain the wishes of the party membership with regard to the matter.

Prof. Herman alludes on several occasions to another aspect of the history of the Mexican Communist Party which might have given such a "self-criticism" session of the Comintern leadership as we have imagined pause for reflection. This was the party's propensity to seek and receive financial aid from the government of Mexico.

Herman notes that in the early 1920's there was a controversy in the party's ranks concerning whether it should continue to accept subsidies from the government of President Alvaro Obregon. Bertram Wolfe has testified to his own inability to dissuade the party leaders from doing so. Subsequently, in the period of the Cárdenas administration, as Professor Herman notes, the Communist Party was again the recipient of benefices from the government. In contrast, it seems unlikely that such aid was given between 1929 and 1934, when the regimes of Presidents Emilio Portes Gil, Ortiz Rubio and Abelardo Rodriguez were persecuting the party.

This situation reflects what for half a century seems to have been a tradition with the successive administrations of the Mexican Revolution. This tradition has been to give some subsidy to virtually every kind of political group in the republic, from far Right to extreme Left. It is not clear to what degree this has been a studied policy to limit the independence of activity of the groups involved, or originates in the fact that almost all administrations have contained influential people of most varied political inclinations, and with control of at least some funds which they could make available to the groups of their preference.

Another factor which might have drawn the attention of our

imaginary Comintern session of self-criticism is the problem confronted by their Mexican comrades in dealing with the Mexican Revolution itself. Herman alludes to this problem, but doesn't give it the
importance I would.

I have already alluded to the fact that the Mexican workers and
peasants generally supported the Mexican Revolution because of what
they thought it was achieving, rather than because of any kind of
Marxist-Leninist ideological commitment. However, the issue goes
farther than that. The Mexican Revolution began seven years before
that of Russia. The revolutionary Constitution of 1917 went into
effect before the Tsar was even overthrown. Elements of that Constitution, say the Mexicans, were copied by the Soviet leaders.

There has therefore been a widespread feeling in Mexico that if
the leaders of one revolution were to learn from those of the other, it
was rather the Soviet chiefs who should learn from those of Mexico,
not the other way around.

This attitude is reinforced by the nationalism which has imbued the
Mexican Revolution since its inception. This nationalism has instilled
the rank and file Mexican with pride in the Revolution itself, as with
other attributes of Mexican nationality. Thus, for large numbers of
Mexicans, the insistence of the Communists, always expressed whether
in loud or more muted terms, that the Mexican Revolution should be
pushed aside, and another movement patterned after that of the
Bolsheviks in October 1917, should be substituted for it, was down-
right unpatriotic.

It seems to me that this disparagement of the Mexican Revolution,
and pushing of the Russian one as the model which the Mexicans
should follow, has been a much more important element in the lack
of success of the Partido Comunista de Mexico than Professor Herman
does. However, on this we agree to disagree.

We do agree fully on the fact that the Communist movement in
Mexico has not been confined to the cohorts of the Partido Communista de Mexico. For four decades or more, Vincente Lombardo
Toledano, who never belonged to the PCM, was probably the country's most distinguished Marxist-Leninist. As Professor Herman demonstrates, Lombardo was a convinced Marxist-Leninist at least from the
early 1930's. By the end of that decade he was allied with the official
Communists in the Mexican labor movement, and throughout World
War Two followed each twist and turn in the international Communist line.

Herman does not carry his story beyond the end of the World War

Two. Therefore, he concentrates principally on the events and factors which led Lombardo into close collaboration with the International Communist apparatus. In the late 1940's, after the period covered by this volume, he became the principal director of the Communist trade union apparatus in Latin America.

However, Lombardo Toledano differed from the leaders of the Partido Communista de Mexico in being an integral member of the Mexican revolutionary Establishment. During the period covered by this book he remained a member of the government party, and his associations were particularly close with President Lazaro Cárdenas; Dr. Herman discusses these associations at some length. Even subsequent to the period covered in this book, when Vincente Lombardo Toledano withdrew from the official government party and set up one of his own—and lost his position in the labor movement—Lombardo did not lose his position within the left-wing part of the Mexican Establishment. His Partido Popular, later Partido Popular Socialista, was widely regarded as the left-wing "loyal opposition" to the government and its official party.

So far, the role of Lombardo Toledano in the history of Mexico since World War One has not been adequately explored. Although some biographies of him have been written, they have not adequately pictured his position in Mexican political life. However, Herman has made a useful contribution to a study of what part Lombardo Toledano did play.

Donald Herman's book is limited to looking at Mexican Communism during the period in which the Communist International existed. This limitation has permitted him to make a more intensive study of the Communist Party, its history and its functioning than might have been possible if he had spread a chronologically wider canvas. It is an important contribution to an understanding of the earlier decades of the Mexican Revolution, and the history of Communism in the Western Hemisphere.

ROBERT J. ALEXANDER

ACKNOWLEDGMENTS

There are several people who made life easier in the preparation of this study. Professor Inis L. Claude, Jr. of the University of Virginia and Professor Martin C. Needler of the University of New Mexico read the early draft of the manuscript. Their comments and "challenges" proved to be most helpful. Professor Robert J. Alexander of Rutgers University read a later draft. Professors J. Lee Kaufman and William C. Baum of Grand Valley State College were kind enough to make valuable editorial suggestions. Miss Emilie Dahan, Miss Kathy Hulst and Mrs. Elaine Duemler were very helpful in typing the manuscript.

Of the many people in Mexico who were most helpful, I must single out two. Rodrigo García Treviño made available his priceless collection of source material, much of it inaccessible anywhere else. My wife, Bluma, a native of Mexico, saw me through the frustrating task of appointments (broken and otherwise), disconnected telephone conversations, and messages that were not delivered. She managed to steer this "gringo" professor closer to "her people." Of course I am solely responsible for the ideas expressed in the study.

DONALD L. HERMAN

CONTENTS

TABLES

APPENDICES

Chapter I

THE COMMUNIST INTERNATIONAL

The First Socialist International was organized by Karl Marx, Michael Bakunin and others in 1864 to unite the Socialist parties and union groups in an affort to improve the lot of the workers. There was general agreement and various resolutions were approved concerning such issues as higher wages, fewer working hours, and improved conditions for the workers. The Second Socialist International was organized in 1889. The major concern then was the tension in Europe and the possibility of war. The delegates of various countries agreed to work against the outbreak of hostilities, and, if war should occur, promised to try to bring it to a speedy conclusion through a policy of non-cooperation with their governments' war efforts.

During World War I, however, most of the Socialist parties supported their respective governments. The German and French Socialists joined their respective armies and the Socialist deputies in the legislatures voted with the majorities to allocate funds to carry out the war effort. The issue of these "war credits," which caused a split within the Socialist movement and led to various conferences throughout the war, did not heal the breach.

Eventually the Socialist movement split into two factions. The majority, who supported their governments during the war, became the right wing; they turned to Eduard Bernstein's theory of evolutionary Socialism,[1] rejecting the tactic of the violent overthrow of the bourgeois state in order to gain power. The minority left wing looked to a revolutionary mass movement in the industrial countries of Europe as the basis for a new international.

Lenin, a leading figure in the Second Socialist International, was infuriated. He had believed that the majority of the Western Socialists would support his position concerning World War I—i.e., to make every effort to oppose the war and, if war did break out, to turn it into a "civil war against the imperialists." [2] He particularly had faith in the German Socialists, who, split primarily over the issue of war credits, had refused to take a position in the conferences during the war.

But Lenin realized he was mistaken; the revolutionary proletariat

1

was a myth, and he concluded that the Western labor movement needed more discipline. He reasoned that the methods by which his organization of professional revolutionaries had conquered Russia must be transferred to the West. Lenin bitterly expressed his views concerning the "patriots" who did not support his position: "I repeat, the experience of the victorious dictatorship of the proletariat in Russia was clearly shown to those who are unable to think, or who have not had occasion to ponder over this question, that absolute centralization and the strictest discipline of the proletariat are one of the basic conditions for victory over the bourgeoisie."[3]

However, it was very difficult for the majority of Western Socialists to accept such a concept since it did not correspond with their experiences. Conflicts arose between those who followed the lessons of Russian revolutionism and those who followed the concepts of the West. The history of the Communist International is largely the story of these conflicts.

Lenin wanted to do away with the Second Socialist International and create a new international reflecting his basic ideas: an international party which should begin as a small body and be under the strictest control of the Bolsheviks, which he had come to regard as the one safeguard of his interpretation of practical and theoretical orthodoxy. Opposition came not only from the right wing Socialists; Lenin's main struggle was with the left wing of the movement.

The revolutionary wing of German Socialism, led by Karl Liebknecht and Rosa Luxemburg, did not want an international controlled by the Bolsheviks, but one based mainly upon the mass parties of the West[4] and which, while definitely excluding the pro-war Socialists and a good many of the wavering elements, would not be preoccupied with orthodoxy.[5] Thus, confronted by strong opposition from even the most revolutionary Western elements, Lenin made very little headway with his idea of a new international during World War I. But pressure to form a new international was exerted by uprisings and strikes in Central Europe, the deaths of Liebknecht and Luxemburg in the German Spartacist uprising of January 1919, the success of the 1917 Bolshevik Revolution, civil war in Russia beween 1918 and 1920, and revolutions in Finland, Germany and Hungary. There was cause for optimism, and revolutionary feeling ran high. The German-Russian peace negotiations at Brest-Litovsk in 1918 were used as a platform to spread the Bolsheviks' ideas of world revolution. In the midst of this turmoil, Lenin realized his opportunity and called for the First Congress of the Communist

International, although it was not until the Second Congress in 1920 that the Bolsheviks were able to give central direction to international Communist activities.

The First Stage, 1919-1920

The history of the Communist International (also called the Third International and, subsequently, the Comintern) is usually divided into six stages, the first of which began with the calling of the First Congress in March, 1919, in Moscow and continued through the Second Congress in the summer of 1920. The many factions that came to the First Congress can be divided into three main elements.[6] First, there were small sects formed in Russia, mostly by war prisoners, and financially dependent upon Moscow. Included in this group were the Hungarian and Austrian parties. The second element consisted of small organizations which had arisen in their respective countries before or during the war, without interference from Moscow but now loyal to the Soviet Union. In this category were the German Spartacists and groups from Holland. Third, a few big mass parties were represented who did not accept money from Moscow and did not obey the Russians in the least. Examples of this type were the Norwegians, the Italians, and the Bulgarians.

Lenin was certainly not in complete control of the various delegations and friendly advice from Russia was often defied during that period even by those considered to be most loyal. Nevertheless, most of the delegates were determined to establish a new international. One strong push came from the old Socialist parties who had held a conference in Berne during the same month with the aim of reconstituting the Second Socialist International.

The First Congress of the Communist International opened on March 4, 1919 with three main considerations. In the first place, imminent world revolution was anticipated and it was the prime purpose of the new International to do everything in its power to assure the speedy and final victory of Communism. Secondly, Lenin wanted to rid the labor movement of the influence of both the "patriots" and "pacifists." Thirdly, he also wanted to overcome those groups which he considered to be 'ultra-left.'

Since the Communists believed that the world revolution was imminent, they considered it the duty of the proletariat to meet the bourgeoisie head-on and bring the struggle to victorious conclusion: "The revolutionary era compels the proletariat to make use of the means of battle which will concentrate its entire energies, namely, mass action, with its logical resultant, direct conflict with the governmental machinery in open combat. All other methods, such as revolutionary use of bourgeois parliamentarianism, will be of only secondary significance." [7]

Thus, the Communists had no intention of waiting for the revolution to unfold; the order of the day was to take the initiative: "The task of the proletariat now is to seize state power immediately. The seizure of state power means the destruction of the state apparatus of the bourgeoisie and the organization of a new proletarian apparatus of power." [8]

The strong optimism of leaders of the Communist International about the imminence of a world-wide proletarian revolution was expressed by Lenin in his concluding speech at the First Congress: "Let the bourgeoisie of the whole world continue to rage, let it expel, put in prison, even murder Spartacists and Bolsheviks, all this will no longer help it. This will only serve to enlighten the masses, to liberate them from the old bourgeois democratic prejudices, and to train them in the struggle. The victory of the proletarian revolution throughout the world is guaranteed. The formation of the International Soviet Republic is approaching." [9]

It is possible more clearly to analyze the optimism of the Communist leaders during the First Congress and the first part of the 1920's by reviewing some of the statements of Georgi Zinoviev, the first president of the Communist International. In an article entitled, "Vistas of the Proletarian Revolution," he set a time schedule for the coming of the new Communist world society: "There will surely be a few isolated defeats for some time to come. Black may temporarily supplant Red here and there. The final victory, however, will be achieved by the Red. And it may be achieved within a few months, nay, within a few weeks. The movement is spreading with giant strides, and it may safely be predicted that in a year's time we shall begin to forget that Europe had ever fought for Communism because by that time all Europe will be Communistic." [10]

Zinoviev went on to state that the proletarian revolution would move from East to West, spread across Europe, and reach North America within a few years: "Capitalistic America and Communist Europe cannot coexist. Or, at least, they cannot coexist for a long time." [11]

At the very outset, then, the members of the Communist International were called upon to participate in realizing the proletarian world revolution, a phenomenon they believed was assured by the forces of history. Lenin stated the ultimate goal of the Communist International: "The Third International has garnered the fruit of the labors of the Second International, casting off the refuse of its opportunist, social-chauvinistic, bourgeois and lower-middle class tendencies, and has set out to achieve the dictatorship of the proletariat." [12]

To denounce the "patriots" and "pacifists," the second main consideration of the Congress, the leaders of the Communist International chose the fiery Leon Trotsky who wrote a manifesto unanimously adopted by the Congress at its last session. The manifesto dealt with the "imperialist war" which was passing into a "civil war" between the classes, criticized the League of Nations as an instrument of international capital, and laid down several revolutionary slogans. The struggle against the Socialist parties which were not loyal to Moscow was spelled out: "Our task is to generalize the revolutionary experience of the working class, to cleanse the movement of the disintegrating admixtures of opportunism and social-patriotism, to mobilize the forces of all genuinely revolutionary parties of the world proletariat and thereby facilitate and hasten the victory of the Communist revolution throughout the world." [13]

Not only were the Communist leaders critical of the right wing Socialists who had supported their individual governments during the war, but they also attacked the left wing Socialists who had been opposed to the war, accusing them of seeking to compromise with their governments in the post-war period. Since this attitude could present an obstacle in the path of world revolution, it was necessary to struggle against all Socialists as well as their "imperialist" governments: "The Independents of Germany, the present majority of the Socialist party in France, the Independent Labor Party in England, and similar groups, are actually trying to re-establish themselves in the position which the old official parties of the Second International held before the war. They appear as before with proposals of compromise and conciliation and hereby paralyze the energy of the proletariat, lengthening the period of crisis and consequently increasing the misery of Europe." [14]

Although no specific action was taken against the social-patriots during the First Congress, the way was cleared to follow up general statements with specific proposals at a later congress.

The third main consideration of the First Congress, the problem of the 'ultra-left,' was spelled out by Lenin. He criticized the "Communist Labor Party in Germany, the Shop Steward Movement in

England, the revolutionary Syndicalists . . ."[15] for not taking advantage of the opportunities for control of the bourgeois parliaments and the bourgeois trade unions for revolutionary activity. Lenin agreed with the critics of parliaments that these institutions were reactionary, but he explained why it was necessary for Communists to struggle within them and meet the enemy in his own camp: "As long as you are unable to disperse the bourgeois parliament and every other type of reactionary institution, you must work inside them, precisely because in them there are still workers who are stupefied by the priests and by the desolateness of village life; otherwise you run the risk of becoming mere babblers."[16]

The Communists had to talk in the language of the masses, and if this required the use of bourgeois parliaments, so be it: "It is just because the backward masses of the workers and the small peasants in Western Europe are much more strongly imbued with bourgeois-democratic and parliamentary prejudices . . . that it is only within such institutions as bourgeois parliaments that Communists can (and must) wage a long and stubborn struggle—undaunted by difficulties—to expose, dispel, and overcome these prejudices."[17]

Lenin used a similar line of reasoning in advocating Communist work in the bourgeois trade unions: "To refuse to work in the reactionary trade unions means leaving the insufficiently developed or backward working masses under the influence of reactionary leaders, agents of the bourgeoisie, labor aristocrats, or 'bourgeoisified workers'."[18]

In encouraging Communist activity in trade unions, Lenin laid down a dictum which was used by leaders of the Communist International throughout its existence: "It is necessary . . . to agree to any and every sacrifice, and even—if need be—to resort to all sorts of devices, maneuvers, . . . in order to penetrate into the trade unions, to remain in them, and to carry on Communist work in them . . ."[19]

One overriding consideration—to reach the masses—had to be accomplished at all costs: "In order to be able to help 'the masses,' and to win the sympathy, confidence, and support of 'the masses,' it is necessary to brave all difficulties . . . and it is imperatively necessary to work wherever the masses are to be found . . . For the whole task of the Communists is to be able to convince the backward elements, to be able to work among them and not to fence themselves off from them by artificial and childishly 'Left Wing' slogans."[20]

During the time of the First Congress of the Communist International, civil war raged in Russia and revolutionary fervor was high; revolution in the advanced countries of Europe was expected. It was believed that the Russian Revolution could not survive if the workers of other countries did not rise against their Capitalist governments. The overriding mission of the International was to encourage and aid the envisioned inevitable revolution in other countries. Therefore, no serious thought was given to problems of organization at the opening Congress. Activities were limited to revolutionary propaganda in the anticipation of new revolutionary outbreaks in Europe.

The high optimism about revolution in Europe continued through the Second Congress of the Communist International, July 19 to August 7, 1920. Although the Soviet Union was struggling for its life, the progress of the civil war seemed more encouraging to the Communists. There was also a great deal of enthusiasm about the campaign in Poland, as the Soviet army was pursuing the Polish army. Every labor disturbance was held to be the beginning of the final struggle which would bring about the destruction of Capitalism. Over-all, the common belief in the imminence of the world revolution largely dominated the proceedings.

There was a more sober attitude, however, compared with that of the First Congress. In a *Pravda* article, Zinoviev now admitted that the term of life given to the Capitalist world in his previous statements was too short: "Yes, perhaps we were wrong; not one year, but two or three will be necessary for all Europe to become Soviet. You still have a short period of grace before you will be destroyed. But if you have now become so modest that you rejoice at these few months of grace, or a few years, then we, in any case, congratulate you on your unusual modesty." [21]

Lenin's theory that the Capitalist stage of development was not inevitable for such backward countries as China and India, which had entered upon the path of progress since the war, was embodied in the resolutions of the Congress: "The idea of the Soviet form of organization is a simple one that can be applied not only to proletarian conditions, but also to feudal and semi-feudal peasant conditions . . . Peasant soviets, soviets of the exploited, are suitable for pre-capitalist conditions also . . . If the victorious revolutionary proletariat organizes systematic propaganda and the Soviet governments give them all the help they can, it is incorrect to assume that such peoples must pass through the capitalist stage of development." [22]

In Lenin's eyes the Socialist revolution failed in Europe because the proletariat itself was not united and especially because it was betrayed by the leaders of the European Socialist movement. He emphasized that dedicated leadership in the vanguard of the proletariat was necessary in order to foster world revolution: "What we shall attain with decisive success (of this there can be no doubt) is the preparation of revolutionary forces, in order to take advantage of the revolutionary crisis which indisputably is at hand, which grows throughout the entire world and which lacks only decisiveness, consciousness, and organization. Communist parties in each country, in touch with all the exploited masses—that is what is lacking." [23]

What best characterized the Second Congress, however, was the introduction by the Russians of the now-famous Twenty-One Conditions.[24] This led to several immediately interesting results. One of these was to attempt to further the reach of the Communist International. Special efforts were demanded to win the support of the peasants and support was also demanded to be given to the emancipation of oppressed and colonial people; propaganda was to be spread among the armed forces, especially against oppression of colonial people; Communists were to attempt to gain control of their countries' trade unions from within; parliaments were to be participated in (this last injunction, to join the enemy and subvert from within, was especially distasteful to the 'ultra-left' who preferred to fight from the base of external Communist structures). The Twenty-One Conditions did suggest that illegal Communist organizations should be set up parallel to legal Communist activity in a country, and reiterated that secret and illegal activity should be used whenever necessary and that it should be combined with the legal activities. Another result of the Twenty-One Conditions was the strengthening of the position of the Communist International, further alienating the 'ultra-left' who preferred autonomous local parties. The work of those involved in trade union activity was to lead to affiliation with the new Red Trade Union International centered in Moscow, rather than the Amsterdam International of Trade Unions.[25]

All parties joining the Communist International were bound by the decisions of the congresses to fight against center tendencies, pacifism, and reformism and remove all persons holding such views. Periodic purges were recommended. All Communist delegates to parliaments must be completely subordinated to the party's central authority. Communist parties must be based on the principle of 'democratic centralism'—the higher party bodies were elected by the lower, but all instructions of the higher bodies were binding on the lower. Members must recognize the authority of a strong party center whose orders must be obeyed in the period between congresses. One condition which was the stumbling block in the ultimate affiliation of the Italian Socialist Party and the Norwegian Labor Party was that all Comintern affiliates had to adopt the name "Communist Party." A hint of future directions was given in the resolution that all Soviet Republics must be supported by Communist parties in the struggle against counter-revolution. Such support should include the urging of workers to refuse to transport arms or equipment destined for the enemies of a Soviet Republic.

In the next months the Twenty-One Conditions were considered by Socialist parties and trade unions throughout the world. Splits occurred within the major European groups—the French Socialist Party did accept the Twenty-One Conditions, but a minority, under Leon Blum, seceded; German Socialists and Independents could not accept them; there was trouble in Italy; and purges and splits took place in other parts of the world. Thus, Lenin took a giant stride toward giving guidance to and securing centralized control of the International (hereafter referred to as the Comintern).

The period 1918-1920 gave birth to international Communism. The strong feeling that the Russian Revolution would be followed quickly by successful revolutionary movements in the major countries of Europe gave way during the Second Congress of the Comintern to somewhat more cautious pronouncements of imminent revolution. This caution was only natural after the severe setbacks of the defeat of the Communists in Hungary and the failure of the German Spartacists. Some degree of revolutionary sentiment, however, still pervaded the entire period.

The Second Congress prepared the way for the direction of international Communism by the Comintern. The Twenty-One Conditions not only split the Socialist parties and the Western labor movement, but established a pattern to guide the future activities of the Communist movement. The Communist Party of the Soviet Union was not yet in control of the international movement, but the seeds had been planted: "The Communist International has proclaimed the cause of Soviet Russia as its own. The world proletariat will not sheathe its sword until Soviet Russia is one member in the World Federation of Soviet Republics . . ." [26] Such was the situation on the eve of the Third Congress of the Comintern.

The Second Stage, 1921-1927

Historical events paralleling and affecting the development of the Comintern were decisive. The Communist movement in Asia was very uneven and although prospects appeared bright in the early 1920's with gains in China, Java, and Japan, the defeat of the Chinese Communists in 1927 was a catastrophe for the Comintern. Revolutionary feeling declined in Europe, and further defeats in Bulgaria, Germany, and Poland were experienced by the Communists. The death of Lenin in 1924 precipitated power struggles within the Communist leadership and the progressive industrialization and economic development of the Soviet Union resulted in a New Economic Policy (N.E.P.).

All this had an effect on the development of the Comintern. The Second Congress and its Twenty-One Conditions had seen the Comintern begin to direct the international Communist movement. In 1921, the Third Congress and the tactic of the 'United Front'—the first of several Comintern 'lines'—was the beginning of a new stage in the history of the Comintern in which it assumed the central leadership of international Communism.

The Third Congress of the Comintern opened in Moscow on June 22 and lasted until July 12, 1921. The Communist leaders who were present were quick to appreciate the meaning of the non-revolutionary world about them. Perhaps their understanding was best expressed by Trotsky: ". . . History has given the bourgeoisie a fairly long breathing spell . . . The revolution is not so obedient, so tame, that it can be led on a leash, as we imagined. It has its ups and downs, its crises and booms." [27] Trotsky went on to say that the proletarian revolution cannot fix a certain date beforehand or carry through the revolution within a given time. Thus, it appeared that a new policy of practical politics would have to be established and this was provided in the report on the tactics of the Comintern submitted by Karl Radek.

Radek argued that if, as Trotsky's analysis showed, the Capitalists had won a respite, the best preparation for action was real revolutionary propaganda; premature revolutionary attempts could retard the progress of the international Communist movement. The Comintern's new tactics, as laid down by the Third Congress through Radek's formula, would involve enlisting the masses in the struggle against Capitalism in the trade unions, the underground organizations, and in demonstrations: "The Third Congress is now addressing a call to the Communists of all countries to follow this path further and to do all they can, in order to unite greater millions and millions of workers in the ranks of the Communist International. The power of Capitalism can be broken down only when the idea of Communism will be embodied in the tremendous impetus of the greater majority of the proletariat, led by Communist mass parties encircling the fighting proletarian class in an iron Solidarity. 'To the masses' is the first slogan addressed by the Third International to the Communists of all countries." [28]

The symbol for the shift in Comintern tactics was the United Front. The Communist tactic of the United Front signified cooperation with non-Communist workers' organizations in two variations—'United Front from below' and 'United Front from above'.[29] The first, openly directed against Socialist leaders, aimed at winning the Socialist masses away from them. The arguments combined the need for workers' unity on the one hand and violent abuse of Socialist politicians on the other. The second, more subtle, variation ostensibly included cooperation with both the Socialist masses and leaders. Although the latter were not openly denounced, the aim was still eventually to undermine their authority and to gain control of worker organizations.

In the early 1920's the Comintern had not yet so clearly defined the two variations; but that the tendency during this period seemed to be towards the 'United Front from below' tactic can be substantiated by the following statement: "Communist parties . . . must exert every effort to overcome completely the influence of the treacherous Socialist leaders on the working class by means of extensive campaigns, and to rally the majority of working masses to the Communist banners." [30]

It is interesting that Zinoviev, the first president of the Comintern, seemed to have no difficulty in moving from his earlier statements of imminent world revolution to expressions of patient preparation for the coming struggles: "Conquest of the majority of the working class for Communism. Systematic, determined, and persistent preparation of the working masses for the coming struggles. Careful work in the creation of illegal organizations. Patient, indomitable work for the arming of the workers. The establishment of strong, independent Communist parties, purified of opportunists, centrists, and semi-centrists. Above all . . . conquest of the trade unions . . ." [31]

The Comintern tactic of the United Front was not readily accepted by the Communists of the West. Many felt that the Comintern leaders were purposely pushing the method of proletarian revolution into the background. That it was a retreat was not denied. However, one must think in terms of the New Economic Policy which was just getting underway in the Soviet Union, and to which Lenin referred as a "deliberate retreat to State Capitalism." Trotsky developed the theme and considered the United Front and the New Economic Policy within the same framework: "At the Third Congress the overwhelming majority called to order those elements in the International whose views involved the danger that the vanguard might, by precipitate action, be shattered against the passivity and immaturity of the working masses, and against the strength of the capitalist state. That was the greatest danger . . . In so far as there was a retreat, it ran parallel with the economic retreat in Russia."[32]

Thus, the Third Congress with its coupling of the New Economic Policy and the United Front saw international Communism move to come under the control of the Comintern.

The Fourth Congress of the Comintern met in Moscow from November 5 to December 3, 1922. As far as the International Communist movement was concerned, the Congress was not of great importance as many of the slogans of previous congresses were again stated in somewhat different terms. Lenin repeated that Communists must be prepared to think of the necessity of retreat. The importance of the United Front was stressed; the working class had to be united and therefore the leaders of the Comintern did not think it advantageous to form competing Communist unions even though many unions throughout the world were expelling their Communist members. Instead, every effort was to be made to bring the expelled members back into the non-Communist labor organizations.[33]

Zinoviev's speech to the Executive Committee of the Comintern showed how far he had retreated from his earlier position. What had become clear, he said, was that although the bourgeoisie was demonstrably incapable of ruling, the proletariat was not yet ready to take its place. The International had been described as an International of action, but it would require years to accomplish the action. Radek echoed this more pessimistic tone: in a later speech he said that "the broad masses of the proletariat have lost belief in their ability to conquer power in any forseeable time . . . the conquest of power as an immediate task of the day is not on the agenda."[34]

The trend toward greater emphasis on the importance of the Soviet Union continued. Bukharin stated that it would be proper for Moscow to seek a military alliance with a bourgeois state for defense.

He added that "the proletarian state should and must be protected not only by the proletariat of this country, but also by the proletariat of all countries."[35]

Several events took place between the Fourth and Fifth Congresses of the Comintern.[36] Lenin had died and the Communist leaders—Stalin, Trotsky, Zinoviev, and Bukharian—were involved in a struggle for power. Economic questions of reorganization and industrialization were rapidly taking precedence over purely political problems in the minds of the new Soviet leaders. N.E.P. meant that projects for economic development within the Soviet Union required help from the outside in the form of capital and technical assistance and the result of this was the necessity of a rapprochement with the Capitalist countries, requiring a revision in attitudes. Generally, domestic preoccupations seemed to be getting the upper hand over problems of purely international politics.

When the delegates to the Fifth Congress of the Comintern met in Moscow from June 17 to July 8, 1924, they were faced with the problem of developing a new tactic which would allow for greater flexibility. Social reality for the Communists presented two possibilities: the slower and more protracted development of the proletarian revolution could not be excluded; on the other hand, the ground under Capitalism was believed to be so undermined, and its contradictions were developing so rapidly, that it was believed that the breakdown of Capitalism in a given country might take place at any time in the not too distant future.[37] This set the stage for a new tactic based on the experience of the Communist Party of the Soviet Union. The immediate background was the disaster of the attempted Communist revolution in Germany in 1923. A new panacea was established for the international movement—'Bolshevization'.

The term generally signified that the Communist parties of the world must be reorganized on the model of the Communist Party of the Soviet Union. Several basic features were involved.[38] The party had to be a real mass party—that is it should maintain the closest possible contact with the masses. The party had to be revolutionary —Marxist in its orientation, with flexible tactics. It was to be a centralized party, permitting no fractions or tendencies, in which the lowest unit would be the "cell," and the power of the secretaries would be strengthened. The emphasis was to be placed on systematic and persistent propaganda and organization, particularly in the bourgeois armies. Zinoviev made it clear that Bolshevization of the Communist parties involved using the experiences of the Communist

Party of the Soviet Union, especially that party's growing struggle against 'Trotskyism:' "The Bolshevizing of the parties of the Comintern is making use of the experiences of the Bolshevik Party in the three Russian revolutions (as well as the experiences of the other best sections of the Comintern), and applying them to the concrete situation of each particular country . . . In the Soviet Union the Bolshevizing of the Party at present consists in the ideological fight against Trotskyism as a 'justifiable' tendency in the C.P. of Russia." [39]

What then was the significance of this new tactic to international Communism? In the first place, Bolshevization seemed to be a repetition of many old slogans under a new title. There was certainly nothing new about such ideas as a mass party, centralization, or a revolutionary Marxian spirit. The words themselves were not very important. Personnel shifted in some of the parties as the new tactic was soon followed by purges, at first against the followers of Trotsky and then against the 'left' in general. As a result, the Stalinist position was generally strengthened. The French and German parties were affected in this manner as the lines become more clearly drawn between the 'Stalinists' and the 'Trotskyites.'

The most important aspect of Bolshevization for consideration here is the effect the tactic had on the Comintern, which continued to use the slogan of the United Front. By this time the idea of 'United Front from below' had been clearly established: "For the Comintern, the main purpose of the United Front tactics consists in the struggle against the leaders of counter-revolutionary Social Democracy and in emancipating the Social Democratic workers from their influence." [40] The tactic of the United Front became less important with the implementation of Bolshevization and its concentration on tighter party discipline. Collaboration with Socialist workers and the elimination of fractions within the Communist parties did not go hand in hand. The greatest effect, however, was that the central leadership of the international movement, assumed by the Comintern after the Third Congress and the tactic of the United Front, was now effectively subjected to the control of the Communist Party of the Soviet Union which had become under Bolshevization the model and guide of international Communism. The Comintern would continue to exist, but as an agent of the Russian leaders.

The most signifiicant developments during the four year period between the Fifth and Sixth Congresses were connected with the new doctrine of Socialism in one country and with Stalin's power struggle with the opposition. The contest between different personalities in the Soviet hierarchy is an interesting study in itself,[41] but rather than be concerned with the political maneuvering within the Communst Party of the Soviet Union, the emphasis here will be on the significance of this new doctrine for the Comintern.

During the Fifth Congress of the Comintern in 1924, emphasis was still placed on the immediacy of the struggle between Capitalism and the proletariat. In 1925, however, it was officially acknowledged that the Capitalist world had entered upon a period of provisional stabilization and it was realized that world revolution was not on the horizon. Under these circumstances, it was only natural that the Soviet Union should emphasize its own development.[42]

The doctrine of 'Socialism in one country,' which was accepted officially by the fourteenth Soviet party congress in April of 1925 as "the aims of the Comintern and the Russian Communist Party," [43] was influenced by various factors. The Soviet Union was ready to begin its first Five-Year Plan and Stalin wanted to maintain good relations with the outside world by reducing the threats to other governments. In addition, Comintern efforts in the East—towards which the Soviet Union, in its historical pattern, had turned after defeat in the West—had failed; Stalin therefore turned inwards to the 'Socialism in one country' doctrine. Parenthetically, as one aspect of the struggle within the party, Zinoviev, who opposed the new doctrine, was replaced by Bukharin. Zinoviev was also in the opposition in the U.S.S.R. after 1925.

The significance for the Comintern, as the second stage in its history drew to a close, was the increasing emphasis placed on nationalism in the Soviet Union; the Comintern would now carry the new message for the international movement—that world revolution could best be promoted by strengthening the position of the Soviet Union. But the implications for the Comintern went beyond this; 'Socialism in one country,' the doctrine of Stalin and his ally Bukharin, meant that control of the international Communist movement shifted from the Communist Party of the Soviet Union to the personal control of Stalin. Bukharin was ousted early in 1929, as leader of the Right Opposition.

The Third Stage, 1928-1934

During the third stage, corresponding to the first Five-Year Plan in the Soviet Union, Stalin found it necessary to disgrace his rightist opponents, both in the Russian party and in the world movement.

Thus, the Comintern embarked on a new 'left' policy, but the result was to weaken many of the European Communist parties. There was further weakening of the Communist movement inasmuch as the world depression generally reduced the economic and political power of the working class. One might think that increasing misery would turn many to Communism and it probably did in some cases, but in Germany, for instance, it was Hitler who profited more from the economic depression than did the Communists. The Sixth Congress of the Comintern, July 17 to September 1, 1928, addressed itself to several problems and presented a new line for the international Communist movement to follow.

The Comintern leaders analyzed the development of Capitalism and divided it into several periods.[44] The first period, the revolutionary phase up to 1923, was characterized by an acute crisis of the Capitalist system and direct revolutionary action by the proletariat. The civil war in the U.S.S.R. was brought to a victorious conclusion and the Comintern was consolidated. The first period ended with a series of severe defeats for the Western European proletariat and the beginning of the general Capitalist offensive, culminating in the defeat of the German proletariat in 1923.

The second period (1924-1928) was one of partial stabilization of Capitalism: a 'restoration' process of the Capitalist economy, the development and expansion of the Capitalist offensive and a weakening of the proletariat by severe defeats. The Soviet Union, however, was strengthened by building up Socialism, and the political influence of the Communist parties over the "broad masses of the proletariat" continued to grow.

Events around the time of the Sixth Congress (1928) led to a further consideration of world affairs by the Comintern leaders. The conviction that the Soviet Union was in immediate danger of invasion after the war scare with Great Britain[45] was repeated by the Sixth Congress of the Comintern and became accepted as dogma by the European Communist parties. War against the Soviet Union came to be considered one of the symptoms of the 'Third Period' of Capitalism: "This Third Period, in which the contradiction between the growth of the forces of production and the contraction of markets become accentuated with particular force, will inevitably give rise to a fresh series of imperialist wars: between the imperialist states themselves, wars of the imperialist states against the U.S.S.R., wars of national liberation against imperialism and imperialist intervention, and to gigantic class battles." [46]

Therefore, it was necessary during this Third Period, to revise the theory of the partial stabilization of Capitalism, since the breakdown of such stabilization was seen as a likely cause of war, especially against the Socialist state. Thus a new militant revolutionary policy would be needed to protect the Soviet Union against the onslaughts of Capitalism.

Some of the features of the more militant revolutionary policy of the Third Period included the replacement of Bukharin by Manuilsky in 1929 as spokesman for the Third Period and as president of the Comintern, the continued use of general strikes, and the pretense that a proletarian revolution was coming.

One of the several essential features of the Third Period was the attack against the Social Democratic parties and the Socialist elements of the trade unions, and the leaders of the latter were severely criticized: "In foreign affairs the Social Democratic and reformist trade union leaders in the imperialist countries are the most consistent representatives of bourgeois state interests. They support this state, its armed forces, its police, its expansionist aspirations and its unprincipled hostility to the Soviet Union; they support its robber treaties and agreements, its colonial policy, its occupations, annexations, protectorates and mandates . . ."[47] Attempts were to be made to create union confederations under Communist party control. Virtually every Communist party organized such a captive labor movement during the 1929-35 period.

The Communists also attacked Social Democracy and compared it to Fascism, at first identifying the two as different sides of the same coin[48] and later stressing their parallel roles to the point where the distinction was almost obliterated by the term "Social-Fascism."

During the latter part of the 1920's and into the early part of the 1930's, the uncompromising hostility to democratic and reformist movements built up an unrelenting attack upon "Social-Fascism": "The Fascists are nationalists, imperialists, war-mongers, enemies of Socialism, enemies of democracy, stranglers of the independent labor movement, worker's assassins, and so on. The Social-Fascists are acting as a rule like the Fascists, but they do their Fascist work not with an open face, but behind a smoke screen, as done in war. This belongs to the nature of Social-Fascism: imperialist policy in the name of internationalism, capitalist policy in the name of Socialism, abolition of the democratic rights of the toilers in the name of democracy, abolition of reforms in the name of reformism, assassination of the workers in the name of labor politics, and so on."[49]

Toward the end of the second stage in the history of the Comintern, with the doctrine of 'Socialism in one country,' there was a shift to the 'right' and not too much emphasis was placed on the 'United Front from below.' The second of the important features resulting from the 'line' of the Third Period, however, and a shift to the 'left' was the stressing of the slogan by Comintern publications:[50] "The Sections of the C.I. must answer this challenge of the world bourgeoisie by intensifying to the utmost their Bolshevik work, by hastening the revolution of the broad masses, developing and leading the class struggles of the toilers on the basis of the United Front from below, by leading the working class to mass political strikes, winning over the majority of the working class and directing the whole movement of the exploited classes and the oppressed peoples along the channel of the world Socialist revolution." [51]

The immediate purpose of the Communist movement was defined during the 'Third Period' as a continuous struggle against the imperialists in all spheres. This included defense of the Chinese revolution and of colonial uprisings. Above all, the Soviet Union had to be defended at all costs.[52]

Perhaps the outstanding feature of the Third Period was the strong emphasis placed upon the Soviet Union as the most important factor in world politics. Since it was considered to be the international driving force of world revolution and the living example of Socialism towards which the world proletariat was striving, the interests of the Soviet Union and the international working class movement were considered to be identical.[53]

The danger of imperialistic aggression against the proletarian dictatorship served a double purpose in Soviet philosophy. It kept alive the militant spirit of the Five-Year Plan and established a most useful link with the theory of world revolution, the complete abandonment of which no Communist would ever concede. But what effect did the overriding issue of defense of the Soviet Union have upon the Comintern? It seems that the Comintern had been converted from the militant and uncompromising general staff of the world revolution into an international organization for the defense of Soviet Russia.

None of the tactics of the Third Period, however, lessened the threat of war in the eyes of the Comintern leaders. Not only had Hitler come to power in 1933 but the Japanese threat from the East had been described as probably the dominant foreign-political reality to the leaders of the Soviet Union at that time: "The reactions of Stalin and his associates to events in Europe during this period will not be intelligible unless this sense of extreme danger on the eastern frontier of their power is borne in mind."[54]

The continued threat from the West and the East brought about another shift in thinking. The Soviet leaders started to make efforts toward "collective security" in order to maintain the peace, a peace which was vital to the interests of the Soviet Union if it was to build up its industrial base during the Five-Year Plans. Diplomatic relations were established with the United States in 1933; the Soviet Union joined the League of Nations in 1934; the Franco-Soviet Pact was signed in 1935.[55] The Comintern also was called upon to support the national interests of the Soviet Union. The Third Period came to a close through the dictates of Soviet foreign policy, and Communist delegates were called to Moscow for another congress and the establishment of a new 'line' for international Communism.

The Fourth Stage 1935-1939

The new Comintern policy resulted from the Communist analysis of the causes of the rise of Fascism, which was appearing as a new "terrible threat to the proletariat": "Fascism was able to come to power primarily because the working class, owing to the policy of class collaboration with the bourgeoisie pursued by the Social Democratic leaders, proved to be split, politically, and organizationally disarmed, in the face of the onslaught of the bouregoisie. And the Communist parties, on the other hand, apart from and in opposition to the Social Democrats, were not strong enough to arouse the masses and to lead them in a decisive struggle against Fascism." [56]

The Comintern proceeded to lay down certain steps to be followed by all Communists to combat the Fascist danger. The first was the utilization of the United Front, whether from above or below: "It is imperative that unity of action be established between all sections of the working class, irrespective of what organization they belong to, even before the majority of the working class unites in a common fighting platform for the overthrow of capitalism and the victory of the proletarian revolution. But it is precisely for this very reason that this task makes it the duty of the Communist parties to take into consideration the changed circumstances and to apply the united front tactics in a new manner, by seeking to reach agreements with the organizations of the toilers of various political trends for joint action on a factory, local, district, national, and interntional scale." [57]

Instead of regarding the Social Democrats as "Social-Fascists,"

Communists were to seek them out as allies, and could even join them in election campaigns to present a common ticket against Fascist candidates.[58]

The second step, following the formation of the United Front, was to be the establishment of a People's Front (Popular Front): "We must advance from the proletarian United Front to the Anti-Fascist People's Front by means of the determined defense of the demands of all the toiling masses, especially of the working peasantry and at the same time of the urban petty bourgeoisie. All their organizations still under the influence of the bourgeoisie at the present time must be enlisted for the Anti-Fascist People's Front." [59]

To prevent confusion by the terms United Front and People's Front, Dimitrov pointed out that the two can overlap in practice: "It is a waste of time to worry about whether the United Front must come first and then the People's Front or vice versa. The proletarian United Front and the Anti-Fascist People's Front are closely bound up with one another by the dialectics of life, merge into one another and are not divided from one another by any Chinese wall. The United Front is the foundation and the leading force of the People's Front. But at the same time the further development of the proletarian United Front depends to a great extent on the successes of the People's Front." [60]

Third, the Communists saw the possibility of a government either by a United Front or a People's Front and that this development might be a new step in the path toward the dictatorship of the proletariat. The theory was expressed by Dimitrov: "Fifteen years ago Lenin called upon us to focus all our attention on searching out forms of transition or approach to the proletarian revolution. It may be that in a number of countries the United Front government will prove to be one of the most important transitional forms.[61] Dimitrov went on to say, however, that this was not an indispensable step.

Fourth, the Congress reversed another policy of the Third Period, and called for trade union unity: "We stand for one International of trade unions based on the class struggle. We are for united class trade unions as one of the major bulwarks of the working class against the offensive of capital and Fascism. Our only condition for uniting the trade unions is: Struggle against capital, struggle against Fascism, and international trade union democracy." [62]

Finally, efforts were to be made in each country to overcome the split of 1919-20, and to form a single party of the proletariat: "The interests of the class struggle of the proletariat and the success of the proletarian revolution make it imperative that there be a single party of the proletariat in each country . . . . The Communist parties must, in reliance upon the growing urge of the workers for a unification of the Social Democratic parties, firmly and confidently take the initiative in this unification. The cause of amalgamating the forces of the working class in a single revolutionary proletarian party, at the time when the international labor movement is entering the period of closing the split in its ranks, is our cause, is the cause of the Communist International." [63]

The new 'line' was generally put into practice with the dropping of violent attacks against the democratic parties and continued attempts to form close alliances not only with the Socialists, but with 'bourgeois' democrats, and occasionally with conservative and even semi-Fascist groups as well. The climax of it all was reached in attempts to merge the Communist and Socialist parties. In the course of these attempts, the independent Communist trade unions were actually dissolved. Thus, the idea of a proletarian revolution receded far into the background; nationalism was now the new tactic of the various Communist parties. The Communists became the "champions of democracy"[64] and in France and several other countries, through the Popular Front, their influence increased.[65]

In 1936 the eyes of the world focused on Spain where the battle between Fascists and non-Fascists was drawn. The Soviet Union became deeply involved and the new tactic of the Popular Front was put to a severe test.

The Comintern publications placed a great deal of emphasis on the Spanish Civil War and stressed two main themes. The first was all possible aid must be given to the forces opposing Franco: "In the threshold of the New Year, we can say without any exaggeration . . . there is not now any higher duty for the international proletariat, for the people of all countries, for all honest elements of mankind . . . than increasing aid for the Spanish people in every way, with the aim of ensuring their victory." [66]

In the second theme, the leaders of the Comintern tried to identify the cause of the Spanish Republicans with the world proletariat: "The Spanish working class, headed by the People's Front Government, are the leading force of the armed people . . . . and with their bodies are defending not only the liberty and independence of their own country, but also the interests of the entire working class of the world and the general cause of democracy and peace." [67]

This is a relatively moderate statement when one considers previous positions taken by the Comintern leaders, such as incitement to revolution or transforming the struggle into a "civil war against the imperialists." In this case, however, the Communists wished to appear as democrats; they would interfere in Spanish domestic affairs in order to save democracy. In addition, the Communists attempted to use Soviet aid to Spain to gain Communist control over the republic.

Concomitant with the interest in the Spanish Civil War was the bitter denunciation of Fascism, particularly that practiced by Nazi Germany: "The most reactionary variety of Fascism is the Fascism of the German type. German Fascism plays the role of a bailiff in international counter-revolution, of the leading incendiary of imperialist war, of the instigator of the crusade against the Soviet Union." [68]

The Soviet propagandists would often draw contrasts between life under the Nazis and life in the first proletarian state: "No profounder antagonism exists than that between the country of the Nazi dictatorship and the land of the proletarian dictatorship. The Nazi dictatorship is the champion of the most unbridled capitalist reaction and of the most bloody suppression of the workers, peasants, national minorities, and the whole people." Therefore all revolutionaries were called upon to struggle against the common enemy: "It is the duty of every revolutionist to concentrate the fire of our struggle against National Socialism as the leading warmonger and as the deadly enemy of the Soviet Union and of the proletarian revolution. Those who fail to grasp this duty fail to understand the nature of the struggle between reaction and revolution today." [69]

Throughout the years, the leaders of the Comintern and of the Soviet Union had tried to create a central point of attraction for Communism. During one period, emphasis was placed on the Comintern as the general staff of world revolution. At a later stage the focal point was to be 'Socialism' as defined by the Soviet leaders. But toward the latter part of the 1930's, all other considerations were pushed into the background as the Soviet Union itself took the center of the Communist stage. The President of the Comintern, Dimitrov, put it this way: "The historical dividing line between the forces of Fascism, war, and capitalism, on the one hand, and the forces of peace, democracy, and Socialism, on the other hand, is in fact becoming the attitude toward the Soviet Union, and not the formal attitude toward Soviet Power and Socialism in general . . . the attitude toward the Soviet Union which has been carrying on a real existence for twenty years already, with its untiring struggle against the enemies, with its dictatorship of the working class and the Stalin Constitution, with the leading role of the Party of Lenin-Stalin." [70]

As the fourth stage in Comintern history drew to a close, the leaders of the Kremlin were forced again to re-evaluate the world situation, to think in terms of another policy which they believed would enhance the national interests of the Soviet Union. The Fascist states seemed to be growing stronger and the democratic non-Fascist states weaker. German rearmament was progressing rapidly, and German troops were permitted to reoccupy the Rhineland with impunity. British appeasement at Munich and the triumph of Franco in the Spanish Civil War posed severe problems for the Soviet leaders to think about. The policy of "collective security" was a failure. Added to these factors was the growing strength of the Japanese in the Pacific. Within the Soviet Union, Stalin had practically destroyed the governing structure of the country through purges; this, according to Kennan, "affected adversely both his qualifications as an ally for the West and the ability of Russia, independently, to stand up to Hitler's power." [71] The leaders of the Kremlin realized that a European war was on the horizon. How could the Soviet Union stay out of the war and yet be in a position to gain strategic territory? The answer seemed clear to Stalin: a rapprochment with the Fascist powers.

The Fifth Stage, 1939-1941

The Fifth Period, known as the time of the Nazi-Soviet Pact, lasted for only twenty-two months. The Soviet Union made gains in territory during this time, but the various Communist parties suffered loss of influence in their respective countries. Those who had been encouraged to be violently anti-Nazi were suddenly forced to help the Germans by sabotaging the war efforts of the Western nations.

The German-Soviet Treaty of Non-Aggression was signed on August 23, 1939, followed by another treaty the next month. Shortly after the signing of the non-aggression treaty, Molotov delivered a speech to the Supreme Soviet on "The Meaning of the Soviet-German Non-Aggression Pact." He emphasized that it was in the Soviet people's interest to improve relations with Germany and to overcome the efforts of Western European politicians to incite friction between the Soviet Union and Germany: "Stalin hit the nail on the head when he exposed the machinations of the Western European politicians who were trying to set Germany and the Soviet Union at loggerheads . . . . Only yesterday the German Fascists were pursuing a foreign policy hostile to us. Yes, only yesterday we were enemies in the sphere of foreign relations. Today, however, the situation has changed and we are enemies no longer." [72]

The line which the Comintern used to 'explain' the war was that it was imperialist; that is, the fault lay with the ruling circles of England and France. The Soviet Union, according to this line, was trying to end the war: "It was not Germany that attacked France and England, but France and England that attacked Germany, taking on themselves responsibility for the present war. After the outbreak of hostilities Germany made peace proposals to France and England, and the Soviet Union publicly supported Germany's peace proposals, since it thought and still thinks that a quick end to the war would radically ease the situation of all countries and peoples. The ruling circles of England and France rudely rejected both Germany's peace proposals and the Soviet Union's efforts to bring the war quickly to an end." [73]

If they couldn't avert the war, at least the Soviets, according to their 'line,' were trying to keep the war small: "The imperialist countries failed to avert a military clash. The sharpening of capitalist contradictions which gave rise to the second imperialist war has placed several major European nations in a state of war, dooming millions of working people to privations, suffering and death for the interests of the bourgeoisie of their countries . . . . The imperialist war which flared up in the heart of Europe has been localized because of the Soviet-German Pact, its scope limited and the theater of war narrowed." [74]

According to Dimitrov, the 'United Front from above' of the Popular Front period could no longer apply if the proletariat were to bring the war to an end soon. Instead, the workers must form the 'United Front from below.' The leaders of the Comintern, however, found no difficulty in justifying such actions: "The Soviet people demand that the frontier of the Soviet Union shall be secured, and therefore they demand that, should it be necessary, the people of Finland shall be saved by timely and prompt intervention by the Soviet Union from the sad fate which befell the population of Poland, who were plunged into a senseless war by rulers of inglorious memory." [76]

Finally, it can be observed that the Comintern traveled the full cycle and became an instrument of the Soviet dictator: "The cause of the international Communist movement is indissolubly associated with the name of Comrade Stalin . . . the Communist International is the International of Lenin and Stalin . . . . [77]

The period of the 'imperialist war' did not last very long. On June 22, 1941, the Soviet Union was invaded by Germany. It was necessary to drop the tactics of denouncing the Capitalist countries of the West and to come to an agreement with them in order to face the menace of the invading German armies. A new 'line' would be needed now.

The Sixth Stage, 1941-1943

To be more accurate, the Sixth Period might be extended to the end of World War II and further. Certainly the history of international Communism is a part of the present. The period immediately after World War II might also be considered as part of the stage of the Cold War. However, the concern here is with the history of the official Comintern, and the analysis in this chapter is only pertinent as long as that organization was in existence.

When the Soviet Union was forced into World War II, it was necessary for the leaders of the Comintern to redefine again their view of the world conflagration. The "imperialist war" had now become a "peoples' war" or "great patriotic war." "Thus the war has already had three phases and may have more yet. . . . From its beginnings in one quarter of the globe, it has become a war of all peoples against Fascism . . . ." [78]

In many respects, Soviet participation in the war marked a return to Popular Front period, with important variations.[79] The Comintern had suspended the class struggle; the charge of imperialism, leveled against the Western powers during all previous stages, was dropped; strikes were no longer regarded as legitimate tools in the hands of the working class. In addition, Communist units played a prominent and often leading role in underground movements.

At the same time the Communist parties did not fail to press special aims of the Soviet Union. When, in 1943, the Western powers believed that establishment of a second front against the German-occupied European continent would be militarily premature, this policy did not coincide with the wishes of the Soviet leaders. Through its diplomatic and military representatives, the Soviet Union pressed for a second front; the Communist groups attempted to create public pressure in the same direction; the Comintern did not hesitate in taking up the call: "We must raise the campaign for the speedy opening of the Second Front and carry it forward in spite of all the howls of the appeasers. Every day, every moment counts. From every organization and meeting must come the call to the government: Speed the Second Front!" [80]

In 1943 the Soviet leaders decided it would be in the best interests of the Soviet Union to dissolve the Comintern. They viewed the strengthening of the wartime alliance as essential for the successful defense of the Soviet Union. Cooperation between the Allies would be easier without the existence of an international Communist organization which sought to overthrow the Capitalist governments. In all probability, the decision was also influenced by the pressure of the United States. The dissolution of the Comintern would also be an indication that the Soviet Union was prepared to cooperate with the United Nations in the post-war period. Furthermore, the Communist leaders in Moscow probably were thinking that the Comintern might prove to be an obstacle to Soviet penetration in Eastern Europe after the war and it also was necessary to create the maximum amount of sympathy for the Soviet Union within Eastern Europe.

On May 22, 1943, without the formality of calling a congress, the Presidium of the Executive Committee of the Comintern issued a resolution proposing dissolution. The resolution declared that the supporters of the Comintern were now free to concentrate their energies on the whole-hearted support of the struggle against the Axis. The political maturity of the Communist parties was now an established fact: "The whole development of events in the last quarter of a century and the experience accumulated by the Communist International convincingly showed that the organizational form of uniting workers chosen by the First Congress of the Communist International answered conditions of the first stages of the working class movement. However, by the complications of the problems in separate countries, it has become a drag on the further strengthening of the national working class parties." [81]

Conclusions

At the beginning the mission of the new Communist International was to hasten and bring to a successful conclusion the "imminent" world revolution. The Twenty-One Conditions did result in the splitting of the Socialist parties and the labor movement of the West to establish a pattern for future Communist activity. The split which was an incident grew, however, to a lasting reality, and the working class was henceforth divided. Thus strength was sapped from the forces of proletarian revolution at the outset and the Communist International failed as an organ of world revolution.

As an instrument in Russian factional struggles, the Comintern proved to be more meaningful. Under Stalin's control, it had a shift to the left and was used as a personal weapon in the dictator's successful struggle for power against the 'right' of Bukharin and Rykov. Only within this context can the Comintern 'line' of the Third Period be fully appreciated.

In its final stage, the Comintern was seen as an instrument of Soviet foreign policy. Only in this view can the abrupt changes of the official 'line'—from the Popular Front to the Nazi-Soviet Pact and then to the tactics of the Peoples' War—be accommodated. There is a dilemma, however, when Soviet foreign policy determines the general path of international Communism. During one period, the Soviet leaders may believe it is in their interest to seek closer cooperation with the world at large. This may be followed by another period in which the Soviet Union pledges to support world revolution by all means at its disposal. The strength of individual Communist parties may suffer by supporting internally unpopular shifts in Soviet foreign policy which are determined by Soviet national interests.

How then may the Comintern be viewed? Can one apply the simple categories of success or failure? For the revolutionary of the Trotsky variety, the Comintern failed because it did not bring about world revolution. A Stalinist or supporter of Soviet foreign policy, however, would appreciate the usefulness of the Comintern in the evolutions of the Soviet state.

Yet one can probe deeper into the problem. Up to this point the analysis has been chiefly concerned with the Comintern from the point of view of its tactical theory. In order to add more substance and depth to a study of international Communism, however, one must combine theoretical and practical aspects while interpreting the development of the movement within particular countries. In the final analysis, it is the daily struggles in many specific Communist movements which spelled success or failure for the Comintern. With this in mind, we shall now examine the case of Mexico and the Communist International.

CHAPTER II

THE MEXICAN ENVIRONMENT

Mexico experienced one of the few genuine revolutions in Latin America, one which re-made the country's society. The Revolution of 1910 and its consequences produced a radical environment which was important in two respects to the development of the Communist movement. In the first place, much of the country's national outlook, as molded by the Revolution, coincided with the Communist position and it was not difficult for the Communists to take many of the revolutionary slogans as their own. In the second place, the form which the Communist movement was to take was in turn affected by the environment in which it developed. One could, for example, in view of the history of the vehement Church-State struggle in Mexico, expect the Communist party there to stress its anti-Church position more strongly than, say, the party in Uruguay, where the relations of the Church to public authority had never been a significant political issue.

There is no question but that the Mexican political soil seemed to be fertile ground for the Communists. There was considerable anti-Americanism and anti-clericalism in the country. In addition, there was a recent history filled with force and violence, a burgeoning labor movement, and great interest in the question of land reform. In this context it is possible to see how the Communists attempted to identify themselves with Mexican experience and bring their position more in accord with the national outlook in order to gain adherents.[1]

Anti-Americanism

The general attitude toward the United States has been expressed in relatively simple terms: "The bogey of American aggrandizement hovers in the background, forming the basis of one of the most important elements in the sentiment of Mexican nationality—the need of resistance to foreign absorption." [2] During the nineteenth century, half of the country's domain became part of the United States: Texas, California, New Mexico, Utah, Arizona, Nevada, and part of Colorado. This has been a ready-made propaganda instrument for Mexican Communists. Their official newspaper played up the anti-American theme at every opportunity: "The great 'Sister Republic' (?) of the

North took away from us by force more than half of the national
territory in 1848, and now is taking away from us petroleum and more
other things, by means of commercial treaties, and enslaves us economically . . . ." [3]

TABLE I

PRESIDENTS OF MEXICO, 1876-1946

President	Years in Office
Porfirio Diaz	1876-1880
	1884-1911
Francisco de la Barra	1911
Francisco I. Madero	1911-1913
Victoriano Huerta	1913-1914
Venustiano Carranza	1916-1920°
Adolfo de la Huerta	1920
Alvaro Obregón	1920-1924
Plutarco Elías Calles	1924-1928
Emilio Portes Gil	1928-1929
Pascual Ortíz Rubio	1929-1932
Abelardo Rodríguez	1932-1934
Lázaro Cárdenas	1934-1940
Manuel Avila Camacho	1940-1946

°It may be argued that the term of Venustiano Carranza started in 1914.
However, the period 1914-1916 was one of anarchy in Mexico. The troops of
Venustiano Carranza, Emiliano Zapata, and Pancho Villa occupied the capital
in turn. The Carranza forces did not have effective control of the country until
1916. Furthermore, during the period 1914-1916, the various military leaders
appointed their own candidates to occupy the Presidency for short periods of time.

Because General Porfirio Díaz gave substantial concessions to and
sought investments from the United States, England, and countries
in Western Europe, he became identified with foreign interests and
was heavily criticized by Francisco I. Madero, the first President
after the Revolution of 1910, who declared: "Our policy of Exterior
Relations has always constituted an exaggerated condescension toward
the neighbor Republic of the North, without considering that between
Nations, the same as between individuals, each concession constitutes a
precedent and many precedents come to constitute a right." [4]

With the Revolution, Mexico's latent nationalism turned into "a
violent protest against the outsider and the things he stood for." [5] Her
defiance of the threat implicit in the reality of United States power made
it virtual political suicide for any revolutionary leader to give the impression he was placating the powerful neighbor to the North.

Bitter conflicts developed between the two countries. Ambassador

Henry Lane Wilson apparently often acted without instructions from his government and in efforts to impose his will "mediated" among the opposing revolutionary forces and succeeded in having Madero overthrown; "but the cost to him, the United States, and Mexico . . . (was) incalculable." [6] President Woodrow Wilson tried to establish what he considered to be "good government" in Mexico: United States forces were sent to Tampico; American and Mexican troops had a pitched battle in Veracruz with casualties on both sides; and troops of the United States entered the country in an attempt to secure the border against the raids of Pancho Villa.

President Venustiano Carranza expressed the government's position with bitter public attacks on the United States, referring often to the invasion of territory: "Unfortunately, in the history of our relations with the United States of America . . . the authorities of said country have judged it necessary or convenient to invade our territory . . . they have accomplished it, . . . violating the rights of a friendly people." [7] Thus the Communists found it easy to criticize American intervention and simultaneously support the official position of the government: "For Wilson's policy in action is a consistent policy of intervention to control Mexico politically for the benefit of American capital; ultimately to go to war if the desired control cannot be fully realized by less expensive means. It is precisely the Wall Street policy." [8]

The road to the doctrine of non-intervention was paved by United States invasions, conflicts with American oil companies over the possession and ownership of oil properties as a result of the provisions of the Constitution of 1917 (conflicts which were not settled until the administration of Lázaro Cárdenas in the 1930's), and threats of further intervention.

President Carranza would accept no form of intervention, mediation by other Latin American countries or compromises with the United States, in order to obtain recognition of his government (*de jure* recognition was finally given to the Carranza government by the United States on August 31, 1917). He also refused to recognize the Monroe Doctrine because he considered it an attack against his country's sovereignty and independence. This was his position as a revolutionary general, and he stated it as President to the Congress on September 1, 1919: "The guiding ideas of international politics are few, clear, and simple. They are reduced to proclaim: 'That no country ought to intervene in any form and for [sic] motive in the internal affairs of

another.' All ought to submit themselves strictly and without exception to the universal principle of non-intervention. . ." [9]

Linn A. E. Gale, a member of the Executive Committee of one of the
two Communist parties which existed for a few years during the
Carranza administration, attempted to explain why American intervention worked against the realization of Communism in the country.
One could conclude that the doctrine of non-intervention was in the
interests of both the Communists and any government which was trying to consolidate its power: "Lenin's position on the independence
of small nations and on the possibility of their attaining Communism
without passing through the stage of capitalism is precisely that which
Gale has consistently taken in regard to Mexico. If the country can be
kept from being swallowed up in the mighty American empire of
finance-capital, its transition into Communism will be comparatively
easy. Thus there is a scientific economic reason for opposing intervention in Mexico, quite aside from the natural working class sympathy
with an oppressed people and the humanitarian impulse against un-
necessary bloodshed." [10]

Cárdenas' expropriation of foreign oil properties precipitated the
most recent major crisis with the United States, even though it was
with oil interests rather than the United States government. Although
President Roosevelt, through the "Good Neighbor Policy," had turned
to persuasion rather than force, expropriation was considered to be a
crucial step on the road toward Mexico's freedom from "economic
imperialism." The Communists fully supported the government: "The
expropriation of the mineral oil is the boldest and most effective step
which has been taken by our revolutionary regime towards the national
liberation of Mexico." [11] In addition they implied that the theory of
Communism justified the bold act of the popular Mexican President:
"The nationalization of oil resources is not a Socialist, but rather a
consistently democratic measure. To be sure, even in the process of
social revolution, there may be cases where the proletariat "buys
out" the exploiters, as Lenin stated in a polemic against the leaders
of the Second International. But in Mexico we are dealing this time
with an act which fits into the framework of bourgeois-democratic development." [12]

The anti-Americanism expounded by the Anarchists under Ricardo
Flores Magón was not very different from that of the Communists:
"The Mexican people see in the North American plutocracy the worst
enemy of their liberties; . . . they have realized well that the persecution and tortures of which we are the object in this country are to

the desire of the great North American millionaires; that the conditions of tyranny and barbarity, which make it possible for the wicked [to realize] their rapid enrichment, subsist in Mexico . . ." [13]

Thus, if the Communists hoped to win adherents from the ranks of Anarchism, while at the same time trying to identify themselves with the national outlook, they had to emphasize the anti-American theme. In addition, as we shall observe in subsequent chapters, anti-Americanism also coincided with several of the Comintern "lines."

Anti-Americanism was also an attitude of the people, but the identity of these "people" is unclear. An ex-official of the Communist party active in the early 1920's told the writer that he believed the "people" in question were the workers and the intellectuals.[14] He felt that the peasants, as a group, actually had a good impression of the United States through the influence of former "braceros" who had spent some time working in the country. The industrial workers, on the other hand, not having had any direct contact with the United States, were more receptive to the anti-American orientation of Communist propaganda. José C. Valadés felt that the strongest influence in fostering anti-Americanim was (and is) the Mexican intellectual. Since the United States has closed its doors to works published in Mexico or there have not been sufficient translations into English, there had been very little understanding between the intellectuals of both countries, and neither group has had an appreciation of the problems which its counterpart's country has had to face. Herein lies the crux of the anti-American attitude.

Anti-Clericalism

Although the country's persistent anti-clericalism was primarily a struggle against the Church as an organized power rather than against religion *per se*, it was not difficult for the Communists, with an ideology opposed to religion and any organized Church, to take advantage of the issue by identifying their position with those forces opposed to the Church.

The anti-clerical tradition is old. As early as 1644 the conservative "Ayuntamiento" (municipal government) of Mexico City complained to the King that the real property owned by the Church amounted to half of the value of all the property in New Spain.[15] During the wars of independence against Spanish power the loyalty to the crown of the ecclesiastical hierarchy, as distinguished from the parish clergy, laid the foundation for the anti-clerical struggle which was to follow: "Neutrality might have saved it from the charge of allegiance to foreign imperialism which, during the last hundred years, has so frequently been hurled against it." [16]

The Church-State struggle was halted during the Díaz era. When it broke out again during the Revolution of 1910, it was over a new description of the nature of the social order. The concepts of the French Revolution (individualism, liberty, and equality), were opposed to the Church and what it represented—a corporate body whose acts seemed contrary to liberty and equality.

There was also a struggle for political power between the conservative forces who promised "order" and maintenance of the status quo, and those who would use European ideas to remake the society. The Church supported the conservative forces and, as a result, it consistently stood behind the wrong man and the wrong causes. Thus, the Church backed Augustín de Iturbide as Emperor of Mexico, and the dictator Antonio López de Santa Anna against the liberal forces of Benito Juárez. The Church worked for French intervention and encouraged the monarchy of Emperor Maximilian. And since the position of the clergy was strengthened during the period Porfirio Díaz was in power, the Church stood behind the dictator and opposed the Revolution of 1910.

These activities of the Church presented the Communists with a ready-made issue. They were able to utilize the facts of history to portray the clergy as perennial allies of "reactionary" forces, in contrast to the Communists who supported the "progressive" forces of the country. This theme was used often during the Comintern's Third Period: "The Church, yesterday the cruel defender of the colonial regime of the Spanish, today will be an instrument of agitation and of propaganda for American imperialism; the Church, which for centuries was the representative of the feudal-large estate order, today will know how to represent the interests of the capitalist class, of the exploiting patronal class; the Church, internal instrument in order to maintain the popular masses submissive and in ignorance, will initiate again and with double force, its task to destroy in the heart and mind of the masses the little consciousness that the Revolution has given them." [17]

During the revolutionary struggles of the twentieth century, the Church continued to align itself with the conservative forces against the liberals. The clergy opposed the administration of President Francisco I. Madero because it feared any possible educational or agrarian reform which might weaken its power. Thus, there was clerical support for General Victoriano Huerta against the Madero government, and the Church was subject to bitter attack by General Venustiano Carranza, who was trying to overthrow the opportunistic General Huerta.

But the Carranza forces did not oppose the clergy merely because of its opposition to their cause: "The revolutionaries also feared, not the actual but the potential, and somewhat imaginary, opposition of the clergy to the adoption of a comprehensive reform program. Memory of the Church as the traditional arch-opponent of democracy and Liberalism persisted in their minds, and it became very necessary, therefore, to anticipate the inevitable clerical reaction. In short, anti-clericalism had become a tradition in Liberalism." [18]

By identifying their opposition to religion and the Church with the liberal tradition, the Communists were able to offer an ideological appeal to many middle class liberals: "We should not only combat the priest and the fanatic, but we must also combat religion, which as Lenin justly said, is 'the opium of the people' . . . . The organization of the anti-clerical campaign in the country has been insufficient until now. Therefore, the task of resolving the problem from the ideological point of view touches us." [19] Another use of the anti-clerical theme was that by identifying the Church with the Capitalist state, the Communists were able to emphasize their arguments for overthrowing the state.[20]

The subordination of the Church to stricter governmental control was realized under President Carranza in the Constitution of 1917, through Articles 3, 27, and 130. Religious instruction would be allowed under government "vigilance." Church buildings were to belong to the nation, and religious charitable enterprises were to be abolished. Political and property rights of individual clerics were limited. The religious clauses were not enforced, however, by President Carranza or by his successor, President Alvaro Obregón, who wanted to consolidate their political positions and refrained from stirring up additional opposition.

President Calles, however, decided to enforce them, provoking a political crisis. In the spring of 1926, the bishops publicly opposed the religious articles (3, 24, 27, 130 and others), and stated that Catholics should organize to change the Constitution. President Calles then issued a decree putting the religious laws ino effect, closing all religious schools, expelling all foreign priests, and ordering all priests to register with the government.[21] The Mexican episcopate replied by ordering all priests to abandon the churches, and from July 30,

1926 until June 27, 1929, there was no official mass in Mexico. Furthermore, the "Cristero" rebellion broke out in a number of states on behalf of the Church; it dragged on for three years and cost many thousands of lives.

During the Cristero rebellion, the Communists tried to place themselves in the camp of "legitimacy," supporting the government and the Constitution of 1917: "The Unitary Trade Union Confederation declares that it hopes the Government maintains its attitude before the disobedience of the Roman clergy, not accommodating differences in any form but hoping for the support of this attitude to the constitutional disposition of Article 130 and the regulations issued before the conflict." [22] They also formed an Anti-Clerical League with locals throughout the country, called for anti-religious instruction in the schools, anti-religious literature, and full cooperation with the government in fighting the rebels.[23]

Church-State tension persisted. The Portes Gil government had brought about a partial settlement with the Church, but in 1931 renewed conflict during the administration of Ortíz Rubio led to more deportations of priests. This tension lasted until the mid-1930's, which were difficult times for the Mexican government. The influence of Fascism was increasing in the world; President Cárdenas had recently sent General Calles out of the country and was trying to rally his forces for internal unity. In addition, there was a great deal of pressure from United States public opinion concerning the difficulties of the Church.

While the Cárdenas policy was conciliatory toward the Church, it was only made for the sake of expediency. His true feelings perhaps were stated when talking to a group of peasants during the electoral campaign for the Presidency: "The advice which you have received has been that you maintain an attitude of obedience, of submission, that you fall upon your knees and kiss the hands of those who render you no service whatever. . . ." [24] One would never hear President Cárdenas utter the words of his successor, President Avila Camacho: "Yo soy creyente" (I am a believer).

The belief that the strong religious convictions of the Mexicans and other peoples of Latin America present a strong barrier against the influence of Communism[25] is not valid when one considers the religious nature of the Mexican people and the type of anti-clerical struggle which took place. The Mexican man is a nominal Catholic; he will go through the customs of his religion and will attend Mass on Sunday in order to appease his wife. One need only speak to a variety of

men on the subject to reach this conclusion. It is true that the women
are more religious than are the men, but political events are determined
by the men. Furthermore, the anti-clerical struggle did not take place
in the villages, where the people might be expected to be more
religious: "When the battle between Church and State came to a head,
it was fought out by the literate in the city and town, between the
middle class intellectuals, mainly lawyers on the one side and priests
on the other. The lawyers won the battle. The mass of the Indian
communities remained at the margin, without understanding what
the strife was about . . . . Anti-clericalism in Mexico has always been
a middle class doctrine . . . ." [26]

Where do the leaders of a Communist movement come from? The
answer is, of course, the middle class. This was true in Russia and,
as we shall see, in Mexico. The anti-clerical struggle was very
meaningful to the small, but politically powerful, middle class. The
anti-clerical theme, its degree of emphasis peculiar to the environment, was an important Communist propaganda device in attracting
adherents from this segment of the population.

The Labor Movement

The rapid growth of the labor movement in the increasingly in-
dustrialized twentieth century, influenced by the ideologies of Anarchism, Syndicalism, Socialism, and Communism brought the workers
face to face with the modern world. Labor had new demands which it
wanted realized in a hurry; the workers were prone to listen to any
voice which would promise fulfillment of their desires.

Two main themes could be distinguished through the various ideological currents of the labor movement. In the first place, various
groups called for "Direct Action" tactics: violence in the form of
strikes, uprisings, a continuous class struggle, without legal political
activity or cooperation with the government.

In the second place, other groups advocated "Multiple Action":
political activity and, in some cases, cooperation with the government,
holding the strike in reserve with the anticipation of realizing labor's
demands through other political and more peaceful means. The Communists sometimes advocated "Direct Action" and sometimes "Multiple
Action," as they saw possibilities of advantage to the Communist movement. Thus, through flexible tactics, the Communists were able to
parallel the main themes of the developing labor movement.

"Direct Action" was advocated by one of the first labor organizations,

the Great Circle of Workers of Mexico, which existed between 1870-
1880. Its leaders called for a social revolution as the final means of
attaining Socialism and forbade the organization from belonging to
political parties, although individual members could participate in
politics.[27]

Another direct action group which came into existence in 1900,
the Mexican Liberal Party of Ricardo Flores Magón, called the workers
to armed rebellion. It used the name of Socialism, but in reality its
leaders were Anarchists who would put an end to all authority:
"Listen to the 'Regeneration' Anarchists who advised us in every
tone, not to follow leaders but to take possession of the land, of the
water supplies, of the forests, of the mines, of the factories, of the
workshops, and of the means of transportation, making all that the
common property of the inhabitants of the Mexican Republic and
consuming in common the product." [28]

Other Twentieth Century labor groups have also advocated "Direct Action." At its inception in 1912, the House of the World's
Workers (Casa del Obrero Mundial) "was dedicated to a policy of
non-political, direct, and even violent action, with emphasis on the
general strike and sabotage." [29] The Confederation of Labor of the
Mexican Region (Confederación del Trabajo de la Región Mexicana),
created in 1916, was another of these groups, although under General
Obregón it shifted to an alliance with, if not subordination to, the
government. One of the more influential labor organizations formed
in 1921, the General Confederation of Workers (Confederación General
de Trabajadores, or C. G. T.), sustained for many years "the thesis
of 'Direct Action' and non-intervention in political-electoral questions." [30]

The Communists attempted to use the accepted labor tactics and
the slogans of "Direct Action." Thus, often failing to gain control
of the C. G. T., they criticized its leaders for lacking the necessary
revolutionary ardor to lead the class struggle.[31] In 1928, during the
Third Period of the Comintern, the Communists were able to juxtapose
a Comintern "line" with an acceptable labor orientation, by forming
their own trade union: "The Unitary Trade Union Confederation of
Mexico (Confederación Sindical Unitaria de México, or C. S. U. M.)
will be completely against all compromise with the petty bourgeois
government which struggles desperately to maintain the control which
until now it had continued exercising over the proletarian organizations
of Mexico. The Unitary Trade Union Confederation of Mexico considers frankly that the petty bourgeois pseudo-revolutionary govern-

ment has already crossed over to the enemy camp and is each day oriented more toward Fascism." [32]

Borrowing a leaf from the Syndicalists, the Latin American Trade Union Confederation to which the Mexican Communists adhered, would often, during the Third Period, call for a general strike when Communists were called upon to struggle against the outbreak of war.[33] Also, when the Communists called for a revolution against the government, as they did during the Third Period of the Comintern, their ideology was coincidental with the early orientation of the labor movement, i.e., the Anarchists of the Mexican Liberal Party, several years before there was a Communist Revolution in Russia: "The Communist Party calls for the abolition of the imperialist yoke; overthrow of the bourgeois-Junker government and the setting up of a revolutionary workers' and peasants' government on the basis of Soviets of workers,' peasants,' and soldiers' deputies; confiscation of all big undertakings belonging to foreign capitalists; confiscation of the land of the big landowners, the state and the foreign capitalists, and its free distribution among the working peasants." [34]

The second main theme in the labor movement, "Multiple Action," also appeared in the nineteenth century, although the term was not used frequently until the turn of the century. In the summer of 1878, the Mexican Socialist Party was formed in the city of Puebla, and shortly afterwards began to publish a periodical called *The Social Revolution*. The first issue explained the purpose of the new party: "The Mexican Socialists, upon constituting themselves in a party, resolve: To struggle through organizing all the sympathizing elements with the end, in the shortest possible time, to conquer through the legal manner the political power of the Republic and to implant the law of the People, whether by the members of the party or because the Federal Government may adopt it through necessity. . . . The members of the party will call themselves Communists, in order to be distinguished from those who do not accept that the proletariat is constituted as a class party." [35]

During the first decades of the twentieth century, the House of the World's Workers, the dominant factor in the labor movement from 1912-1918, turned from "Direct Action" to "Multiple Action." After the assassination of President Madero, General Huerta actively opposed the organization and it was suppressed in 1913. The workers' leaders then decided to seek some type of accord with the forces of General Carranza. As a result, a pact was signed in which General Carranza promised the workers future support of their unions (including funds) once he had established a government. The workers, on their part, recruited six "Red Battalions" which fought with the Carranza forces in the Revolution. Although, as President, Venustiano Carranza was not sympathetic with the demands of labor, the agreement was important for the development of the labor movement. For one thing, the workers moved away from the Anarcho-Syndicalist tactics of "Direct Action" and decided to cooperate with the forces of General Carranza and, subsequently, with his government, in order to realize their aims. In addition, a pattern was set by which the labor movement would become a political arm of the state.

Other labor groups turned to "Multiple Action." The manifesto of the Socialist Labor Party, founded by Luis N. Morones and several others on February 20, 1917, stated the tactics: "We, who have always avoided taking part in political disputes have decided to widen, by means of MULTIPLE ACTION, our system of action." [36] The manifesto went on to state that the party would present workers' candidates for elections.

In Saltillo, Coahuila, during May 1918, Luis N. Morones formed a second group, the Mexican Federation of Labor (Confederación Regional Obrera Mexicana, or C. R. O. M.), which dominated the labor movement until 1928 and presented a strange mixture of Marxism in theory and "Multiple Action" in practice. The Marxist Constitution of the C. R. O. M. repeated many sections of the *Communist Manifesto* and called for the class struggle, the socialization of industry, and the replacement of the Capitalist by the Proletarian states. As late as 1933, the C. R. O. M. program called for the creation of the "Karl Marx Workers' Superior School" in Mexico City.[37]

In practice however, the Action Group of the C. R. O. M. decided to cooperate with the government, and many of the labor organization's leaders held high governmental posts. Since 1928, however, when the C. R. O. M. lost governmental favor through its refusal of support for the candidacy of ex-President Obregón as successor to General Calles as President, it has never been able to regain the leadership of the labor movement.

In the 1930's the leadership vacuum of labor was filled by the person and the ideological beliefs of Vicente Lombardo Toledano. Under his leadership, the newly-formed Mexican Confederation of Workers (Confederación de Trabajadores de México, or C. T. M.), joined the official party under President Lázaro Cárdenas. The two men were very close in their views of the labor movement. We shall return to Lombardo Toledano and his influence on the labor movement in a later chapter.*

It was not difficult for the Communists to shift their tactics. "Direct Action" coincided with the early revolutionary fervor of the Comintern, which culminated in the Third Period; "Multiple Action" coincided with the tactics of the United Front and the Popular Front. Like the proponents of "Multiple Action," the Communists also found it advantageous to participate in elections. In the 1920's they presented their own candidates and in the era of the Popular Front they supported the candidates of the government: "We shall work to obtain a great popular mobilization in the next elections, to assure the triumph of the candidates of the Popular Front, the triumph of General Manuel Avila Camacho, and (to see) that it represents the triumph of the revolutionary program of the people. . . ." [38]

Not only were the Comunists strong supporters of the Cárdenas government, but Comunists were permitted to participate in certain state governments and even allowed to make electoral alliances to support the "left" of the official government party. [39] Thus, the Communist position was in accord with the doctrine of "Multiple Action" and, in some cases, seemed to go beyond: "The C. T. A. L. (Latin American Federation of Labor) guaranteed the economic cooperation which the countries of Latin America have contributed to the cause of the United Nations, agreeing not to exercise the right to strike for the duration of the war. . . ." [40]

Although the two main themes of the labor movement—"Direct Action" and "Multiple Action"—are somewhat opposed, the Communists were able to shift flexibly from the one to the other to broaden their appeal to the workers. Moreover, there was, in the labor movment, no pattern such as the Church-State conflict, which determined the limits of maneuverability for the Communists. On the contrary, the terrain was unsettled and the Communists attempted to put their flexible tactics to the utmost advantage.

The field of labor offered several other good opportunities for Communist penetration. In the first place, the labor movement was partly a political one. It has been observed that the state created the trade union movement: "The C. R. O. M. was a child of the

---

*Many of the early labor groups existed only for a few years. Some were dissolved and others were incorporated into the larger organizations. Several of the early labor and Socialist leaders became prominent in the C.R.O.M., the C. G. T., and the C. T. M.

Obregón and Calles governments and the C. T. M. was a creature of later administrations." [41] It has been observed, too, that the trade union movement has been built up by the state to increase its own power, causing the two to become interwoven in their outlook and in the interpretation of their interests. A proper understanding of the Communist movement must therefore consider the question of ideological influence. As we shall see at a later point in this study, the C. T. M. was more influential during the administration of President Cárdenas than the C. R. O. M. appeared to be during the Obregón-Calls administrations. The C. T. M. was one of the main pillars of the President's strength. The analysis then leads to the question, which will be answered in a later chapter, of what the ideological orientation of the C. T. M. and its leaders was.

Another opportunity for the Communists was provided by the state of flux of the labor movement. Anarchists, Syndicalists, Socialists, and Communists were all competing for the allegiance of the workers. They all supported the claims for higher wages, fewer hours, and better working conditions. The average worker would follow those leaders who could offer him the most, and leave difficult ideological considerations to the intellectuals. Furthermore, since some of the main labor groups such as the C. R. O. M. and the C. T. M. were strongly inbued with Marxist theory, it was not difficult for the worker to view his interests through a Marxist interpretation. All groups, including the Communists, spoke to him of the evils of Capitalism and of the exploitation of man by man: "While the capitalist order exists, the exploitation of man by man will exist, for which the Unitary Trade Union Confederation of Mexico, through the conduct of the organizations adhered to it, will struggle to destroy the present order of exploitation by implanting a better society in which humanity may definitely be freed." [42]

Regardless of the many opportunities the Communists had to develop their strength in the labor movement, they were not successful in the early part of the twentieth century. Perhaps the reason is partly explained by the fact that Mexico was predominantly agrarian and that the country had had its own non-Communist revolution. As we shall observe, the Communists were of some real influence in organized labor only within the C. T. M. during the Cárdenas period.

Force and Violence

Mexico has experienced the throes of violent upheaval throughout most of its history. There have been three revolutions: 1810, the War of the Reforma (1857-1860), and 1910. Rebellions, barracks revolts (cuartelazos), assassination, and violence became almost a way of life throughout most of the period before World War II.

From the time the royal authority was dissolved and independence was a reality, the armed forces controlled the political development of the country, contributing to violence and disorder. There were good reasons: "The army was the chief gainer from the general dissolution. The weaker the organized community became, the stronger was the army; the weaker the centralized army became, the stronger were the smaller units within the army." [43]

When Augustín de Iturbide led his troops into Mexico City and subsequently made himself Emperor Augustín I, a pattern for violence in politics through competing irresponsible army officers was made which was to last for more than one hundred years. Mexico finally became a republic, but even then military adventurers such as General Santa Anna were able to make and unmake governments throughout most of the nineteenth century. General Porfirio Díaz bought off most of the military leaders to obtain army support for his government, and after Díaz was overthrown, not only were there separate armies under the control of different revolutionary generals, but the army was a society apart completely beyond civilian control, until President Obregón attempted to bring the various factions under the control of the government and to create a standing professional army. The process was finally completed during the administration of Avila Camacho. After 1920 no army revolt was successful and in the 1940's civilian supremacy was established in the political sphere.

The stubborness of governing groups also contributed to political violence. This elite and its adherents had access to the only available income through jobs, commissions, franchises, and prerogatives and would not absorb the new leaders of the younger elements and allow them to share in the spoils of politics. Violent transitions were the only means of governmental change. No efforts to break the cycle of government-by-revolt were made until President Calles attempted to bring the conflicting interests into one official party.

Many of the revolutionary leaders were assassinated, including Generals Emiliano Zapata and Pancho Villa, Presidents Francisco I. Madero, Venustiano Carranza, Adolfo de la Hueata and Alvaro Obregón. Presidential succession through rebellion lasted until 1920, when General Obregón became the last President to assume office through a successful revolt. Nevertheless, revolt accompanied succession crises in

1923, 1927, and 1929. There was also an uprising during the administration of Lázaro Cárdenas.

During the first decades of the twentieth century, the country suffered from what has been called a legitimacy vacuum, with no "stable patterns of legitimate political behavior, (and) no alternatives. . . to the dominance of personality, the absence of public spirit, and the rule of force." [44] The focus of loyalty and faith was the individual leader, not the political and social institutions. The basis of legitimacy—popular sovereignty, jurdical and social equality—was not part of the reality.[45]

The Constitution of 1917, promulgated during the Carranza administration (1916-1920), began a change which eventually brought institutions and policies into the realm of legitimacy. President Obregón (1920-1924) started to implement the land reform and social welfare provisions of the Constitution and encouraged labor organizations. It took many years, however, for the constitutional provisions to become a part of the social and political reality.

The Communist ideology of violent revolution against the bourgeois state corresponded not only with one of the main themes of the Mexican labor movement—"Direct Action"—but with the general environment such as revolutions, struggles between army officers, assassinations, violent transitions of power, and frequent rebellions. The Communists were merely one of several groups of "revolutionaries" and their slogan of revolution became a familiar battle cry for the mass of the people. To reach a wider audience, the revolutionary slogan "dictatorship of the proletariat" [46] was, at the Latin American Communist Congresses of 1929, changed to the "government of the workers and peasants": "The Communist Party of Mexico must be capable of coping with the great tasks imposed upon it by the historical situation. In close connection with the Parties of the imperialist countries, and under the leadership of the C. I., it must exert all its force in order to overthrow the bourgeois rule and set up in its place the government of the worker and peasant masses under the leadership of the Communist Party." [47]

Many years later when constitutional provisions were not realized in practice, the Communists supported the workers and peasants when they refused to lay down their arms because of unsatisfied grievances after the Revolution. This was in hopes that they could gain power by assuming leadership of guerrilla forces in the chaos consequent to a "legitimacy vacuum." "When elements of a still revolutionary character seek the support of the peasants and workers of Latin America, we must put down as one of the minimum organizational conditions, the right of those workers and peasants to separate armed detachments under their own leadership, with their own program, and maintaining the status of guerrilla forces in the general struggles that take place. . . . This tactic has been applied with some success in Mexico, and as a result, whole sections of the peasantry are armed today, and in spite of the repeated efforts to disarm them, they retain their arms." [48]

Communist ideology and tactics coincided with much of the national outlook as expressed in the force and violence of the Revolution of 1910. The Communists attempted to portray themselves as a revolutionary party trying to gain adherents in a country which was experiencing a genuine revolution. The appeal of Communism might have been strong for those who were disillusioned with their own revolution.

Nevertheless, the Communist movement probably would have assumed a violent form through its own volition inasmuch as the Mexican Communists were deeply committed to the Comintern's policy of unceasing struggle and violence. During the period of the Popular Front in the mid-30's, as we shall see in a later chapter, the Communists shifted their tactics and began to cooperate with the government. Coincidentally, this was also a period during which the governments moved further away from force and violence in the settlement of disputes and approached a greater degree of political maturity.

During most of the period under consideration in this study, there were two elements which could have made the terrain propitious for the development of Communism as a totalitarian movement. For one thing, the political and social environment was one of chaos in which there was no respect for authority. The Constitution of 1917 was not implemented to any degree and rebellion was an accepted instrument of social and economic change. A contemporary philosopher has related the decline of authority to the development of the Nazi and Soviet regimes. We submit that the same criterion can be applied to the Mexican example with equal validity: "The rise of the Fascist, Communist and totalitarian movements, and the development of two totalitarian regimes, Stalin's after 1929 and Hitler's after 1938, took place against a background of more or less general, more or less dramatic breakdown of all traditional authorities. Nowhere was this breakdown the direct result of the regimes or movements themselves, but it seemed as though totalitarianism, in the form of regimes as well as of movements, was best fitted to take advantage of a general political and social atmosphere in which the validity of authority itself was radically doubted." [49]

A second factor which helped the Communists was the general dissatisfaction which often followed the rule of military governments. It was not so much that the Communists failed to infiltrate the army and therefore failed in the country as some would indicate,[50] as much as that the Communists could call for a revolution against any regime, even when the regime seemed to have the support of the army. The recent revolution in Cuba proves that such a tactic can be successful: "The Workers and Peasants Revolution, the great question which is presented with compelling character to the workers, the Indians, the peasants. . . . To initiate the first battles against the military juntas; to struggle for the revindications of the workers of the city and of the field, for the conquest of the land by the peasants and Indians, for the trade union and political organization of the proletariat. For struggle, for insurrection, and for victory."[51]

Social and Economic Problems—the Land

It is highly probable that social and economic problems, chiefly the question of land, turned some people to Communism as a salvation. The extreme poverty of the country, the great lack in the fields of public health, sanitation, literacy, education, and housing did not allow for simple or immediate remedies.

In addition, the insufficiency of the railroads resulted in various parochial markets, preventing the formation of a national market and a single nation. The enormous amount of capital required to correct the railroad's shortage of rolling stock and equipment[52] would have meant foreign investment, and it was politically unwise for any administration to try to attract foreign capital. Support for the Revolution involved opposition to foreign interests.

A chronic problem for Mexico and all of Latin America has been inflation. Paradoxically, the period of increased economic activity since 1941 brought about a worsening of conditions for the population at large. Both external and internal causes were involved. The country had an export surplus during the war and a capital inflow unaccompanied by goods ("refugee" capital from Europe and local capital which had come back from Europe for greater security). Within the country there were increased military expenditures, public works outlays, more investments in industry, and wage increases. All these factors led to higher prices and less real income for the industrial and agricultural workers, which caused a lowering of standards of living. The result was social tension and unrest.

This was a more dangerous period than many realize: "In 1943 a short crop of corn caused the price of this basic item in the diet of the Mexican people to skyrocket, and led to public protests, even riots, in all parts of the country." [53]

The country also had the dual problem of most of Latin America—growing population and limited resources. Mexico's "population boom" got underway after 1920, as order was restored somewhat and the reorganization of economic, political, and social life was begun. By 1940 the population of 1870 had doubled as the result of a rising birth-rate and a falling death-rate. The agricultural yield, however, had remained fairly constant. In addition, the agricultural resources had been deteriorating for centuries: "Since the Conquest the desert area has increased and the remaining soils have been impoverished." [54] Excluding irrigation, approximately seven per cent of the land in Mexico is arable, as contrasted with approximately 21 per cent in the United States. The lack of arable land and the low yield of what there was, produced a land-hunger in the nineteenth and early twentieth centuries similar to that which preceded the Russian Revolution of 1917. The people expected the Revolution to satisfy this hunger.

In their attempt to gain revolutionary power the Communists used the economic and social problems of the country to influence the "conscience stricken" intellectuals as well as the poor masses. Their promises of quick methods of eradicating illiteracy and disease, for accelerating economic development, and for raising living standards, had a strong attraction for some of the educated, politically conscious individuals who composed the small but growing middle class. Although they drew members from many income ranks, there were relatively more from the middle than from the lower.

The Revolution had neither a Lenin to become the center of revolutionary doctrine nor a clearly-expressed ideology. When, early in the Revolution, President Madero developed his *Plan de San Luis Potosí,* he saw his mission as political; viz., restoring the Constitution of 1857 and imposing democracy. He simply was unaware of the forces built up by centuries of economic oppression. The voices—few at first—that called for economic emancipation grew louder and, making the issue of land paramount, changed his political slogan—"Effective Suffrage; No Reelection"—into a call for agrarian reform—"land and liberty." The revolutionary leaders who followed Madero were forced to face the social and economic issues of the time.

One leader who recognized the importance of the land question was Ricardo Flores Magón. Around the turn of the century, his Liberal Party began to publish a periodical called *Regeneración*. One of its articles, published February 11, 1911, showed a great deal of foresight in recognizing the type of revolution the country was to experience: "We poor people need a social revolution and not a political revolution, that is, we need a revolution which places in the hands of all men and women, the land which until today has been the exclusive patrimony of a few spoiled people of fortune." [55]

The cry for land persisted in the Revolution. Writing some twenty years after Magón's article in *Regeneración*, the Communists called attention to the land problem: "The conclusion is, without question, that the central problem in Mexico is the land problem, the level which moved the rural masses in the bourgeois Revolution of 1910, and which will move them again in the coming Workers' and Peasants' Revolution." [56]

Another leader, Emiliano Zapata, in all probability influenced the agrarian programs of Carranza, Obregón, Calles, and Cárdenas. It is difficult to overestimate the influence of this man who became a symbol for the landless peasant: "The significance of Zapata is indicated by the fact that 'agrarismo' has become almost synonymous with 'Zapatismo'." [57]

Zapata's ideas were incorporated in the *Plan de Ayala*, published on November 28, 1911.[58] Article 6 of this plan called for giving the land back to the "villages or citizens who have their titles to these properties, of which they have been deprived by the bad faith of our oppressors, and . . . maintain these at all costs with arms in their hands." [59] Article 7 stated that only one third of the land would be taken and paid for. Article 8 added that those who opposed the plan would have the remaining two thirds of their land nationalized.

The Communists tried to identify themselves with national heroes such as Zapata. One of the issues of *El Machete*, the Communist party newspaper, had the following headline: "THE COMMUNIST PARTY WILL CONCLUDE THE WORK OF ZAPATA." [60] The Communists used such slogans to emphasize their stand that the Revolution could be brought to a successful conclusion only under their leadership.[61]

The turning point from the purely political and military phase of the Revolution to a broadened economic and social movement was General Carranza's decree of January 6, 1915. Because the Carranza forces ultimately established themselves in power, this decree became the first legal source of the agrarian program of the Revolution. The heart of the decree is the third article: "The people who, needing them, may lack communal lands, or who may not be able to gain their restitution through lack of titles, through the impossibility of identifying them or because they may have been transferred legally, will be able to obtain a sufficient portion of the land in order to be provided with the basic necessities, the indispensable land for that effect, which is found immediately contiguous to the interested people, being expropriated by . . . the national Government." [62]

The essence of this now-famous decree is incorporated in Article 27 of the Constitution of 1917. The Carranza administration seemed nevertheless to be somewhat out of sympathy with the agrarian (and labor) principles of the Constitution. The President continually neglected agrarian demands and moved very slowly in developing an active land program, as indicated by Table II, which shows the amount of land distributed by the various administrations.

In order to identify themselves with the grievances of the peasants and to attract followers, the Communists would criticize any administration in the case of the land question: "In order to contain the revolutionary drive of the masses, Carranza fabricated the Law of January 6, the Constitution of 1917 and, within it, Article 27 which was to realize the restitution . . . of communal lands. But in practice neither one nor the other law was fulfilled." [63]

Alvaro Obregón, the first President who turned toward the social and economic requirements of the Revolution, started to implement the land reform and the social welfare provisions of the Constitution. The rate of land distribution, however, was only gradually accelerated during that period. Table II shows not much difference between the amount of land distributed by the Obregón government in four years and that distributed by the administration of Portes Gil in one year.

President Calles saw the Revolution as progressing through two avenues—encouragement of the labor movement and persecution of the Church—thus, though he continued land reform there was to be no drastic change in land tenure during his administration: "By reason of the relation between the population and the expanse of the Republic, as well as on account of the state of culture in which the masses are found and the slight resources which they possess, it would be foolish to destroy the productiveness of the land. I speak and fight for the compliance of the agrarian policy of the Revolution, for in this lies the revindication of the right of the people to live. To satisfy this necessity, the breaking up of the large estates which are yet intact and which because of their size and the system under which they are worked constitute a monopoly of the soil, must be brought about through evolutionary proceedings, amply planned and studied, backed by a firm system of agricultural credit and by the organization of cooperative societies by the small farmers." [64]

While President Calles did distribute more land than his predecessor, Alvaro Obregón, much more could have been given to the peasants, as indicated by the period 1935-45 of Table II.

The Communists spoke for many of the peasants when they pointed out that the accomplishments of the Revolution did not live up to its promises: "The Revolution of 1910 had as a fundamental task the dissolution of the property of the large estates and the handing over of all the land to the peasant class. And the Revolution of 1910 has not fulfilled this task." [65] Furthermore, when the Comintern line of the Third Period, begun in 1928 toward the end of the Calles administration, demanded a more militant anti-government stand, the Communists were able to center slogans around the land question. One headline of El Machete read: "IF THE GOVERNMENT DOES NOT WANT TO HAND OVER THE LAND TO THE PEASANTS, THE PEASANTS SHOULD TAKE IT WITH THEIR OWN FORCES." [66]

TABLE II

AREA OF LAND DISTRIBUTED UNDER THE AGRARIAN
PROGRAM BY INDIVIDUAL PRESIDENTS, 1916-1945°

Venustiano Carranza	1916-1920	166,571
Alvaro Obregón	1921-1924	1,124,672
Plutarco Elías Calles	1925-1928	2,979,878
Emilio Portes Gil	1929	1,003,124
Pascual Ortiz Rubio	1930-1932	1,638,124
Abelardo Rodríguez	1933-1934	864,926
Lázaro Cárdenas	1935-1940	17,890,577
Manual Avila Camacho	1941-1945	4,951,388
Total		30,619,321

°The information is based on figures given by Nathan L. Whetten, *Rural Mexico* (The University of Chicago Press, 1948), p. 125. The time periods do not refer to Presidential years in office. Frequently, the term of one President would end and that of another would begin during the same year. Therefore, Table II refers only to the full years of land distribution. Table I gives the years the individual Presidents spent in office.

After the high point of land distribution for one year was reached by the Portes Gil administration in 1929, the succeeding years, as indicated by Table II, were marked by a continuous decline in the redistribution program until the administration of Lázaro Cárdenas who often expressed his thoughts about land distribution while campaigning for the Presidency in 1934: "If I am elected President, there will be no one who can stop me until the peasant has received the best land and the state has given him all financial, moral and material aid possible. . . . On the banners of the Revolutionary movement in which we have been fighting and in which I have had a personal part since 1913, it is written that lands . . . shall be given to the peasants." [67]

Table II indicates that during President Cárdenas' administration, more than twice as much land was distributed than under all the previous governments combined. President Cárdenas emphasized the development of the collectivized *ejido*, in which the land was owned by the village and cultivated by the peasants in common.

However, after reaching a peak in 1937, during which more than 5,000,000 hectares were distributed, the land distribution program was considerably slowed down by the Cárdenas administration in the years 1938-1940 for a variety of reasons: "The decline from 1937 was probably due partly to the fact that the available haciendas for expropriation were becoming scarce and partly to the social and economic confusion resulting from such a sudden and widespread altering of existing land-tenure relationships. . . . Tremendous problems confronted the administration: The new communal lands needed organizing; agricultural credit had to be provided; boundary disputes required settlement." [68]

Even though the Cárdenas government distributed a tremendous quantity of land compared to other administrations, when the rate of land distribution decreased sharply during the latter part of the administration it became vulnerable to Communist criticism as they continued in their effort to identify themselves with the peasants' struggle for land. [69]

During the administration of President Avila Camacho, the land reform of the Cárdenas government was not reversed, nor was it extended very far. Communal lands and the medium-sized small private holdings continued as the basis of land reform but as shown in Table II, the rate of land distribution under Avila Camacho was considerably slowed until 1945, when less than 600,000 hectares were distributed. The administration needed to stimulate the production of food and war materials for World War II and President Avila Camacho, therefore, gave guarantees of "no nationalization" to the remaining private landowners: "We shall continue sustaining the agrarian conquests in order that the worker of the field may be free, owner of a modest destiny but his own; the land has been given to him, now we shall continue fortifying him economically; we shall protect small property because there, where the Revolution finds the land already well distributed, it does not have any reason to affect the modest proprietors. . . ." [70]

The government also deemphasized the agricultural program in favor of producing many manufactured goods which could no longer be purchased from the United States because of the war. Industrialization intensified during this period and was clearly the heart of the government's economic policy by the end of 1946.

Although the Communists supported the candidacy of Avila Camacho as President, throughout his administration they continually emphasized their theme that his land policy was not in the interests of the peasants: "Equally serious to the Mexican Revolution is the agrarian crisis. During the years of the Cárdenas regime, the program of land distribution was carried forward at a faster rate than ever before. Large estates were confiscated from their feudal and foreign imperialist owners and handed to the peasantry. Recently, however, agrarian reform has completely slowed down. A manifesto of the Communist Party charges that the distribution of land has been completely discontinued since last autumn. Moreover, under a recent presidential decree, hundreds of peasants are being forced to give back their communal lands . . . to the big landowners." [71]

The quantity of land distributed was only part, although the most important part, of the land problem. In addition there were also the problems of agricultural credit, adequate machinery, the size of the plots, and the quality of the land. The government did not establish a national bank of Ejido Credit until 1936. As late as 1945, the bank was making loans to only about 14 percent of those who worked the communal lands.[72] Most of the funds seemed to go to the north and north Pacific regions though most of the population was concentrated in the central region. In 1950, there were still over 70,000 landless peasants who were not on communal land. Many others had uneconomical plots smaller than 10 hectares. In addition, there was the problem of the land itself: "A jolting lesson, brought home clearly, is a basic consideration, 'Mexico has poor land, and little of it.' The fundamental problem of poverty could therefore not be solved by the right distribution of land, which was the main slogan in 1910." [73]

Although the Communists emphasized the question of land distribution in their propaganda, they did not hesitate to point out other shortcomings of the agrarian program: "The Plenum of the Central Committee of our Party considered that the two principal obstacles for the development of our national economy are first, the subsistence of the great agrarian property, which impedes the flourishing of agriculture and is the fundamental cause of the poverty and backwardness of our country; and second, the system of archaic credit, which does not correspond to the revolutionary character of our institutions of Government." [74]

That agrarian reform was a major achievement of the Revolution cannot be denied. However, one cannot equate the agrarian reform of the Revolution with a lessening of the appeal of Communism, as has been suggested.[75] The desire of the peasants for land was used as a rallying point many years after the first land reform, and the often-used Communist slogan of "all land to the peasants" coincided with that desire.

In addition, the Communists furthered their propaganda aims by identifying themselves with the Revolution: "The Communist Party, as inheritor of all the revolutionary tradition of its people, from Hidalgo to Cárdenas, is assigned as a task that of contributing decisively to the definite overthrow of those who are opposed to the development of the liberating movement, initiated in 1810 and still not terminated, that of contributing to the consummation of the economic (and political) independence of Mexico and to the total liberation of the Mexican people." [76] Although the effort was not successful, it did have propaganda value.

Conclusions

The various themes discussed in this chapter showed a coincidence of the national outlook with the Communist position. Both the Communists and many non-Communist intellectuals opposed American imperalism and the Church. The main ideological currents of the labor movement were consistent with the shift in Communist tactics, which reflected the changing policies of the Comintern. The Communist belief in violent revolution as the road to power fitted in with the tradition of force and violence. The acute social and economic problems made Communism attractive to certain segments of the population; the Communists were able to utilize the land-hunger of the peasants as a strong propaganda weapon. The emphasis which the Communists placed on certain slogans was peculiar to and determined by the Mexican environment.

In addition, three main factors prevailed. In the first place, the country was not unified from within. The force of anti-Americanism for latent Mexican nationalism was offset by the pervasive violence. The

"Pax Porfiriana" (i.e., the relative peace under the regime of Porfirio Díaz) disintegrated soon after the turn of the century, and for the most part the armed forces were involved with internal rebellions and not with an external threat which could unify the country.

In the second place, middle class intellectuals promoted anti-Americanism and led the anti-clerical struggle. It was the middle class intellectuals, as represented by Vicente Lombardo Toledano, who assumed the leadership of the labor movement and generally sought means to alleviate the social and economic conditions of the country.

In the third place, many of the hopes of the Revolution were not fulfilled. It cannot be denied that the Revolution did attain certain positive achievements: political reform, establishment of unions, incorporation of the Indian into national life, initiation of industrialization, etc. However, the reform of the landholding system was only partially realized in practice, and chronic social and economic problems persisted through the end of World War II. In addition, the industrialization which developed rapidly under President Avila Camacho did not benefit the mass of people, workers or peasants, due to inflationary pressures on the economy.

Because the social and economic problems, in the main, were not solved by the Revolution, one might conclude that the peasants, as well as some workers, would be attracted to Communism. But this was not necessarily the case. It is very difficult for Communist and non-Communist groups to organize the agricultural workers in Latin America: "because they are not so concentrated into one spot; because the rural areas are out of the mainstream of national life; because agriculture is less productive than industry and presents fewer possibilities of workers' gaining through organization; . . ."[77] We shall see, presently, the difficulties the Communists faced in their efforts to organize the peasants.

However, the failures of the Revolution were important in bringing certain middle class intellectuals into the Communist fold, although the middle class as a whole was not affected to any great degree. Many of the Communists, youths who were active in the early years of the Communist movement in their country, were disillusioned with the Mexican Revolution and considered the Russian Revolution of 1917 as the ideal.[78] These were the indigenous elements that cooperated with the foreign "agents" to form the Communist movement of Mexico.

CHAPTER III

BEGINNING OF THE MEXICAN COMMUNIST MOVEMENT

Although the Comintern did not recognize an "official" Communist party from Mexico until 1922, the first stage of the Communist movement in the country began about 1917. In that year a small group which considered itself "Communist" was organized. Between 1917-1922 the first foreign "agents" appeared, various Communist organizations were formed and Communist periodicals were published. By the end of 1927 meetings were held in Moscow between representatives of the Comintern and a few Latin American Communists. However, Moscow did not present a "thesis" for Latin America or develop an organized program until the Sixth Congress of the Comintern in 1928. As we shall see in the next section, the Mexican Communist movement arose from personal and ideological interests which had little if anything to do with Communism at the outset.

The First Foreign "Agents"

One of the first foreign agents was Manabendra Nath Roy, who came to Mexico in 1918. Since the Comintern was created in 1919, Roy was not sent as an agent of the international Communist organization as some writers have claimed.[1] An Indian nationalist who had been struggling against the British in India, he escaped to the United States but was soon forced to leave and fled to Mexico.[2] Strongly anti-British, Roy turned to the Soviet Union to get help but he did not become an important Comintern agent until after he left Mexico in 1920.[3]

The case of M. N. Roy is an example of the Comintern's opportunism during its first years. Without an efficient apparatus in 1919-1920, the Comintern recruited sympathizers by espousing the cause of those whom it believed could be useful—even Indian nationalism and opposition to the British. The response of many of these agents was to support the Comintern and Moscow's position without taking orders, similar to the "fellow travelers" of today.

A few months after Roy arrived in the country, an American named Linn A. E. Gale appeared. A deserter from the United States army, Gale had fled to Mexico to escape the American authorities. Gale never had direct contact with Moscow and the "Communist" party which he helped form was never recognized by the Comintern. Both he and Roy joined the Mexican Socialist Party for a time. Gale advocated his anti-American ideas through a magazine called *Gale's;* Roy espoused his anti-British views through a periodical called *El Socialista.*

Other foreigners arrived during that period: José Allen, Frank Seaman (Charles Francis Phillips), Fort Mayer, M. Paley, Michael Borodin, and others. Some were Anarchists and others Communists; with the exception of Borodin, probably none were sent by the Comintern, and only a few became important even for a brief time in the Communist movement in Mexico.

Moscow's overriding concern during the period from 1918-1921 was the Allied blockade against the Soviet Union imposed after the latter had surrendered to Germany during World War I. Contacts were made and agents were sent to create a propaganda campaign which would break the blockade and obtain commercial relations for the Soviet Union. In Mexico the plan was to put pressure on the United States with a campaign against "Yankee Imperialism." The plan also included the establishment of a Communist party and other Communist-controlled organizations. In 1918 José Allen, Felipe Carrillo Puerto (who subsequently became Governor of Yucatán), and others created a "Latin American Bureau of the Third International." They also formed a Red Marxist Group (Grupo Marxista Rojo) which was a propaganda arm for the "Bureau."

The National Socialist Congress

Various groups and individuals came together in September, 1919, in an attempt to form one political party of the proletariat. Present were representatives of the Socialist Labor Party, organized by Luis N. Morones in 1917, representatives of the Mexican Federation of Labor (C. R. O. M.), Socialist and labor groups from different states throughout the country, and others.[4] Individuals representing various degrees of the left attended—among them José Allen, Frank Seaman, Manabendra Nath Roy, Linn A. E. Gale and Luis N. Morones.

Dissension was rife. Gale spoke bitterly against Morones and opposed his seating, but was overruled by the majority. Gale also opposed the efforts to control the Congress by Roy and his followers, who made up a majority of the National Committee.[5] It soon became evident that the Congress was split into three groups. The left wing wanted to create a Communist party which would adhere to the

Comintern (the First Congress of the Comintern was held in March of 1919). This group included Roy, José Allen, Frank Seaman, and others. The right wing group, composed of Morones and his followers, wanted to form a Socialist party similar to those which adhered to the Second International. Then there was a third current headed by Gale who was seeking recognition for his group from the Comintern. The resultant confusion among these groups was probably caused by the clash between Gale and Roy for control of the Congress.

The resolution which was approved by the Congress and allowed for electoral activity and the class struggle called for the dictatorship of the proletariat:

"As we are in favor of political action in cooperation with industrial Communism to unify the activity of the working class, we do not deny the value of the vote and the success of electing candidates to public positions, but always provided that this may not divert the action of the effective struggle of the classes." [6] Such political action must "propagate the idea of the overthrow of capitalism by means of industrial conquest of political power, until arriving at the transistory establishment of the dictatorship of the proletariat."

It might be pointed out that this resolution of a "Socialist Congress" generally accorded with the orientation of the First Congress of the Comintern. Moscow expected that world revolution would take place in the immediate future and that the dictatorship of the proletariat would replace the Capitalist state. Furthermore, participation in elections was in agreement with Lenin's call for Communist activity in bourgeois parliaments.

Almost immediately after the Congress, the Mexican Socialist movement split into three parts: One group was led by Gale, another by Roy. The third group consisted of the remainder of the Mexican Socialists who either stayed in the Socialist party or joined the Mexican Labor Party formed by Morones a few months after the Congress ended. Contrary to the experiences of most of the Socialists in other countries, the split in the Mexican Socialist movement was not a result of the promulgation of the Twenty-One Conditions, which actually took place several months later, but stemmed from groups competing for power.

Although ideological differences seemed to play a secondary role, the three groups tried to justify their disagreement on policy grounds. Those who remained in the Mexican Socialist Party re-affirmed their support of the Second International and refused to apply for admission to the Comintern.

Gale designated his group the left wing of the Mexican Socialist Party and referred to Roy and his followers as the right wing.[7] He accused Roy of failing to repudiate the Second International and for not following Moscow until very late in the game when the National Socialist Congress was almost over.[8] Once the Congress terminated, Roy and Gale formed their own organizations.

Two Communist Parties

A few days after the National Socialist Congress ended, Roy succeeded in having Gale expelled from the Mexican Socialist Party.[9] Gale and his faction then held a meeting in Mexico City (toward the end of September, 1919) and formed the Communist Party of Mexico (Partido Comunista de México). The executive committee consisted of Gale, Enrique H. Arce, George Barreda, Fulgenico C. Luma, Sr., Adolfo Santibañez, C. F. Tabler, Dmitri Nikitin, J. C. Parker, and A. P. Araujo.[10]

In the meantime, Roy was having a great deal of difficulty trying to convince the Mexican Socialists to change the name of their party and seek admission to the Comintern. His efforts ended in failure and he was subsequently expelled from the Mexican Socialist Party.

Toward the end of 1919 or early in 1920, the Communist Party of the Mexican Proletariat (Partido Communista del Proletariado Mexicano) was formed in the city of Tacuba.[11] Whether Roy took a direct part in forming the party, or whether it was formed by his followers after Roy had left Mexico[12] is unclear. José Allen, the first Secretary General, led the establishment of the new party, along with Frank Seaman and Manuel Díaz Ramírez; Allen, Felipe Carrillo Puerto, and Elena Torres were members of the first executive committee. This was the party which was subsequently accepted by the Comintern.

The Communist Party of the Mexican Proletariat followed the orientation of the Comintern rather closely before its formal adherence to the international Communist organization in 1922 and its acceptance by the Comintern. This can be observed in the party's Constitution: "In order to realize its aspirations, the Mexican Revolutionary Communist Party considers indispensable the establishment of Socialism of the state under the Dictatorship of the Proletariat, as a prior step in order to arrive at National Communism, the base of Universal Communism." The Constitution also followed Lenin's dictum in recognizing the usefulness of political activity: "To cooperate with bourgeois political parties when it may be necessary, but never to become sub-ordinate to them. . ." [13]

After the Third Congress of the Comintern, which met in Moscow during the summer of 1921, the party followed Radek's emphasis on agitation and organization, and his caution against premature revolutionary attempts. The First Congress of the Communist Party of the Mexican Proletariat, which took place from December 25-31, 1921, approved the following resolution:

"The Communist Party of Mexico (i.e., of the Mexican Proletariat) recommends to the workers not to take part in the riots which are prepared by diverse political groups, because the participation of the workers in these riots cannot but weaken the forces of the Mexican proletariat, which ought to guard these forces for the Social Revolution. The Communist Party of Mexico will indicate to the workers the opportune moment in order to enter the combat and to take advantage of the political moment, transforming it into a proletarian revolution." [14]

The Communist Party of Mexico, organized by Linn A. E. Gale and others, differed from the Communist Party of the Mexican Proletariat in two respects. In the first place, evidence points to the fact that the party had a working relationship with the Carranza government. Gale denied that his magazine, *Gale's,* was printed by the government printing office.[15] He wrote extensively, however, of an interview he had had with President Carranza in December 1918, which showed the President to be sympathetic toward his ideas. During the interview, Gale expressed his anti-interventionist views (i.e., anti-Americanism) to the President and asked if the government would be able to donate paper to the magazine. President Carranza assented to the request, and *Gale's* received "small" quantities of paper from the government.[16]

Gale and his party subsequently reacted favorably to the Carranza government: "The Mexican government is, to be sure, more tolerant of differing opinions and permits far more freedom of speech and press than the black reactionary regime of Wilson, Wall Street, Palmer, and Burleson." [17] This praise of President Carranza and his government contrasts sharply with the views of other "agents" who were in Mexico and sympathetic to Allen's Communist party. One of these foreigners, Irwin Granich, also a deserter from the United States Army, wrote of the "white terror" of President Carranza and the shooting of peasant leaders by government troops.[18]

The extreme anti-American attitude of Gale and his Communist

Party of Mexico coincided with the Carranza government's doctrine of non-intervention: "The Communist Party is naturally opposed to intervention in Mexico. It does not want Mexico made into a doormat for American imperialism. It believes the Mexican masses can work out their own destiny better than a few men in Wall Street. And it is eternally and everlastingly against the shedding of working class blood in another capitalist war . . . Intervention in Mexico has been postponed. Wall Street has tested American sentiment and found it too hostile to the project for another war . . . A wave of indignation has swept the United States that makes even the hardened despots of Imperialism tremble and crouch." [19] Gale and the Communist Party of Mexico also used the friction between the Carranza government and the United States oil companies to strengthen their anti-American position: "Big Business in the United States always wanted Mexico, but now it is a matter of absolute necessity from a commercial standpoint. It must have Mexico's oil—all of it." [20]

Why did the Carranza government favor, and in all probability support, the Communist Party of Mexico under Gale and his associates? President Carranza shared some of Gale's anti-American feelings. As a revolutionary general, he had seen his country invaded by American troops. As President, he was at the head of a government which came into conflict with certain powerful economic interest groups of the United States. It appears that the President perceived it advantageous to utilize a Communist party to give a wider propaganda base to his anti-American views. Gale and the other leaders of the Communist Party of Mexico welcomed governmental support in order to further their own ends. This was a case in which Communism, in the form of a group which considered itself to be a Communist party, was aided in its development through the impact of local conditions which had nothing to do with the Comintern.

The Communist Party of Mexico, under Gale, differed from the Communist Party of the Mexican Proletariat in its involvement in the activities of the Mexican branch of the Industrial Workers of the World (I. W. W.), an Anarcho-Syndicalist organization which worked for the realization of "Industrial Communism" in which all power would be in the hands of the people organized into branches of industrial unions. The I. W. W. refused to join the Comintern, however, because it rejected the idea of a political party and would not take part in parliamentary activity.[21]

Because the leaders of the Communist Party of Mexico believed that the I. W. W. would become the backbone of the revolutionary

movement in the country,[22] they actively cooperated with it and both
Gale and Tabler were on the I. W. W.'s executive committee. At the
National Socialist Congress, Gale and his faction had wanted to organize the I. W. W. in Mexico and "take concrete economic action,"
but were opposed by Roy, Frank Seaman, and their followers.[23]

For a while the Communist Party of Mexico, probably through its
close ideological agreement with the I. W. W., found itself opposing
the views of Lenin. During the First Congress of the Comintern in
March of 1919, Lenin had criticized "ultra-left" party branches partly
because of their refusal to take part in parliamentary activity. One
year after this Congress, the Mexican Communist party was still rejecting electoral and parliamentary activity "except in very rare in-
stances." [24] It was not until two years after the First Congress of the
Comintern and after Gale had been deported by the Mexican government, that the party agreed that parliaments should be utilized by
Communists as Lenin had stated.[25]

This does not mean, however, that the Communist Party of the
Mexican Proletariat, established by José Allen and others, was not
influenced by Anarchism and Anarcho-Syndicalism. On the contrary, the resolutions of its First Congress showed that these were the
predominating ideas: "The party should be be a-political, it should
not participate in any elections however important they may be, it
should not obey the laws of the country and has to combat them, it
should adopt direct action (terrorism and sabotage) as the essential
form of struggle." [26] But the influence of Anarchism and Anarcho-
Syndicalism in the early years of the life of a Communist party was
one thing (the Communist Party of the Mexican Proletariat was not
unique in this respect); active cooperation and participation in the
activities of the I. W. W. was another. Furthermore, Gale and his
associates tried to influence the workers through the I. W. W.; José
Allen and his associates attempted to lure away the workers by
creating a Communist labor organization which competed with the
I. W. W. for the allegiance of the workers.

The beginning of the end for the Communist Party of Mexico
was the assassination of Venustiano Carranza in May of 1920. The
provisional government under Adolfo de la Huerta deported several
foreign Communists who were members of the Communist Party of
Mexico, notably Tabler and Gale.[27] The latter was sent back to the
United States as a deserter. The succeeding administration under
President Obergón continued the expulsions, including foreign Communists who were members of the Communist Party of the Mexican

Proletariat such as José Allen and Frank Seaman.[28] The Communist Party of Mexico ceased to exist following the deportation of many of its leaders. But the Communist Party of the Mexican Proletariat survived the expulsion of its most prominent leaders. It was reorganized and became the Communist Party of Mexico.

The Appearance of New Foreign Agents

A new group of foreign agents, several sent by the Comintern, entered Mexico in the years 1920-1921. The blockade against the Soviet Union was still in force. Although by the fall of 1920, a Bolshevik victory seemed assured in the Russian civil war, there was still fear that the Capitalist countries, particularly Great Britain perhaps joined by the United States, would launch an all-out attack. To offset this possibility, Moscow had been pushing Bolshevik propaganda in various parts of the world. The mission of the Comintern agents was to divert the attention of the United States to the troubles in Mexico and thus make the Americans reluctant to join Great Britain in any large-scale military operation against the Soviet Union. The United States might also be inclined to withdraw from the blockade and the joint military effort against the Bolsheviks.

Michael Borodin, the Comintern agent sent to Mexico in 1920,[29] asked for Roy's cooperation in developing a Communist party acceptable to the Comintern in return for their support of Hindu independence.[30] His approval of Roy's party rather than Gale's meant that the Communist Party of the Mexican Proletariat was subsequently accepted by the Comintern. Borodin and Roy, as Mexican representatives, returned to Moscow for the forthcoming Second Congress of the Comintern in the summer of 1920.[31]

There were several factors in Borodin's decision to encourage Roy's party instead of the one formed by Gale, Tabler and others. In the first place, Gale's party was probably too close to the Carranza government to suit the Comintern leaders. Secondly, the Comintern doctrine of "democratic centralism" was not compatible with concurrent membership in a Communist party and the Anarcho-Syndicalist I. W. W. Furthermore, Gale had deserted the United States Army and was a man without a country. In contrast was Roy, a Hindu nationalist, who could be useful in any future Communist designs on India.

In 1921, the Comintern emphasis was on Communist organization and preparation. Sen Katayama and Luis Fraina (Lewis Corey), Comintern agents well-known in Communist circles, were sent to organize the incipient Communist movement. A person by the name of Natacha Michaelowna also appeared on the scene. In addition several Latin American Communists entered the country—Sebastian Sanvicente, José Rubio, Felipe Recinos, Antonia Sánchez, Leopold Hormachea, Genaro Laurito, and others.

These emissaries tried to organize the Mexicans to take part in election campaigns. But the Mexican Communists, still under the influence of Anarchist ideas, at first refused to have anything to do with such tactics. Katayama and Fraina were, however, well-financed and the Mexicans were persuaded to go through the motions. Posters were made, reports were issued and meetings were held; but much of the money was "lost" and the Mexican Communists never did participate in an electoral campaign.[32]

The agents themselves also contributed to the failure of the mission, which shows how little the Comintern leaders understood about the Mexican scene. It is true that Fraina tried to organize the electoral campaigns, but the contribution of Katayama to the purpose of organizing the local Communists was negligible. They fought over money; they did not speak Spanish; and they were generally out of touch with Mexican political reality.[33]

The record of the first foreign "agents," those who appeared of their own volition and those who were sent by the Comintern, was rather spotty. The work of Allen and Roy was probably the most effective of all the foreigners during that period. Fraina was so disgraced that he never returned to Moscow.[34]

These first groups of "agents" were active from 1918 through the beginning of 1922. They spent a great deal of money to finance propaganda and organize the Communist movement as best they could. Nonetheless, their efforts to infiltrate the labor movement ended in failure. Furthermore, their main purpose, supporting the international position of Russia, did not contribute in any appreciable way to the lifting of the blockade, the withdrawal of foreign troops from Russian soil, or the subsequent rapprochement between the Soviet Union and the Western powers.

The Labor Movement

The early activities of the Mexican Communists in the labor movement were not fully in accord with the thinking of the Comintern leaders. During the First Congress of the Comintern, in 1919, Lenin criticized the "ultra-left" for not participating in the "reformist" trade unions. At the Second Congress of the Comintern, in 1920, one of the Twenty-One Conditions made it mandatory for Communists to work within the existing trade unions in their countries in order to gain control. At this time at least, the Comintern leaders were not in favor of creating Communist trade unions.

The Communists in Mexico, however, tried to create their own trade union. The first Communist labor organization, formed in September of 1920 and fairly active in the Federal District, was the Communist Federation of the Mexican Proletariat, oriented toward the Anarcho-Syndicalist position prevalent among the local Communists during the early 1920's: "It repudiates political action, insists upon industrial organization, denounces government job-holding on the part of union leaders, attacks the A. F. of L. Its purpose is summed up in direct action and recognition of the Third International." [35]

In addition, the Communists also tried to cooperate with other groups in the labor movement, a tactic more in accord with the orientation of the Comintern, which even before the First Congress had let it be known that Communists should form a bloc with other "revolutionary" elements in the labor movement, i.e., the Syndicalists.[36]

In the CROM convention of 1920 the Anarchist, Syndicalist, and Communist factions tried and failed to defeat Morones and his Action Group. The following year, February, 1921, these dissident groups sent delegates to a Great Red Radical Convention (Gran Convención Radical Roja) convoked by José C. Valadés, Manuel D. Ramírez, and others which gave birth to a new labor organization—The General Confederation of Workers (Confederación General de Trabajadores, or CGT).[37]

The Anarchists, Syndicalists, and Communists struggled for control of the CGT. The Communists brought the Red Marxist Group and the Communist Federation of the Mexican Proletariat into the new labor organization. It looked as if they might gain control of the CGT, and they succeeded in having it adhere to the Comintern. However, the Syndicalists continued to gain strength at the expense of the Communists. In the first congress of the CGT, September, 1921, the Communists were defeated and immediately withdrew from the organization. Affiliation with the Comintern was thus ended, and the CGT turned instead to the Syndicalist international being formed in Berlin, the International Workingmen's Association.[38]

During the first period of their activity through 1927, the Communists failed to make any perceptible headway in the labor movement. They created their own labor organization in 1920 and joined the CGT in order to aid their efforts to control the latter organization. But after their failure in the CGT, the Communists did not try to organize any new labor groups for many years. Their analysis of the labor movement brought them to one conclusion—the CROM controlled the majority of the organized workers. They subsequently decided to make a greater effort to infiltrate the ranks of the CROM. In addition, they wanted to try once again to capture the CGT with greater emphasis placed on influencing the rank and file.

These new tactics were more in accord with the orientation of the Comintern. During the winter of 1922, the Fourth Congress of the Comintern called on every Communist party to do everything it could to prevent the splitting of the trade unions, to restore trade unity where it had been destroyed, and to try to have the trade union movements of their countries adhere to the Red Trade Union International.[39]

During the Third Congress of the Communist party, in April of 1925, a decision was make to form Communist nuclei in the CROM and the CGT.[40] Although the Red Trade Union International did succeed in making contact with the CROM,[41] this did not lead to its affiliation with the international Communist labor organization. Nevertheless, the Communists continued in their efforts to penetrate the labor momevent from within, particularly in the CROM—"Communists must enter the CROM and remain in the organization at all costs; if Communist members were expelled, they should make every effort to be readmitted." [42] As we shall see presently, the Communists also turned to the slogans of "United Front of all Workers" and the "Government of Workers and Peasants."

The Peasants

The Comintern handed down general guidelines for Communists to follow in regard to the peasants. One of the Twenty-One Conditions stipulated that special efforts should be made to win the support of the peasants. Communists were cautioned, however, against forming separate peasant parties which might not be allied with the proletariat.[43]

The Communists of Mexico were more successful with the peasantry than with the labor movement during most of the 1920's. In fact, their influence with the peasants through the first part of 1929 was probably stronger than at any other time prior to the end of the second world war. But this was temporary and the Communists were unsuccessful in their efforts to bring the majority of the workers and peasants together under their leadership.

In 1923 the Soviet leaders formed the Peasant International. That same year the League of Agrarian Communities of Veracruz (Liga de Comunidades Agrarias del Estado de Veracruz) was formed under the leadership of Ursulo Galván, a prominent Communist. In its congress of December, 1924, the League resolved to join the Peasant International.[44]

For the next two years the Agrarian League of Veracruz attempted to bring about a national organization of peasants. Galván traveled throughout the country enthusiastically inviting peasants to the Communist banner: "What is perhaps even more important is the decision to send him (Ursulo Galván) to all parts of the country to organize the rest of the peasants with a Communist program, to unify them in a single national organization and to unite them to the Peasant International. He has already begun this propaganda trip and is being enthusiastically received everywhere. As Mexico is predominantly an agrarian country, peasants cannot be overemphasized." [45]

In 1926, the efforts of Galván and his followers in Veracruz proved to be successful. The Agrarian League of Veracruz, together with similar leagues in fifteen other states, formed \The National Peasants' League (La Liga Nacional Campesina). Galván became president of the League and it joined the Peasant International.[46]

Prior to the era of the Popular Front, which began in the middle 1930's, there were changes in the Comintern "lines"—United Front, Bolshevization, the Third Period, and so forth—but the overall view was one of agitation and insurrection against the forces of the bourgeoisie. The Comintern leaders considered the peasants an integral part of the continuing struggle.

In 1923 a letter was sent by the Comintern to the Communist party to suggest various tactics for the Communists to follow. One of these concerned the peasants: "In a country where 75% of the population consists of poor peasants, the working class can carry through a proletarian revolution successfully only by allying itself with these peasants and recognizing their interests as its own class interests. At this very moment, the peasants are being threatened by the Government. Obregón, with the tacit support of all the left bourgeois and petty-bourgeois parties, is trying to deprive the peasants of their arms. The slogan of the Government: Our national forces guarantee land to the peasants, is nothing but the beginnings of petty-bourgeois democratic betrayal. To counteract this, the Communists must proclaim that the only guarantee the peasants have for the security of their land is the weapons they hold in their own hands. Therefore, fight against bourgeois militarism and demand that the peasants be armed." [47]

The advice was taken. During the Third Congress of the party, April, 1925, the leaders called for "a fight against the disarmament of the peasants, which the federal government is attempting to carry out." [48]

The political terrain was fertile for arming the peasants. In 1923, the Obregón administration sought the support of the workers and peasants in putting down a revolt in behalf of Adolfo de la Huerta. Galván went to a congress of the Peasant International in Moscow and returned with instructions to raise a peasant army and oppose the revolt.[49] The workers and peasants supported the government and the revolt was crushed. (We shall analyze further the Communist tactic of supporting the government against armed revolts at a later point in this chapter).

Although the Communists made headway in the peasant movement through most of the 1920's, their effectiveness with the peasantry during that period was limited for two main reasons. In the first place, there were other organizations which were competing for the allegiance of the peasants—the National Agrarian Party, the CROM and the Mexican Labor Party. Other non-Communist organizations, which also tried to attract the peasants, were formed in later years. In the second place, the government increasingly satisfied the peasants' hunger for land which reduced the influence of the Communists with the rural population. The Communists were well aware of the impact the government land program had on the peasants: "In predominantly agrarian countries, the Communist Parties have especially difficult tasks to face. In Mexico, there is a petty bourgeois, semi-socialist government which is actually distributing land to the peasants. The peasants are partially reconciled and not so open to our propaganda."[50]

Developments in Yucatán

Other than possibly the Federal District, it was in Yucatán that the Communist influence was the strongest because of the work of one man, Felipe Carrillo Puerto, a member of the Latin American Bureau and one of the early organizers of the Communist Party of the Mexican Proletariat. He was a federal deputy from the state of Yucatán as well as president of the Socialist party of that state and of the Socialist

Party of the Southeast (Partido Socialista del Sureste). From 1922 until his execution during the de la Huerta revolt in 1923, Carrillo Puerto was Governor of Yucatán.

A federal deputy from Yucatán, Carrillo Puerto as a militant Communist, often delivered fiery speeches to the Chamber of Deputies: "We want no more Congressmen, Presidents, churches, bourgeois governments. . . Soviets and Communism are what we want. We do not ask them. We are going to have them, peacefully if we can, otherwise if we must. It would be better to dynamite the National Palace, the home of the Catholic archbishop, and the cathedral than to permit the will of the masses to be thwarted." [51]

In another instance Carrillo Puerto once described a fiesta in Yucatán: "Now they were living easily and well, some of them were studying Marx, all of them were hearing of Debs and Lenin; and on May 1st every Yucatán pueblo and town was wrapped in red, and the workers sang the Marseillaise and the Internationale at the jolly three-day fiesta that was held." [52]

The Socialist Party of Yucatán, under the leadership of Carillo Puerto, was not a true Socialist party. On the contrary, as the following excerpt from one of its early documents shows, its propaganda was strictly Communist:

WORKERS:
PREPARE FOR THE COMMUNIST REPUBLIC!

"The workers of the World already conscious of their situation, judges of their history and of the economic phenomena which generate laziness and misery, are prepared to establish the empire of equity by means of the dictatorship of the proletariat. That the industries may belong to the working people; that the land is cultivated in collectivity; and that the workers administer the factories and workshops . . . are the general propositions of the Government of the soviets. In order to reach this noble object of Communizing society, it is necessary to be bolshevik. . . a revolutionary worker, not democratic, not socialist-parliamentarian." [53]

Under Yucatán Governor Salvador Alvarado, Carrillo Puerto was encouraged to recruit peasants and workers into Communist-oriented Leagues of Resistance (Ligas de Resistencia) throughout the state of Yucatán. In August, 1921, the Leagues of Resistance of Yucatán were federated with those of the state of Campeche and the territory of Quintana Roo during the Congress of Izamal. The Central League of Resistance of Mérida, Yucatán, gained control of the enlarged federation and also of the Socialist Party of the Southeast. Carillo Puerto became president of the party and the various speakers at the Congress urged members of the Leagues to take note of Karl Marx's observation that "the emancipation of the proletariat is the work of the proletariat itself." [54]

Carrillo Puerto left the Communist party when he became Governor of Yucatán in 1922. However, he continued to encourage the development of the Leagues. There is no indication that the influence of Communism abated appreciably in Yucatán during the period he was chief executive of the state.

The Communist penetration in Yucatán was not a direct result of the activity of the Comintern. On the contrary, Carrillo Puerto's principal advisor, Robert Haberman, formerly from New York and a member of the Socialist party in the United States, was definitely hostile to the Soviet Union.[55] It is possible that Carrillo Puerto may have come in contact with agents who were sent by the Comintern, but basically he was a revolutionary who was stirred by the Russian Revolution of 1917.[56]

Soviet Diplomacy

In 1924 Mexico became the first country in Latin America to establish formal relations with the Soviet Union. The two countries broke diplomatic relations in January of 1930. The following analysis of Soviet diplomacy will be carried forward until the breaking of relations in 1930. This goes slightly beyond our first period of Communist development, which ended approximately in 1927. For the sake of continuity, however, the writer has decided to discuss this first period of Soviet diplomacy in its entirety.[57]

In 1924, shortly before the first Soviet minister arrived, the Commissar for Foreign Affairs of the Soviet Union, Chicherin, broadcast a speech in Moscow in which he tactlessly stated that Mexico would henceforth provide a base of operation for the Soviets in Latin America. President Calles immediately replied that the new Soviet Legation would have to respect international law and the sovereignty of the country. This, of course, created an inauspicious environment for the arrival of the first official representative from the Soviet Union.

The First Secretary of the Soviet Legation, Petskovsky, provided additional basis for the ill feelings which developed between the two countries. He attacked the CROM whose leader, Luis N. Morones, was in the Calles cabinet. He also antagonized the CROM by supporting the strike of railway workers, which was declared illegal by the government and not supported by the railway unions under Morones' control. When the Moscow railway workers donated 50,000 pesos to the strike fund, the authorities took the move as a deliberate affront, since government officials knew that no foreign exchange was granted without the recommendation of the Soviet Minister in Mexico City.[58] From then on, relations between the CROM and the Russians were very bitter.

During the two years Petskovsky was in the country, the periodical of the Communist party, *El Machete*, founded in 1924, increased in size four-fold. The Soviet Legation became the center for Communists and other labor groups opposed to the CROM. Front organizations were launched: Friends of the Soviet Union, the Anti-Imperialist League and the Young Communists. In addition, an attempt was made to attract the intellectuals to the Communist cause. Anti-CROM labor leaders, artists, writers, and lawyers were given free trips to the Soviet Union. On their return, they were encouraged to publish their impressions of the first Socialist state.

By 1926, however, the Soviet leaders realized that Petskovsky was causing too much friction with the government. He was replaced by Madame Alexandra Kollantay, the first Soviet ambassador to Mexico. This brilliant and cultured woman tried to put an end to Soviet meddling in local affairs, and it was the impression of ex-President Portes Gil, writing several years later, that friction between the two countries subsided during her stay.[59] Nevertheless, most officials snubbed Madame Kollantay because of the activities of her predecessor. The government began to persecute Communists and suspected Communist sympathizers; the Soviet Embassy was raided and its guests arrested. Madame Kollantay left in 1927.

Dr. Alexander Makar, the next Soviet ambassador, promised the government that he would refrain from political activity within the country. Portes Gil felt, however, that the new Soviet ambassador did not try to ease the tension between the two countries and that the Soviet Embassy had become a center of political restlessness and propaganda. Many Mexicans attended meetings in the Embassy and were then sent to various parts of the country to incite the people. Portes Gil also contended that Dr. Makar gave the Communists money, accompanied by instructions to attack the government.[60]

Eventually, the repression by the government of the local Communists resulted in protests, probably organized by the Comintern, outside Mexican legations abroad. When the Mexican government protested, the Soviet leaders answered that actions within Mexico were caused by the Comintern, not by the Soviet government and that demonstrations against Mexico in other countries were caused by the Communist parties, not by the Soviet government.[61] The Russian government's reply may not have been entirely accurate, however. A report from the Department of the Interior of the Soviet Union had come into the possession of the Mexican government. The report gave detailed instructions for provoking agitation and revolution—money, arms, and names of public officials to be assassinated.

On January 23, 1930, under President Ortiz Rubio, the government broke relations with the Soviet Union. The Mexican note placed the blame on the Soviet government: "The Government of Mexico knows perfectly that this propaganda against the institutions and the National Revolution has been prepared and directed from Russia. It also knows that the Russian Communist groups do not work nor can they work independently, because any political organization of that country is subject to the soviet government." [62]

The Communists vehemently denied the charges: "It was the threadbare excuse that these demonstrations (by workers in the U. S. against Ortiz Rubio on his recent U. S. trip) were 'ordered by the Russian (sic!) government' because certain pernicious 'Russians' had been deported, that the Portes Gil government (i.e., the administration of Oritiz Rubio) announced the breaking of relations with the Soviet Union within about 24 hours after (Ortiz) Rubio had returned from the U. S. As a matter of fact, not a single Russian 'revolutionary' had been deported, though many Latin Americans had been, most of them Cubans. The stupidity of the excuse hid the real reason: that the United States imperialists had ordered the break." [63]

The development of Communism during the period 1924-1929 was primarily in the hands of Soviet diplomats who were more effective than the earlier Comintern agents in developing the Communist movement. For example, they controlled the finances; funds did not pass through the hands of several individuals and become "lost." Perhaps the most important factor, as far as the composition of the Communist party was concerned, was the success of Soviet diplomacy in attracting a small number of middle class intellectuals to the Communist banner.

Events came to a head between Mexico and the Soviet Union in the period 1928-1929, which coincided with the initiation of the Third Period of the Comintern. In all probability the more militant orientation of the Third Period to the left contributed to the breaking of relations. However, the diplomatic blunders of the Soviet representatives, i.e., antagonizing influential labor officials, crude interference in the internal affairs of the country, and so on, would probably have resulted in a breaking of relations sooner or later.

A by-product of Soviet diplomacy was the intense persecution of the Communists which continued without abatement until the administration of Lázaro Cárdenas. One cannot say with certainty that the Mexican governments would have been more tolerant toward the Communists had the Soviet officials shown more prudence in their dealings within the country. However, it is clear that the various administrations were more sensitive to the activities of the Communists as a result of their experiences with the representatives of the Soviet government. This led in turn to restrictions which inhibited the development of the Communist movement as a whole.

Development of Communist Tactics and Comintern "Lines"

Early in 1922, many of the artists formed a "union," the Revolutionary Trade Union of Technical and Plastic Workers (Sindicato Revolucionario de Obreros Técnicos y Plásticos). Within a year, most of the members joined the Communist party, including Diego Rivera, José Clemente Orozco, David Alfaro Siqueiros, and others. Their organ, El Machete, became the official party paper.[64] The editors were Xavier Guerrero, Siqueiros, and Diego Rivera. Upon joining the party, the artists' "union" issued the following statement of principles:

"We believe indispensable the overthrow of the old social mechanism now in power; we believe that to arrive at this goal the producing and creating classes have the right or rather the obligation to employ whatever means of action necessary for the execution of this end.

"We recognize as the only effective means for this the temporary dictatorship of the proletariat . . . In short we wish to substitute from the very foundation the government of the producers for the government of the exploiters." [65]

The strength of the artists during the '20's was shown in the 1923 convention, when the three editors of El Machete were elected to the Executive Committee, lacking only one member of making a majority of that body. Since the Communists had failed in their efforts to penetrate the unions in the party's first year of existence, they turned to the party bourgeoisie for support: "From a party of vaguely revolutionary politicians, the Mexican Communist party was now converted into a party of vaguely revolutionary painters." [66]

Regardless of the levels of population from which the party tried to recruit its members, it was not able to attract any sizeable number. The party did not have over 500 members during the 1920's, and in 1925, the Communists themselves admitted to having no more than a few hundred adherents.[67]

The tactics of the Communists vis-à-vis the various administrations and presidents differed according to the period and the circumstances. They supported a presidential candidate only to criticize him as president; they supported and criticized a president during the same term of office; they alternately praised one president and criticized another.

As previously indicated, the leaders of the Communist party, as distinguished from Gale and his group, criticized President Carranza: they attacked his policies in opposing the Agrarian Leagues of Yucatán; they were opposed to his choice of a successor.[68]

At first, the Communists praised General Obregón[69] but praise turned to scorn as the new President began to deport many Communists and have others thrown in jail. The Comintern leaders strongly criticized the President: "Obregón exploits the possibilities of radicalism and the atmosphere of the sham socialism in the fight for his share of the booty gained by the common exploitation of the Mexican workers and peasants. He either flirts with the proletariat or has their revolutionary leaders shot down in the streets, according as the state of negotiations demands." [70]

The Communists of Mexico, in accord with the Comintern leaders, were almost unrelenting in their criticism of the President: "It was only after his power was thoroughly consolidated that he began to show himself a true reactionary, breaking strikes, throwing workers into jail, suppressing radical meetings and deporting all foreigners active in the Communist and Syndicalist movements." [71]

Nevertheless, however critical the Communists may have been of the Obregón administration, they supported him against the de la Huerta revolt. The Communists continued to follow this tactic through the end of the second world war—support the government in power against a threatened or actual revolt. From time to time, the Communists themselves called for a revolution which would install the dictatorship of the proletariat. But they would not support any other group which threatened the government by revolt.

The main reason the Communists supported the governments against rebellion was ideological. They viewed the Revolution of 1910 as a "democratic-bourgeois" revolution which would bring Capitalism and eventually lead to Socialism, i.e., of the Communist variety. In addition, the national governments were generally anti-foreign, particularly anti-American. Thus, the Communists were able to support bourgeois nationalism as a stage in the historical process leading to Communism.[72] It was in this sense that they viewed Alvaro Obregón: "General Obregón represents the right wing of the national petty bourgeoisie . . . and is the representative of those elements who aspire to national reconstruction, to industrialization of the country at the base of the creation of the national capitalism and of a strong national bourgeoisie independent of foreign influence." [73]

The Communists maintained, and correctly so, that the revolt of the de la Huerta forces was not so much against the administration of President Obregón as against the President's proposed successor, General Calles. Furthermore, they claimed that the supporters of the revolt were the rich landowners, the Capitalists, and the Fascists. In opposing the de la Huerta revolt, they also utilized the anti-American theme in calling for the people to support the government.[74]

Through the years, the Communist party increasingly shied away from the Anarcho-Syndicalist position due to the pressure of the Comintern. For example, the leaders of the Comintern decided that the Mexican Communists should participate in the presidential election of 1924. Therefore, before the election, the following instructions were sent by the Comintern: "It is already apparent that the overwhelming majority of the workers and peasants will support . . . Calles. If the whole working class participates in this struggle, the Communist party must not stand aside and look on; it must fight with the others, for Calles today means protection for the masses from reaction and clerical domination. But it is the duty of the Communists to combat the illusions of the masses as to the ability of the Calles Government actually to give this protection . . . In spite of this, the Communist party must participate in the elections on the part of Calles . . . certainly not as enthusiastic followers of the government . . . as this tactic is merely a necessary halting place on the road to the Workers' and Peasants' Government, on the road to the proletarian revolution and the dictatorship of the proletariat." [75]

Shortly after the Comintern letter was received, the Communist party issued the following declaration dated September 9, 1923:

"The National Committee of the Communist Party of Mexico . . . declares formally: . . . the immense majority of the Mexican population being the peasants and . . . the workers, that the Government of Mexico should emanate from those forces which are the true people, . . . consequently the Communist Party of Mexico will support for the candidacy

of the presidency of the Republic the one who unites the majority of
the peasant and worker communities.

"The Communist Party of Mexico declares ... (also) that the peasant
and laboring forces, being the majority of the population of the country
(and) from whom in justice, the Government ought to emanate, the
workers who individually or corporatively abstain from voting, will
support effectively the bourgeoisie with the force which they take
away from the workers' parties, and thus, with the pretext of anarchism,
are only traitors to their brothers of their own class and to the country to which they belong as citizens." [76]

Thus, the Communists supported the candidacy of General Calles
to succeed Alvaro Obregón as President.[77] The Communist attitude
toward the Calles government showed the difficult position in which
they placed themselves. They felt that the central point in the tactics
of the party should be the struggle against American imperialism.[78]
In a sense this would signify support of the government: "We must
be prepared to lend solid support to Calles in his struggles against
American imperialism . . ." [79] However, if the administration came to
an understanding with American interests, as in the case of the oil
companies, then the government was to be criticized for capitulating
to American imperialism. The latter was the Communist attitude during
the Third Congress of the party in April of 1925: "Expose the Calles
government as the left arm of American imperialism, the right arm of
which is fascism and intervention. Slogan: The labor government is
the gendarme of the Yankee bankers and petroleum companies." [80]

The Communists' task was difficult, if not impossible. How does
one support and oppose a government at the same time and reconcile
this with Communist ideology? The dilemma was succinctly presented
in an *Inprecorr* article: "The young CP of Mexico has great tasks
before it. It must gather together the revolutionary forces and must
unite them with the masses which are under the influence of the petty
bourgeoisie and the Reformists. It must support the Government in its
struggle against reaction and against American imperialism and must
at the same time endeavor to intensify this struggle. On the other hand
it must combat the policy of cooperation with the bourgeoisie, the petty
bourgeoisie, the Utopians, and the open treachery of the Reformists." [81]

The Communists supported the Calles government, as they had done
during the administration of Alvaro Obregón, against an attempted
revolt in 1927 under Generals Francisco Serrano and Arnulfo Gómez.
The Mexican Communists sent a telegram to the *Daily Worker*, the
periodical of the American Communists, in which they requested

"agitation in behalf of the Mexican proletariat in its struggle jointly with the government." The American periodical then went on to comment: "The foregoing telegram, in harmony with all reports from Mexico, is taken as indicating the policy of the Mexican Communist Party in the present crisis . . . As against the present counter-revolutionary attempts of agents of U. S. oil speculators allied with the whole landlord and clerical group of reaction . . . the Communist Party of Mexico calls upon the working class and peasantry to resort to arms in defense of the Calles government and urges the workers and farmers of the United States to support the Calles government against the counter-revolutionary reaction." [82]

On the other hand, the Communists criticized the administration for supporting the CROM and opposing "revolutionary trade unions," [83] and continuously attacked Luis N. Morones, leader of the CROM and an official in the Calles cabinet. The Communists also used their most common propaganda weapon against a Mexican government: they criticized its land distribution program.[84]

The Communists supported General Obregón, too, in his attempt to become President a second time. Indicative of their opportunism was their attitude toward possible candidates of the government: "Still not having the indispensible cohesion nor the necessary direction, the working and peasant masses cannot now undertake the preparation of an independent struggle for the conquest of power. Therefore, and before the efforts of reaction and of the clergy to overthrow the government of the petty bourgeoisie, it is a duty of the proletarian class to support the candidature of the national bourgeoisie and petty bourgeoisie . . . the candidature of General Obregón; Generals Gómez and Serrano who represent the interests of reaction, . . . (are) of the conservative classes." [85]

Normally, the Communist party followed the orientation and "lines" of the Comintern very closely; however, in the case of the United Front, the Comintern was the source of some confusion among the Mexican Communists. The line of the United Front was officially declared by the Comintern at its Third Congress in the summer of 1921. The Mexican Communists were slow in picking up the new slogan; the fact that their party was not officially recognized by the Comintern until 1922 might have contributed to their hesitation.[86] The leaders of the Comintern then decided to send a letter, cited above, to the Communist Party of Mexico explaining various tactics which the Communists should follow. The explanation of the United Front was, however, confusing because in one paragraph the Communists were called upon to cooperate with the "reformist" labor and peasant leaders, and in another paragraph they were instructed to liquidate these leaders:

"The tactic of the United Front is the revolutionary fight of the Communist Party to win the wide organized and unorganized working and peasant masses for a common struggle for common demands. The Communist Party therefore openly turns towards the leaders of the reformist, syndicalist, and so-called independent trade union organizations and requests their participation in a joint Committee of Action. The same thing applies to the Laborites and the Agrarian Party. The object of the Committee of Action is organized centralization of the fight for definite demands. The Committee of Action does not bind any of the participating parties or trade unions to its political agitation and propaganda, or to its activities in general. Above all, the right of criticism of every Party will be fully preserved.

"The liquidation of the social-reformist leader cliques and of the petty-bourgeoisie, anarcho-syndicalist ideology, is the purpose of the fight for the United Front." [87]

The Communist party confirmed the tactic of the United Front during its Second Congress in 1923.[88] The party criticized the non-Communist peasant and labor leaders and, as the Comintern had done in the early 1920's, tended toward the "United Front from below": "The spirit of unification is rapidly opening a path in the workers movement of the country. The cry of 'United Front!' . . . has found an echo in all the places where the workers' conscience feels the necessity of taking form in an organization of decisive and pugnacious force, and the proletarian masses, both of the CROM and of the CGT, vilely betrayed in their conflicts by the personal interests of the sold-out directors, in these moments want the United Front and are disposed to impose it." [89]

The leaders of the Comintern thought in terms of a three-stage process: United Front—Workers' and Peasants' Government—Dictatorship of the Proletariat. Thus, they pointed out to the Mexican Communists that the United Front was merely the first stage (albeit an important one) in the overall process which would lead to the ultimate victory of Communism:

"Closely connected with the question of the United Front is the slogan of the Workers' and Peasants' Government. This slogan must take root in the profound and often unconscious conviction of the wide masses that only by the closest union of the industrial working class with the working peasantry can the exploitation and oppression by the large estate owners and by the industrial magnates be brought to an end. The Communist Party knows that only the dictatorship of the proletariat can finally shatter the power of the capitalist social order. But the Workers' and Peasants' Government may be the final halting place on the road to the proletarian dictatorship. The Communist Party must therefore formulate the question of the Workers' and Peasants' Government in a concrete form. The Workers' and Peasants' Government is a coalition of workers, peasants, exploited employees, and members of the petty-bourgeoisie against the parties of reaction and of the big bourgeoisie. The Workers' and Peasants' Government is the declaration of war of the masses to the capitalist social system. The Communist Party must make the halting place of the Workers' and Peasants' Government a period of preparation and organization for the proletarian dictatorship. The Workers' and Peasants' Government means civil war. But only the proletarian dictatorship can guarantee the victory of the workers and the peasants." [90]

The Communist party reacted favorably to the interpretation of the Comintern. Its leaders also saw the United Front as a step along the path to the Workers' and Peasants' Government. Following is a manifesto of the Communist party, published shortly after the unsuccessful de la Huerta rebellion against the government of President Obregón in 1923:

"It is only that the government of Mexico still is not a government of the workers and peasants. A government benevolent to the workers and peasants—yes, but a government of the workers and peasants, that [is] not yet. That is the next task of the revolution. That is the whole program of the Communist Party. . .

"The Communist Party invites the peasants and workers, who wish to make a government in Mexico exclusively of the workers and peasants, to enter into its ranks. The Communist Party invites the Agrarian and Labor Parties to form with it a united front to achieve the government of the workers and peasants.

"Peasants and workers of the world, unite! Forward to the government of the workers and peasants in Mexico. Forward to the government of the workers and peasants in the entire world." [91]

In the summer of 1924, the Fifth Congress of the Comintern handed down the new "line" of Bolshevization. During the Third Congress of the Communist Party of Mexico, which terminated on April 13, 1925, a considerable amount of time was spent discussing Bolshevization and its significance for the party. Bertram D. Wolfe wrote a summary of the Congress in an *Inpecorr* article entitled: "Bolshevization

and Immediate Tasks in the Mexican Communist Party." [92] Bolshevization for the Communist party meant facing the party's shortcomings
and taking steps to correct them. The following quotation by Bertram
D. Wolfe explains the dire straits in which the members of the party
found themselves:

"Situated in a country of continuous turmoil, loosely called 'revolutionary,' it was nevertheless, until a year ago, one of the most
opportunistic parties in the Communist International. Its opportunism
was due to three factors: Its then leadership, the policy of corruption
by subsidy which characterizes the Mexican government in its dealings with labor organizations, and the absence of a social democratic
party which might absorb the opportunistic elements. The bolshevization of the Mexican Communist Party began somewhat before the
slogan was adopted by the Communist International. At the meeting
of the Enlarged Executive Committee called in April of 1924, one
year previous to the Third Congress of the Party, all of the Executive
Committee, with one exception, was thrown out of office or resigned.
The party had fallen to pieces under its guidance, had failed to take a
resolute communist attitude in the de la Huerta revolt, had no press,
no dues system, no meetings and no longer any of its one-time influence it had in the Peasant movement, principally in the state of
Veracruz. . ." [93]

The new Executive Committee elected by the party at the Third
Congress was composed of Rafael Carrillo as Executive Secretary,
Xavier Guerrero, Bertram D. Wolfe, David Alfaro Siqueiros, Carlos
Rendon, and Manuel D. Ramírez.

The discussion of Bolshevization at the Third Congress of the party
closed by calling for a more militant Communist attitude vis-à-vis
the government and governmental officials. The Communists were
instructed to cease "all political trading with the 'revoluntionary'
politicians of certain states." [94]

Summary and Conclusion

During the first period of the Communist movement, approximately
from 1918 through 1927, a Communist party developed which was primarily middle class in composition. At its birth, the party was basically
Anarcho-Syndicalist in ideology, but it shifted from this position and
began to participate in elections and support particular administrations. However, the further the party moved away from Anarcho-
Syndicalism, the more firmly it became wedded to opportunism.

Regardless of the self-criticism during its Third Congress, the Communist party continued to receive subsidies from the administration. It proclaimed that it would support any presidential candidate of the government, regardless of what reactionary forces he represented or however conservative he might be.

The Communists interpreted the Comintern "line" of Bolshevization and applied it to the peculiar conditions of Mexico. Part of this interpretation signified that the Communists should harden their attitude vis-à-vis the government. But they were not consistent in supporting and opposing the various administrations. Furthermore, rather than assume a more militant attitude toward the various governments, they actually supported them against internal revolts.[95] The only consistency which the Communists displayed, besides opposing insurrections against the Mexican governments, was a rather close following of the Comintern "lines," as exemplified by the United Front.

A good share of the blame for the inconsistent and opportunistic actions must fall upon the Comintern. At the beginning of the period, the Comintern leaders believed that world revolution was imminent. They felt the best way to realize this revolution was to have the Communists seize power immediately, by meeting the bourgeois governments in direct conflict. But when the Twenty-One Conditions were handed down, the Communists were then told to struggle within the bourgeois parliaments and trade unions. The "line" of the United Front coincided with the New Economic Policy within the Soviet Union, but with the advent of Bolshevization the United Front became less important. Finally, the Comintern shifted to the right, away from the advocacy of imminent world revolution and the importance of the Soviet Union was emphasized with the doctrine of "Socialism in one country."

In Mexico, these shifting "lines" and tactics caused confusion in the minds of the Communists and their prospective adherents. Several of the early leaders of the party left its ranks after approximately a year's service—Felipe Carrillo Puerto, José C. Valadés, Francisco Mujica, and others.[96] There is no way of telling how many thought of joining the party but were repulsed by its confusion and inconsistencies. The small number of adherents is some indication of the problem of attracting members. Thus, on the eve of the Third Period, the Communist movement was still in its infancy.

CHAPTER IV

THE COMINTERN DISCOVERS LATIN AMERICA

The next period in the development of the Mexican (and Latin American) Communist movements can be considered to have begun toward the end of 1927 and to have ended in 1935, with the initiation of the Popular Front era. There were two conferences in Moscow, toward the end of 1927 and in the spring of 1928, among representatives of the Comintern, Western European Communists, and Latin American Communists. In the summer of 1928, the Sixth Congress of the Comintern was held. These were followed by two congresses in Latin America in 1929. Many Mexican Communists attended these congresses and actively participated in the assemblies as they developed tactics in preparation for the next stage of Communist development in Latin America.

The Moscow Conferences

In December of 1927, during the Tenth Anniversary of the Bolshevik Revolution, several Soviet officials and Latin American Communists came together for a conference which produced the following Resolution of the First Latin American Trade Union Meeting: "We, the delegates of the unions of Argentina, Brazil, Colombia, Cuba, Mexico, Uruguay, Chile, and Ecuador, who have met in Moscow on the occasion of the Tenth Anniversary of the October Revolution, have joined the Red Trade Union International on December 11, 1927, and after having examined the problem of the situation of the working class and unions in the countries of Latin America, have arrived at the following conclusion: . . . in Montevideo, may be realized a conference of unions of all Latin America, with the goal of constituting a Latin American Trade Union Secretariat. . ." [1]

The above document was signed by Alexander Losovsky for the Red Trade Union International and several Communists representing Western European countries. Among the Latin American delegates who signed was "one delegate from the National Peasants League of Mexico." In addition, the "delegates of the Trade Union of Miners of the State of Jalisco, of the Trade Union of the Petroleum Workers of the State of Tamaulipas, and of the F. O. (i.e., Railroad Workers) of the Transport of Mexico" attended the conference but had to leave before the document was signed.[2]

The December meeting was followed by a second Moscow conference held from April 6-10, 1928. Several Latin American Communists were present, and the Comintern was represented by Losovsky and Humbert-Droz. The delegates from Mexico were from the Trade Union of Miners of the State of Jalisco (David Alfaro Siqueiros) and the Confederation of Railroad Workers of Mexico.[3] A Provisional Secretariat was elected to prepare for the Montevideo congress (as planned in the December conference) and various resolutions were adopted describing the Communist version of conditions in Latin America.

According to the resolutions, the Montevideo congress should work primarily to combat the "exploitation of foreign imperialism (i.e., the United States) and of the national bourgeoisie."[4] Other resolutions spoke for the necessity of well-organized strikes and the importance of the struggle against dictatorships.[5]

The conference also passed a resolution concerning the Mexican Revolution, interpreting it in Communist terms as a petty bourgeois (sometimes called bourgeois-democratic) revolution which had become bogged down in its bourgeois stage. The implication, repeated in more definite terms at the Sixth Congress of the Comintern, was that the Communists had to assume leadership of the revolution and direct it toward Socialist (i.e., Communist) goals.[6]

Probably the most important figure who attended the conference was Alexander Losovsky, president of the Red Trade Union International. He delivered an extensive report, giving his views on the conditions in Latin America and Mexico and proposing several tactics which the Communists should follow.

Losovsky began by pointing out that the Latin American trade union movement was weak in terms of ideology and organization because of two opposing extremes—Anarchism and Anarcho-Syndicalism, which directed the Latin American trade union movement before and during World War I, and reformism as exemplified by the CROM in Mexico. The inability of these extremes to carry out a revolution presented the Communists with an opportunity to make their tactics meaningful by presenting a revolutionary theory.[7]

This did not mean, however, that a social revolution was on the immediate horizon for Latin America: "In Latin America one speaks too much of social revolution . . . there are a certain number of comrades who believe that if the Socialist revolution has not been produced yesterday, it will arrive tomorrow." [8] Losovsky offered other advice for the Latin American Communists: "The social revolution is not today the order of the day in all the countries of Latin America. It is not this question which is presented before you presently, but that of organization of the masses, that of consolidation of our forces, that of attraction to our ranks of the great masses of unorganized. We should also impart a clear ideology to the trade union movement in order to be able to establish just perspectives and powerful organizations. All this ought to precede the social revolution." [9] As we shal see, Losovsky's thinking was not in accord with the general tone of the Comintern congress.

The Sixth Congress of the Comintern

The Sixth Congress of the Comintern, held July 17-September 1, 1928, was important in two respects: It proclaimed the "line" of the Third Period and developed a thesis for Latin America.

Several themes were presented at the Congress.[10] First, it was necessary for all Communists to defend the Soviet Union from attack and oppose the war which the imperialists were preparing. Attacks were also made on Social Democracy and the Socialist elements in the trade unions. The Socialist leaders were identified with "Social-Fascism," and they were to be opposed by the formation of the "United Front from below." If the Communists believed their efforts could best be realized outside of the "reformist" trade unions, they should try to form Communist trade unions. Finally, more emphasis was placed on the general strike as a prelude to the approaching proletarian revolution.

In addition to presenting several themes which were to be followed by Communists during the Third Period, the leaders of the Comintern handed down particular instructions for the Communists of Latin America. This was the first time that the Latin American area received such special attention during a Comintern Congress. A general resolution was passed calling attention to some of the problems in Latin America to which the Executive Committee would address itself: "The Congress instructs the ECCI to devote more attention to the Latin American countries generally and to draft a 'program of action' for the parties in these countries (which among other questions should include the extremely important agrarian peasant question and the question of combating United States imperialism). The ECCI must secure the definite organizations (trade unions, peasant unions); that they carry on proper work among the masses; that they consolidate and broaden the trade unions, unify and centralize them, etc." [11]

One of the leaders of the Comintern, Otto Willi Kuusinen, spoke at considerable length about the role of the Communists in colonial and semicolonial countries. Although he devoted little space to Latin America, subsequent speakers expanded his thesis and concrete resolutions were presented which applied specifically to the Latin American area. Pursuing one of the themes of the Third Period, the Comintern leaders saw Latin America become more important as the United States gained in strength vis-à-vis Great Birtain. In fact, Latin America was considered to be developing into "the principal colonial sphere of Yankee imperialism." [12]

The Comintern leaders at the Congress, with great optimism, believed that what they considered to be the "revolutionary movement of Latin America" would not result in the formation of Capitalist regimes: "the predominating struggle is not that of a national bourgeoisie for independence on a capitalist basis but struggle of the peasants for the agrarian revolution against the regime of the big landed proprietors." [13]

It was felt that the Communists had to play a more active role in Mexico. We shall see how this analysis during the Sixth Congress was translated into agitation and violence by the Mexican Communists: "The prospect of the development of the bourgeois-democratic revolution in Mexico is not progressive transformation into Socialist revolution, the prospect is that the hegemony of the petty bourgeoisie in the revolutionary movement of Mexico will be gradually eliminated and that the role of the Communist Party, of the proletariat, will become a very important role, that of leader of the masses in the second wave of the revolutionary movement. The bourgeois-democratic revolution of Mexico, instead of being led by the petty bourgeoisie, will be led more and more, after the failure of the petty bourgeoisie in power, by the proletariat, by the party of the proletariat—the Communist Party." [14]

As a result of their interpretation of the type of revolution that the Latin American countries were experiencing, the Comintern leaders concluded that the Communists must take part in the "revolutionary mass movement." They might be forced to cooperate with the petty bourgeoisie in struggling against the landlords, the Church, and other elements of feudalism, but this was to be a temporary alliance. The Communists were exhorted to assume the leadership of the revolutionary movements. Their purpose would be to realize the Government of the Workers and Peasants, which, incidently, was the same goal toward which the Comintern leaders attempted to direct the Mexican Communists in their letter of 1923.[15]

Finally, the Latin American Communists were instructed to organize blocs of workers and peasants, in their respective countries, which would include the more advanced revolutionary elements of the petty bourgeoisie. Its purpose was twofold—to separate the masses from the influence of the petty bourgeoisie and, by so doing, to bring a larger number of people under control of the Communist party.[16] During the Third Period, the Mexican Communists placed a great deal of emphasis on a Workers' and Peasants' Bloc.

There were other resolutions and slogans of the Sixth Congress pertaining to Latin America, but those discussed above were the major elements which comprised the Latin American thesis.[17] The instructions for the Latin American Communists were part of the more militant turn to the left of the Third Period. They were warned to be cognizant of the Anglo-American imperialist rivalry, which was particularly acute in Latin America. They were called upon to participate in revolutionary movements and bring them under the control of the Communists and develop the Workers' and Peasants' Bloc. Thus, Latin American was to be one of the battle fields in the orientation of violence and militancy which characterized the Third Period.

There was a significant difference between Losovky's interpretation of the Latin American scene and the militancy which was reflected by the resolutions of the Sixth Congress of the Comintern. There was no doubt when Comintern leaders proclaimed that the Soviet Union was in danger of an imperialist attack, that they were thinking of Great Britain and the United States. Latin America's role was to incite agitation and revolutions to overthrow the "bourgeois" governments which were the tools of "Yankee imperialism."

As we have seen, one of the resolutions of the Sixth Congress called upon the Mexican Communists to replace the petty bourgeoisie in the leadership of the Mexican Revolution for a "second wave of the revolutionary movement." Another resolution of the Congress stipulated that Latin American Communists should "actively participate in the revolutionary mass movements" in order to realize a Government of the Workers and Peasants. Bukharin's speech to the Sixth Congress also followed this line of reasoning: "On the question of tactics in the South American countries there are various currents among us. I cannot deal now with all the controversial points. I would like, however, to emphasize the point that from the viewpoint of struggle against war and against imperialism and in general, from the viewpoint of the development of powerful national revolutions and powerful agrarian revolutions, and which most likely will reveal the tendency to become transformed into social revolutions, the whole gamut of South American problems is assuming increasing significance from day to day." [18]

In all probability, the president of the Red Trade Union International was correct in advising organization, consolidating of forces, and the presentation of a clear ideology for the weak Latin American Communist movement; however, the entire orientation of the Third Period called for violence, agitation, and possible revolution for the Latin American Communists. The Mexican Communists followed the resolutions of the Sixth Congress, not Losovsky's advice.

The difference between Losovsky's report to the Moscow conference and the resolutions of the Sixth Congress of the Comintern were based on different views of the timing of the revolution. The feeling of the Sixth Congress was that it was not necessary for the Communists to wait in order to participate in the revolutionary mass movement. Losovsky also believed the Latin American Communists should play an active role, but only when the time was ripe for a "Socialist" revolution. This seemed to be his thinking in the description of the Mexican Revolution: "In this bourgeois revolution, the working class of Mexico, with the peasants, should create a force against the bourgeoisie and international imperialism; this bloc, these two united forces, should give the land to the peasants, should be converted into a force such as can afterwards, in a moment and propitious situation, go further, from the social point of view, from the point of view of a change in the base of the national economy." [19]

A new phase was to begin for the Communist movement of Latin America and Mexico, and the foundation was laid in Moscow: The Sixth Congress of the Comintern handed down a new "line"; various resolutions and tactics were decided upon for Latin America. The Sixth Congress crystallized, and in some cases modified, decisions of the preceding Moscow conferences which had organized the forthcoming Latin American congresses and the formation of a Latin American trade union organization. Losovsky expressed the awakening of the Comintern to Latin America during the Tenth Plenum of the ECCI:

"I shall say frankly that I discovered Latin America, approximately, on the X Anniversary of the October Revolution. We have there a huge labor reserve, a huge amount of revolutionary energy which is spoiling for a fight against imperialism and against the national bourgeoisie, for the creation of a really united revolutionary International." [20]

The Latin American Congresses

As a direct result of the Moscow conferences and the Sixth Congress of the Comintern, two Latin American Communist congresses were held in South America during May and June of 1929. The first congress concerned Communist tactics in the labor movement and the formation of a Latin American trade union organization. The second congress dealt with the tactics and orientation of the Communist parties of Latin America.

In May, 1929, several European Communists plus delegates from fifteen Latin American countries met in Montevideo, Uruguay. The Mexican delegates represented the Unitary Trade Union Confederation of Mexico, formed during the Third Period, and the League of Agrarian Communities of the State of Veracruz. The Mexican Communists were David Alfaro Siqueiros, Elías Barrios, Samuel Rodríguez Cerrilla, and Valentín Campa.

During the congress, the Latin American Trade Union Confederation (Confederación Sindical Latino Americana or CSLA) was formed. Valentín Campa and Siqueiros were elected to the General Council. The latter also served on the following committees: Executive Committee, Secretariat (Montevideo), and the Sub-Committee of the Caribbean.[21]

The Congress, and the CSLA which its delegates established, were products of the policy orientation of the Third Period. One of the early resolutions clearly stated the role of Latin America during this most recent stage of Capitalist decline: "The world proletariat has entered the third period of the post-war, which is that of its (capitalism's) decadence and its contradictions and most fatal crises and of its definite death, and we should prepare ourselves to march with our forces to the general counter-offensive against capitalism and to conquer it, instituting the regime of emancipation and of proletarian liberation in all Latin America, such as our brothers have already implanted in Workers' and Peasants' Russia." [22]

In many of the resolutions given by the most prominent Mexican delegate, David Alfaro Siqueiros, much emphasis was given to the dominant theme of the Third Period: the expected war against the Soviet Union.[23]

Since the Capitalists were preparing to unleash a series of wars, particularly one against the Soviet Union, all Communists must struggle to oppose the outbreak of war. This could be done most effectively by defending the Soviet Union and Communist organizations of other countries.[24] But if the Soviet Union should be attacked, the workers of the world would know what to do: "during a war against the Soviet state (country of the world proletariat) the workers' organizations must mobilize the proletarian masses in defense of the revolutionary country. . ."[25]

Other resolutions repeated the main slogans of the Third Period: the importance of Latin America in the struggle between English and American imperialisms was stressed; international Social Democracy was depicted as contributing to the war preparations against the Soviet Union.[26] Indicative of the militancy of the Third Period was the call for a struggle against "reformism" and any forms of collaboration or pacifism.[27]

Several resolutions criticized various non-Communist labor organizations in Latin America. The attacks on the CROM were particularly bitter: "The CROM, even in the periods in which the Mexican petty bourgeoisie, within its vacillations, made anti-imperialist gestures, always maintained an 'apolitical' attitude which in reality was of collaboration and capitulation before imperialism. . ."[28]

The congress also addressed itself to the question of the peasants. The delegates were well aware that the proletariat alone could not bring a Communist victory in Latin America. What was needed was an alliance of the workers and peasants. One of the resolutions, based on Siqueiros' report, called for an agrarian revolution: "The principal allies of the Latin American proletariat in the anti-imperialist struggle are the peasants, whose situation cannot be improved radically without an agrarian revolution directed similarly against landowners and the imperialists, whose interests in the countries of Latin America coincide."[29]

The form of the alliance between the workers and peasants, as previously stated in Losovsky's report to the April, 1928, Moscow conference, and during the Sixth Congress of the Comintern was to be the Workers' and Peasants' Bloc.[30]

The main purpose of the congress, the creation of a Latin American trade union organization, was realized in the establishment of the CSLA. Reflecting one of the main themes of the Third Period, the new organization was to be a United Front of all revolutionary workers: Communists, Anarchists, Anarcho-Syndicalists, revolutionary Syndicalists, and workers without a party.[31] In fact, it consisted almost exclusively of Communist controlled groups.

Mexico was very important in the proceedings of the congress. Not only were several Mexican Communists members of committees established by the congress, but one of the statutes of the CSLA designated Mexico as the base of one of the important sub-committees in charge of propaganda for the Caribbean and Central American areas.[32] As noted previously, Siqueiros was one of the members.

In addition, several resolutions were passed pertaining to Mexico, most of them extremely critical of the Mexican government: "Thus in Mexico. . .a government clearly petty bourgeois, called pro-labor, a product of various popular revolts against feudal and imperialist exploitation . . . is yielding rapidly to Yankee imperialism and consequently is attacking the revolutionary movement of the masses in a more and more determined and open manner, definitely passing over to the camp of counter-revolution and imperialism." [33]

A second Latin American Communist congress was held in Buenos Aires in the following month, June 1-12, 1929. The delegates included all the members of the Latin American Bureau, representatives of the Comintern, the Red Trade Union International, the French Communist Party, the Communist Youth International, members from the Communist Party of the United States, and representatives from the Communist parties of fourteen Latin American countries. Mexico was represented by Siqueiros (under the name of Suárez) and an individual called Rosáenz.[34]

In the draft thesis of the congress, the main slogan of the Third Period, the danger of an imperialist war, was once again drawn to the attention of the Latin American Communists: "The VI Congress Thesis correctly states: 'As a result of the squeezing out of British capital, South America is gradually becoming an enormous sphere of influence to the United States.' To affirm that the process is completed means to underestimate the strength of British imperialism, to underestimate Latin America as a source of imperialist conflict and consequently to underestimate the danger of imperialist war."[35]

There were many other resolutions which repeated the slogans of the Moscow conference of April, 1928, the Sixth Congress of the Comintern, and the Montevideo congress of the previous month. The various delegates described the problems in their individual countries: the "reformist" trade unions were criticized and the importance of defending the Soviet Union was stressed again.

During the congress an analysis of the Workers' and Peasants' Bloc brought out the question of Communist control. Victorio Codovilla, the representative of the Latin American Secretariat of the Comintern, and Stephanov, the Chief of the Latin American Section of the Comintern, proposed that the Latin American Communists infiltrate the Workers' and Peasants' Bloc to gain control. Stephanov explained the strategy in the following manner: "It is necessary, above all, to create Communist factions in the center of the workers' and peasants' organizations. . .so that we can have in our hands the whole of this organization (bloc) by means of our stratagem of fractions at the base, with the fundamental condition that the Party can push, recruit, organize the Workers' and Peasants' Bloc to transform it into an auxiliary of the Party's mass actions. . ." [36]

The various resolutions of the Buenos Aires congress indicated that there would be more violence and greater crises in the Latin American countries with the weakening of the petty bourgeoisie. This led to the conclusion that the possibility of realizing a proletarian revolution would be greatly enhanced. [37]

In considering the general tasks and tactics of the Communist parties, the congress proposed three stages to bring about a complete Communist victory in Latin America: initially, the revolutionary movements would be directed by workers' and peasants' Soviets; when the revolutions ended in Communist victories, the Soviets would then be incorporated into the Workers' and Peasants' Governments; this would finally lead to Workers' and Peasants' Republics throughout Latin America. [38]

Several speeches during the congress by Mexican and foreign Communist delegates pertained to Mexico. The foreign Communists, those representing the Communist Party of the United States and the Comintern, called for bold action. Earl Browder, Secretary General of the Communist Party of the United States, criticized the Communist Party of Mexico for not taking advantage of a recent strike to form groups of insurrectional Soviets. Stephanov, representing the Comintern, told the Mexican Communists that the hour of revolution had come: "A regroupment of forces is operating (in Mexico) and it appears absolutely clear that only a new revolutionary action of the mass of workers and peasants, a new violent revolutionary crisis, will impede the complete liquidation of the positions acquired previously by the laboring masses. . .political action of our Party is decisive in this hour. If it knows how to mobilize the masses of workers and peasants for the struggle; if it knows how to lead them, the hegemony in the revolutionary struggle will pass, from the hands of the small bourgeoisie . . . to those of the revolutionary proletariat and peasants. . ." [39]

David Alfaro Siqueiros, speaking for the Mexican Communists, answered the other Communist leaders: "In resumé, comrades, facing the failure of Calles and Portes Gil, no other remedy is left to our Party than to take arms, to organize the armed uprising. . .it is necessary to organize sabotage. . .for imperialism will penetrate the country in order to stifle the revolution. In the event the Yankees dominate the first moment of the organized uprising by our Party, one can destroy their industries, set fire to the petroleum enterprises, etc., and then, we take refuge in the hills where they will never drag us out. . ." [40]

The conferences and congresses which took place in Moscow and Latin America provided the Mexican Communists with a wide range for tactics and propaganda and for instructions for the direction of their movement. In turn, the Mexican Communists reacted strongly to the propaganda and threats posed by the Third Period of the Comintern.

CHAPTER V

THE THIRD PERIOD OF THE COMINTERN

A few weeks before the opening of the Sixth Congress of the Comintern which (among other things) called upon the Communists to form their own trade unions, the periodical of the Communist Party of Mexico was asking the workers and peasants to seek unity within the existing non-Communist organizations: "the Communists ask all the workers and peasants that. . .they establish national workers' unity, in order to prevent the purposes of our enemies from prospering." [1] However, shortly after the Sixth Congress of the Comintern was concluded, the Mexican Communists initiated preparations to form a new labor organization under Communist direction and control.

By the end of 1928 the Communists of Mexico had formed a National Committee for Proletarian Defense and for the Latin American Trade Union Confederation (Comité Nacional Pro Defensa Proletaria y Pro Confederación Sindical Latino Americana). The resolution establishing the committee expressed opposition to American imperialism and governments of "exploitation." [2] The committee soon began to publish a periodical called *Defensa Proletaria* (Proletarian Defense).

The National Committee formed a Committee For A Workers and Peasants National Assembly which organized a congress (January 26-30, 1929) to establish the Unitary Trade Union Confederation of Mexico (Confederación Sindical Unitaria de México, or CSUM). [3] Members of the Executive Committee were David Alfaro Siqueiros, secretary general; Valentín Campa, Elías Barrios and Gastón Lafarga. It was not long before the CSUM adhered to the Latin American trade union organization (the CSLA) established at Montevideo a few months later.

In regard to relations with the non-Communist labor organizations, the orientation of the CSUM was an example of the change produced in this Third Period. The new plan called for the destruction of such organizations as the CROM and the General Confederation of Labor; and to win the workers away from them into the Communist-controlled CSUM, making possible the "United Front from below." The CSUM would then be strengthened to carry on its work in Mexico and to aid the CSLA in organizing the workers in other parts of Latin America. [4]

The unyielding Communist attacks on the CROM were along two main lines. In the first place, the CROM was identified with the government: "Another similar case is that of Mexico, where the government of the petty bourgeoisie in proportion to which it surrenders body and soul to imperialism, tries to free itself from the revolutionary trade union movement, crushing it and repressing it bloodily, while on the other hand, it endeavors to develop a trade union movement clearly governmental and toward the Fascist edge, supported by the national bourgeoisie and imperialism." [5] The leaders of the CROM were also bitterly criticized: "The revolutionary proletariat of Mexico will not permit itself to be suppressed, not even when the reformist trade union leaders, such as Morones and his like, now playing the sorry role of Social Democracy towards the imperialism which is enslaving the masses, lend their aid to that imperialism." [6]

Other positions of the CSUM corresponded with the general Comintern view during the Third Period: the organization would further the class struggle in order to realize a better society for humanity; Capitalism would be opposed at all costs; Yankee imperialism must be opposed wherever it appears. Furthermore, there could be no compromise with the petty bourgeois government.[7]

In 1932 a major split occurred in the CROM when a dissident group, under Vicente Lombardo Toledano, broke with the CROM just before its national convention and later formed its own labor organization.

There has been much discussion as to whether Lombardo Toldeano was a Communist. He denied the charge on several occasions; he never belonged to the Communist party. By his own admission, Lombardo Toledano believed in Marxism-Leninism as a solution for the social problems of Mexico. But he added that one must think in terms of local conditions and not be limited by the dogmatism of the Communist party. In addition, he believed that while what the Soviet leaders had done had been good for Russia, their solutions to the problems in their country might not have been the solutions for Mexico: the country should seek its own way.[8] Lombardo Toledano could perhaps be described as a "national Communist." However, for the purpose of this study any discussion of Lombardo Toledano will be based upon one factor—What, if anything, was his influence in shaping the Communist movement in Mexico as he rose to power in the labor movement?

The factors lying behind the split in the CROM deserve special attention in the light of subsequent Communist development. Lombardo

Toledano told the writer that he left the CROM because many of its leaders were not taking the proper attitude with regard to relations with the government. General Calles moved to the right after the assassination of Alvaro Obregón in the summer of 1928. The CROM leaders, according to Lombardo Toledano, wanted to move slowly and seek means to cooperate with the government. Lombardo Toledano and his followers opposed the growing cooperation between the CROM and the government and decided to break away and form their own organization.[9]

However, this interpretation is open to question. After the assassination of Alvaro Obregón, the CROM leadership and the government parted ways. Many suspected that Morones played a role in the assassination of the ex-President, although no evidence of this was ever proved. The complete break between the government and the CROM has been described by several writers and even recognized by the journal of the Comintern: "The Congress of the Mexican Trade Union Federation (CROM) decided to break completely with the government and to combat the president of the Republic, Portes Giles (i.e., Gil). The Congress further decided to recall all members of the Trade Union Federation from the Federal Government and from the provincial governments, and also to withdraw all delegations from the parity commissions, consisting of representatives of the workers and employers, which were set up to deal with the new Labor Law." [10]

Furthermore, in March of 1931, some of Lombardo Toledano's followers on the CROM Central Committee tried to have him elected secretary general of the organization. This attempt failed, as did other efforts of Lombardo Toledano to become a member of the Action Group.[11]

The factors behind the split in the CROM were a struggle for power and ideological considerations. Lombardo Toledano failed to gain control of the CROM and its Action Group. A similar attempt by another group within the CROM, under Fidel Velázquez, was prevented by the old leadership under Morones. As a result, the followers of Lombardo Toledano and Fidel Velázquez joined forces and left the CROM.[12]

The ideological factor, although more difficult to substantiate, is more important for its impact on the labor movement and subsequent Communist development. According to Lombardo Toledano, he turned to Marxism-Leninism around 1932, the period during which he left the CROM.[13] He was the main person in the formation of a new labor organization, Marxist-Leninist in orientation, which existed side by side with the Communist-dominated CSUM for several years. The Marxist-Leninist ideology continued to grow in labor circles until it reached its pinnacle of success in 1936, during the Popular Front era.[14]

In 1933 Lombardo Toledano and his followers formed the General Confederation of Workers and Peasants of Mexico (Confederación General de Obreros y Campesinos de México, or CGOCM). Although the new organization was clearly Marxist and did not vary greatly from the position of the Comintern during the Third Period, its leaders, particularly Lombardo Toledano, were critical of the Communists.

On October 29, 1933, the CGOCM issued declarations similar to the resolutions passed by the Sixth Congress of the Comintern. For example, they agreed about the peasants: "expropriation of the land without indemification . . . (on behalf of) the peasants and for the restitution of the peasant population. . ." In addition, their views regarding the opposition to war coincided: "against the preparatives of war of any order, from the propaganda which is made in the schools to the organization of industries of war-like products; against wars of aggression and of conquest; . . ."[15]

During the time of the Third Period, Lombardo Toledano often criticized the Soviet Union and the Mexican Communists. Once, as a CROM official, he accused the Communists of operating through orders carried in the valise of the Soviet Legation. When Mexico and the Soviet Union broke diplomatic relations in 1930, Lombardo Toledano supported the position of the government.[16] He attacked the Communists on many occasions: "The communists are groups of agitation. . . they do not represent the working class . . ."[17] He clearly was competing with the Communists and other labor groups for the support of the workers.

On the other hand, Lombardo Toledano tried to persuade the other leaders of the CGOCM to bring the organization more into line with a strong Marxist-Leninist position. Speaking at the First Congress of the CGOCM, he declared: "It is not a question of incorporating workers' representatives into the state, but of recognizing the power of the working class organized against the state; . . . The root of the controversy is that the comrades who oppose the motion uphold the anarchist ideology and believe that all power, merely because it is power, corrupts. I believe the opposite, for I believe that we must arrive at the dictatorship of the proletariat."[18]

For their part, the Communists opposed Lombardo Toledano. They attacked him when he was an official of the CROM: "But simultaneously with this advance, England is forging its weapons of war, and this time Morornes and (Lombardo) Toledano are the willing servants and are coming forward to speak of the 'progressive' role of European capital." [19] Furthermore, when Lombardo Toledano left the CROM the Communists looked upon him as a competitor for the allegiance of the workers: "Particularly dangerous now are such reformist demagogues of the 'left' as Lombardo Toledano, who have left the CROM 'fighting against Morones' and who can canalize the mass discontent, deviating the masses from the mass revolutionary movement." [20]

Summary

Mexican labor witnessed significant changes during the Third Period in the development of Communism. A Communist trade union organization, the CSUM, was formed as the tactics of the previous period, working and remaining in the "reformist" trade unions, were abandoned. The Communists tried to bring those workers under ther control into direct conflict with the non-Communist labor organizations and with the government. In addition, a Marxist-Leninist labor organization, the CGCOM, also came into being. Although its leaders criticized the Communists, the position of the new workers' organization was close to that of the Comintern and the Communist-controlled CSUM.

The Peasants

For a short time the Communists were very successful in the peasant movement. The National Peasants League took part in the assembly which formed the CSUM and subsequently joined the latter.[21] When a Workers' and Peasants' Bloc was formed under Communist leadership, Ursulo Galván brought the National Peasants League into the new organization. Upon entering the bloc, the National Peasants League presented the following program:

"First-abolition of the present Legislative Power, and the consequent suppression of the Federal and Local Councils, substituting for them the Assemblies of Workers' and Peasants' Representatives elected in their respective industrial and agricultural centers.

". . . Fourteenth—Effective nationalization of the large industries: railroads, petroleum, mines, textile factories, etc.

". . . Nineteenth—Dissolution of the large estates and handing over the land to the peasants. The form of occupation, of distribution and work of the land, will be communal or parceled out according to the agreement of the people and the communities of the general assemblies.

"The land and the factories for the workers! Not political insurrection but social revolution! Workers and peasants unite!" [22]

The National Peasants League was a very strong factor within the bloc and Galván became a member of the National Committee.

The peak of Communist success with the peasants lasted only until the spring of 1929. By the summer of that year, only a small group of peasants remained under Communist influence and before the year was out, the National Peasants League and the Communists had split. During the purge of the Communist party (more about this later in this chapter), Galván was expelled from the party and all other Communist organizations. He later resigned from the Workers' and Peasants' Bloc.[23] From 1929 until the end of World War II, the Communists failed in their attempts to bring the mass of the peasants into the fold. During the Third Period, the influence of Galván was the main obstacle in the path of the Communists. After the death of the peasant leader in 1930, the government was able to organize the peasants and brought them under government auspices.[24] Although the leaders of the Comintern had frequently stated that success could only be realized by an alliance of the workers and peasants under Communist control, the door was closed as far as the Mexican peasants were concerned.

Tactics, Agents and Propaganda

When General Obregón was assassinated in 1928, the Communists condemned the act. They had supported his candidacy, and now that he had passed from the political stage, they emphasized the need of forming a Workers' and Peasants' Bloc to continue the advance of the Revolution.[25]

During a conference of Communists, January 24-25, 1929, in Mexico City, a Workers' and Peasants' Bloc was formed in accord with the various resolutions of the Sixth Congress of the Comintern and the Moscow and Latin American gatherings. The thesis of the Communist party was that the bloc was needed to separate the masses from the bourgeoisie.[26]

The program of the Workers' and Peasants' Bloc, as expressed during the January conference, indicated the militant orientation of the Third Period: "This program included the arming of the masses, nationalization of the land, confiscation of the industries with workers' control, and the setting up of workers' and peasants' councils, etc. This program is clearly based upon a perspective of a sharply revolutionary situation in which the leadership must be assumed by the working class." [27]

In accord with the thinking of the Comintern leaders, the Communists did not believe that the Workers' and Peasants' Bloc would be the ultimate stage: "Against the electoral farce of the parties of the bourgeoisie, we oppose the WORKERS' and PEASANTS' BLOC with its program of revolutionary action, of frank and indefatigable class struggle until the implementation of the Government of the Workers and Peasants." [28]

The president of the Workers' and Peasants' Bloc was Diego Rivera. Other officials, besides Ursulo Galván, included Luis G. Monzón, Rafael Carrillo and Hernán Laborde. During the January conference in which it was established, the Workers' and Peasants' Bloc selected Pedro V. Rodríguez Triana to be its presidential candidate.

The close relationship established between the Comintern and the Mexican Communists during the Third Period (as shown by the formation of the Workers' and Peasants' Bloc) was strengthened by personal contacts. Many of the personnel changes within the party were a direct result of the activities of Comintern agents who appeared intermittently in the country from the beginning of the Communist movement through the end of 1945.[29]

In the spring of 1929 the Comintern official, Dimitri Manuilsky, appeared using the name of Comrade "Pedro" to bring about an insurrection of the peasants against the government. A warning was issued that those "Trotskyites" who refused to cooperate would be purged from the Communist party.[30]

During his stay Manuilsky directed the Central Committee of the Communist party as a member of the Executive of the Comintern. Diego Rivera described how Manuilsky tried to "convince" him to accept the tactic of insurrection with the promise of as much work as he might want as a painter of murals in the Soviet Union. Manuilsky also threw in the offer of a professorship in the first Socialist state. In exchange, Rivera was expected to sign a document in which he promised not to attack the general line of the Comintern, nor discuss the internal politics of the Soviet Union, nor try to take part in any political work while in the U.S.S.R.

Diego Rivera refused the offer. He voted for his own expulsion in the final session of the Central Committee because, according to his account, he did not want to be in the "Official Stalinist Party." Manuilsky said that Rivera would be allowed to come back into the party if he consented to sign a manifesto attacking the government.

The manifesto was never published. It would start with "I accuse" and, after its publication, Rivera was to leave the country. According to Rivera, Manuilsky showed him a mandate signed by the highest authority of the Comintern and the Soviet state naming the artist to the posts he wanted in the organizations of art of the Soviet Union. He could fill his own positions.[31]

In March, 1929, another presidential election crisis arose in the form of a revolt by Generals Aguirre and Escobar against the government of Portes Gil. Many of the leaders of the Communist party believed that the time to take power had arrived. Two other Comintern agents, Sormenti and A. Stirner, were helping Manuilsky direct the activities of the Communist party at the time. Under their influence, the decision was made to collaborate with the government in crushing the rebellion and then to turn it into a civil war against the government. Opposed to this decision were several Communist leaders (including Rivera and Rafael Carrillo) who wanted to work at organization and not incite government persecution against the party.[32] Galván was also opposed to the operation but he agreed to lead some peasant detachments against the rebels.

The immediate aim of the Communists was to establish Soviets in the northern regions. According to the plan of the Third Period, however, the long-term goal was to overthrow the government and establish a Workers' and Peasants' Government.[33]

The Communist-inspired insurrection, lacking proper planning and organization, was easily suppressed by government forces led by General Calles. Diego Rivera gave the following description of the Communist insurrection: "The Central Committee agreed to place in, *El Machete* instructions to the peasants for insurrection . . . the edition of the paper was distributed in the capital and the provinces . . . giving the names of those who were to take part in the insurrection . . . In reality this was placing the insurrectionists into the hands of the police by listing their names. The government confiscated the edition . . . many comrades were imprisoned and shot, especially peasants."

Among the prominent Communists killed, were José Guadalupe Rodríguez and Salvador Gómez. The Communists reacted to the failure of the insurrection and the deaths of some of their militants by assailing the government: "The assassination of those two . . . (i. e., José Guadalupe Rodríguez and Salvador Gómez) shows that the Mexican government, which before and during a time vacillated under the pressure of the worker and peasant masses, has already surrendered itself completely to imperialism, which is a fact of real importance which deserves particular attention on the part of all the workers of the continent." [34]

Perhaps the most disastrous effect of the insurrection, as far as the Communists were concerned, was the loss of peasant support. The party could afford to purge Diego Rivera and other members of less prominence. It was able to withstand increased government persecution. The loss of Galván and the peasants, however, was catastrophic.

The Comintern leaders recognized the complete failure of the ill-fated tactics which were used. Manuilsky, upon his return to the Soviet Union, reported to the ECCI: "And we have a very painful experience . . . in Mexico. Here the collaboration of the Communist Party of Mexico with other classes, without a firm Bolshevik line, led to the crushing of the Mexican Communist movement." [35]

The main criticism by the Comintern was that the Mexican Communists believed "imperialism" was united. The Comintern leaders pointed out that, in fact, the British supported the Escobar-Aguirre rebellion while the United States supported the government. The Mexican Communists were also brought to task for their policy of supporting the governments against rebellions. According to the Comintern interpretation, the rebels always represented one of the imperialist powers and the government the other. This meant that the Communists should not seek an alliance, however temporary, with either of these forces. This was the Third Period of Capitalism— the imperialist powers were struggling among themselves and "Capitalist stabilization" had come to an end. Not only were the Communists mistaken in supporting the Portes Gil government against the rebels, but they should never have supported President Callas against a similar rebellion or the candidacy of his chosen successor, Alvaro Obregón.[36] Characteristically, the Comintern leaders criticized the Mexican Communists, but not their own agents.

The conclusion reached by the leaders of the Comintern was that the Communists had to close ranks. The Mexican Communists were instructed to destroy the influence of the bourgeoisie within the party. The Workers' and Peasants' Bloc had to be brought more clearly under Communist control; the proletariat and not the peasants was to assume the leadership of the bloc. The peasants could not be relied upon as a revolutionary force. Furthermore, in the future, the Communists must oppose both the government and rebellions under the leadership of reactionary forces.[37]

The reaction of the government to the increased violence of the Com-

munists was swift and decisive. The Communist-inspired insurrection
was crushed; diplomatic relations were broken with the Soviet Union.
The offices of *El Machete* were closed, and the CSUM and the Communist party were declared illegal (the party was thus illegal from
1929-1934). Many Communists were arrested and sent to the peni-
tentiary of Islas Marias. They were brutally treated and some were
never heard from again.

Many Communists were arrested on the accusation that they were
planning to assassinate General Calles. When an attempt was made
upon the life of Ortiz Rubio, on the day of his inauguration as President, renewed attacks were made on the Communists by the government. Strong measures were taken against the Communists throughout the administration of Ortiz Rubio[38] and Abelardo Rodríguez and
did not cease until Lázaro Cárdenas became President of Mexico. The
Communists considered this period as a "wave of terror": "Following
the resignation of President Ortiz Rubio at the behest of Yankee
Imperialism, and the substitution in his place of General Abelardo
Rodríguez, who in his inaugural speech indicated that he would still
further cement the bonds of friendship with the Northern neighbor
(U.S.A.), the wave of terror took a sharp upward turn. The government made an onslaught on the Communist Party, the Revolutionary
Trade Unions, and the Peasant Leagues in order to prevent further
development of the wave of strikes and struggles of the unemployed
and of the peasants whose conditions have become even worse than
before in the past few months." [39]

Communist propaganda during the Third Period reflected the thinking of the leaders of the Sixth Congress of the Comintern. The main
theme, that a war was being prepared against the Soviet Union, was
repeated often by the Mexican Communists.[40] As a result, they
opposed war in general and participation of Mexico in any war:
"We decided (CPM) to organize the struggle against the participation
of Mexico in the South American war (i.e., the Chaco War between
Bolivia and Paraguay) and against the war itself, linking up this
struggle with the fight against imperialist war in general and against
the preparation of intervention against the Soviet Union." [41]

During the Third Period the Communists cleverly manipulated the
theme of anti-Americanism to serve two purposes: Mexico and the
Soviet Union were depicted as facing the common enemy of American
imperialism; the Communists were also able to attack the government
by identifying it with American financial interests.[42]

The Communists suggested that the government was typically

bourgeois whenever Communists were persecuted and when the government broke off diplomatic relations with the Soviet Union. Throughout the Third Period the Communists interpreted the actions of the government as inevitable in a period in which Capitalist stabilization had come to an end and the revolutionary tide was rising.[43]

In spite of their abortive insurrection and their suppression by government troops, the Comunists did not cease in their efforts to create a revolutionary crisis. Wiser elements within the Communist party probably realized such efforts would be futile, particularly since the party had been weakened by government persecution; nevertheless, the Communists continued to espouse the cause of revolution in accordance with the dictates of the Comintern: "Realizing its immediate tasks, according to the decisions of the Twelfth Plenum (i.e., of the ECCI), our Party will create the conditions for development of the revolutionary crisis in Mexico." [44]

From August 23-26, 1934, the First National Congress Against Fascism and War was held in the country. Various resolutions were passed by the congress, including that of the "United Front from below." The slogan, frequently used by the Communists,[45] was a rallying cry used during the Third Period to help prevent the unleashing of an "imperialist war."

The Communists criticized the various administrations throughout the Third Period. Their attacks on the Calles government were relatively mild (for which they were subsequently criticized by the Comintern), but their attacks upon his successors were harsh. The Portes Gil government was identified with the forces of American imperialism and "counter-revolution." [46] Portes Gil's successor, Ortiz Rubio, considered to be the head of a Fascist government which had capitulated to foreign capital,[47] fared no better under Communist propaganda. The Communist attitude toward President Cárdenas was determined by the "line" of the Third Period; since they had not yet made the transition to the Popular Front era. Even as the Seventh Congress of the Comintern (which proclaimed the tactic of the Popular Front) was drawing to a close, the Mexican Communists were highly critical of the Cárdenas government: "the workers and peasants cannot . . . be content with . . . the government of Cárdenas, which we agree is a great deal different from Callismo . . . . To support it would be to fall into a collaborationist policy . . . contrary to the interests and the cause of the proletariat and of the people." [48]

Overall, the Communist movement received a setback during the Third Period. Most of the tactics followed led to reversals, except in the labor movement, where the Communists did not fare so badly. The previous period of Communist development had had but limited success in influencing the workers. The CSUM was formed in the hope of altering the pattern and it did attract some workers. It might have been more successful if other Communist tactics had not resulted in such a violent reaction from the government.

More significant for Communist influence in the labor movement was the formation of the Marxist-Leninist CGOCM. It is true that the CSUM and CGOCM exchanged propaganda volleys. It is also true that the CROM, although in a period of decline, continued to have the support of the majority of the organized workers. However, by having the CSUM and the CGOCM exist side by side for a few years, it was easier to bring Communists and self-proclaimed Marxists-Leninists into one general labor organization during the succeeding period of the Popular Front. As we shall see in the next chapter, this proved to be the key which opened the labor movement to the Communists and allowed them to enjoy greater success with the workers than at any time through 1945.

However, if the labor movement encouraged some Communists to feel guardedly optimistic, the failures of the rest of their activities cast a dim shadow over prospects for the future. The Mexican Communists were shackled by the tactics of the Third Period. The Comintern agents who appeared led them down the road of disaster, and the exigency of Soviet foreign policy (i.e., to protect Soviet Russia against an impending imperialist attack "by all means") retarded the Communist movement. Any previous success with the peasants was nullified. The Communist ranks were weakened by an unsuccessful insurrection. In addition, the government resorted to more repressive measures than ever against the Communists. If the Communist movement was to survive the Third Period and continue to develop, a change in the methods of operation would be needed.

What would a reversal of tactics and propaganda bring in the forthcoming period of the Popular Front? What would happen if the Communists supported the government for a change? What changes might take place if Communist leaders fully cooperated with other Marxist-Leninist organizations? What might occur if the Communists joined with other groups in a united labor movement? Interestingly—if not unexpectedly—such questions received serious consideration in the next stage of the Communist movement.

CHAPTER VI

THE POPULAR FRONT ERA

The tactics of the Popular Front era which lasted from the Seventh Congress in Moscow in the summer of 1935 until the signing of the Nazi-Soviet pact in August, 1939, were based on one main theme: Facism was to be opposed at all costs and on all levels, whether this signified denouncing the Fascism practiced by Nazi Germany or supporting the forces opposed to Franco in the Spanish Civil War.

Five main tactics were decided upon during the Seventh Congress of the Comintern,[1] most of which were attempted, with varying degrees of success, by the Mexican Communists. Communists were first called upon to make an effort to form a United Front in their respective countries, whether from above or below. They were expected to cooperate with "bourgeois" leaders and Socialists on all levels; the slogan of "Social-Fascism" of the Third Period ceased to exist. Communists were even encouraged to participate in election campaigns. The call for a proletarian revolution, one of the slogans of the Third Period, was dropped; nationalism was to be the new slogan of the Popular Front era. Secondly, the United Front was to merge into the People's Front (Popular Front). Thirdly, it was hoped that the Communists in the various countries would be able to realize a government of the United Front or People's Front. Moreover, Communists were to strive to bring about trade union unity; Communist trade unions had to be abolished. Finally, Communists were to join with other elements to form a single party of the proletariat.

Transition From the Third Period to the Popular Front Era

The Mexican Communists' hostility to the early phase of the Cárdenas administration was the result of following the Third Period tactics, rather than the new Popular Front, which dictated cooperation. As they had in their attacks on previous governments, the Communists tried to utilize the theme of anti-Americanism: "It is necessary to say here, that Cárdenas continues the policy of his Callista predecessors . . . in the question of his exterior relations with Yankee imperialism, a policy of alliance and submission to imperialism."[2] The Communists also used anti-Americanism in attacking the government's Six-Year Plan, a program they subsequently supported. The Plan was portrayed as a project planned in Wall Street and carried out by native exploiters.[3]

During the power struggle between President Cárdenas and General Calles (which resulted in the latter's expulsion from the country), the Communists took a neutral position, as indicated by their slogan: "Neither with Calles nor with Cárdenas." The Communists also tried to isolate President Cárdenas from the masses: "With Cárdenas, no; with the Cardenista masses, yes."

The tactics of the Third Period were not easily discarded by the Mexican Communists. Even during the Seventh Congress of the Comintern, one of their representatives, Serrano, still clung to the idea that a revolutionary crisis was still possible in Mexico.[4]

But when the Communists of Mexico remembered that the Popular Front called for new methods of struggle, they felt it wise to renounce their past tactical sins of the Third Period. This was done by Hernán Laborde, Secretary General of the Communist Party of Mexico, in a speech delivered to the Seventh Congress of the Comintern: "This wrong line prevented us from seeing the favorable conditions which the political situation in the country, from the taking of power by President Cárdenas to the end of 1934, offered us to develop a vast people's movement against imperialism . . . in June, when the clash between Calles and Cárdenas took place, when Cárdenas rejected the statements of Calles by announcing himself opposed to his reactionary proposals and for the right to strike, we saw nothing more than a factional struggle between two bourgeois-landlord cliques, and disagreements on the most adequate methods to liquidate the struggles of the masses and to quiet down the country for the benefit of foreign capital and its national allies. We placed Cárdenas on the same plane as Calles and limited ourselves to saying to the masses: 'Neither with Calles nor with Cárdenas,' and to asserting that the two were against the proletariat. This position was wrong." [5]

The added error of their wrong attitude toward the PNR (National Revolutionary Party) and its Six-Year Plan,[6] which may have cost them the support of the masses, was explained by Laborde in the above-cited speech to the Seventh Congress of the Comintern: "All this explains why the masses could not understand us when we shouted against the National Revolutionary Party and against its governments, calling them 'counter-revolutionaries,' 'lackeys of imperialism,' etc.; and why the National Revolutionary Party has succeeded in retaining a large mass base, notwithstanding its undoubted collaboration with imperialism, while we with our loud slogans on the agrarian anti-imperialist revolution, the workers' and peasants' government, the power of the soviets, have been able to win over only the most advanced sections of the working class and the peasantry." [7]

A new approach, in accord with the tactics of the Popular Front era, was needed. In his speech to the Seventh Congress of the Comintern, Laborde stated that the Mexican Communists "must quickly change the line of the Party and adopt a correct tactic." He proposed a United Front with the followers of President Cárdenas who were in the PNR with the hope that once the government party had been cleansed of "reactionary" elements, the United Front could be extended to the PNR as a whole. When this point had been reached, it would be permissible for Communists to enter the organs of the PNR. [8]

As the United Front merged into the Popular Front, the Communists would be expected to cooperate with all groups in realizing certain basic (i.e., nationalistic) demands such as national liberation and the economic and political independence of the country. To strengthen national unity, the Communist party would support the government—any government—in order to carry out the policies of the Popular Front. [9] Thus, the foundation was laid for the Mexican Communists to be converted from the instigators of proletarian revolution of the Third Period to the nationalists of the Popular Front era.

Serrano's speech to the Seventh Congress of the Comintern, however, reflected the continuing Communist fear of the new President. The Communists did not want their support for his policies to compromise their own independent position. Thus, at the beginning of the Popular Front era, the Communists claimed they would be free to criticize President Cárdenas. [10] However, as we shall see, this conditional approval of the Cárdenas administration was transformed into almost unqualified support before the end of the President's term of office.

Laborde left no doubt in the minds of the delegates to the Comintern Congress the road toward which the Mexican Popular Front would travel: "The people's front will be successful and the victory of the revolution will be possible only if we know how to link ourselves to the broad masses who today follow national-reformism, to organize them through partial struggles towards the revolution, at the same time retaining the organic and political independence of our Party, as the revolutionary Party of the proletariat, and always keeping in view our objectives of agrarian and anti-imperialism revolution, which opens the breach towards Soviet Power and towards socialism."[11]

The Popular Front

The Communist leaders went through two phases in trying to explain to their followers the best methods to be used toward realizing a Popular Front. At first, they hoped to create a broad movement which would include the PNR as one of several groups. However, after the official government party was reorganized and the Party of the Mexican Revolution (Partido de la Revolución Mexicana or PRM) came into being in the spring of 1938, the Communists changed their tactics. They began to think in terms of infiltrating the new party, and, according to their interpretation of conditions, to make the PRM into a Popular Front which would include Communist and non-Communist groups.

In the letter of the Mexican delegation of the Seventh Congress of the Comintern to the Central Committee of the party, cited previously, definite steps were presented in order to realize a Popular Front: "The bourgeois-democratic revolution initiated in 1910 and betrayed by its principal leaders, has not liberated the country from economic domination, nor from the political influence of imperialism; neither has it resolved the agrarian problem (destruction of the large estates and of the semi-feudal survivals and handing over the land to the peasants). In order to place the Revolution again on the march and to realize its anti-imperialist and agrarian goals, it is necessary to create a wide popular movement of masses, which clasps all the people and carries them to struggle against imperialism and reaction, through the economic interests of the people, through national liberation of the country, and through democratic liberties."[12]

The Communists believed that the PNR had to be included in the Popular Front in order to make it meaningful. Therefore, it was necessary to subject the members of the official government party to intense propaganda so that they would become part of a broad national movement.[13]

By no means would the Communists allow the Popular Front to limit them. They frequently pointed out that flexible tactics would always be at their disposal and that any adjustments which might be necessary could be made within the overall framework of the Popular Front.[14]

In order to gain the support of the mass of the people for the creation of a Popular Front, the Communists linked their policies with Mexican heroes and events: "The Communist Party ought to revindicate figures as that of Emiliano Zapata, the most honored and most revered leaders of the peasant masses in the Agrarian Revolution. It ought to convert the 16 of September, anniversary of the Independence, and the 20 of November, anniversary of the Revolution of 1910, into two dates of the popular movement for effective independence, for emancipation, and for the benefit of the people." [15]

The statement by Laborde at the Seventh Congress of the Comintern, that the Popular Front in Mexico would have as its ultimate goals the attainment of "Soviet Power and Socialism," was possibly offensive to some of the Mexican Communists. Although they substituted the phrase "dictatorship of the proletariat" for "Soviet Power," the meaning was still much the same.[16]

Throughout 1937, the Communists proclaimed several tactics, often conflicting, in order to bring an effective Popular Front into being. Early in 1937 they declared that Communists would be allowed to participate in some state governments. They would not be allowed, however, to participate in a higher level until the country had a truly "National Revolutionary Government." [17] The Cárdenas government and the PNR, according to the Communists, did meet their test of "revolutionary."

The "resistance" of the administration and the PNR to follow the Communists in the formation of a Popular Front led them to accuse the President and the official government party of "inconsistency" and "vacillation." [18] It would have been closer to the truth, however, if the Communists had been more self-critical; it was they who were inconsistent in their gropings to find a clear-cut policy during the early years of the Popular Front era.

One of the inconsistencies concerned the role of the Communist party and other groups within the Popular Front. In the summer of 1937 Laborde stated that the Communists would support the Popular Front even though the Communist party was not a participant.[19] A few months later, however, the importance of the role of the Communist party in the Popular Front was stressed: "The actual soul of the People's Front, and of the united front of the proletariat, is represented by the CP of Mexico, with its more than 20,000 members." [20] In 1940 a new Secretary General of the Communist party, Dionisio Encina, told an Extraordinary Congress of the party (which we shall analyze in the following chapter) that the Popular Front had to include the Communist party.

The Communists simply did not know how to fit the new Comintern "line" to the conditions of the country. After a period of self-contradictory trial and error efforts to form a Popular Front policy, the Communists came to the conclusion that the PNR would have to be reorganized to make the Popular Front effective. In his report to Central Committee of the Communist party, Laborde spelled out the problems and the steps that must be taken:

"In Mexico, the National Revolutionary Party is the party of the revolution in power and has the support of all the people's organizations. Having leadership in national politics, this party does not consider it necessary to share its power with other organizations in a united front which would place upon it determinate obligations and restrictions. Therefore, the National Revolutionary Party has been opposed to the formation of the Mexican People's Front and has in return done everything possible to strengthen the support given it by mass organizations and to absorb them transitorily in the electoral campaigns.

"Under these conditions, the People's Front is possible only within the National Revolutionary Party (PRN); that is to say, by transforming the PNR into a bloc-party, in a broad united front, formed by the CTM, the Peasants' Federation, the Communist Party, and all the organizations accepting the common program . . . Thus, there will be a genuine People's Front, only with another name and carried out in accordance with the peculiar conditions of the country." [21]

A few weeks after Laborde called for the transformation of the PNR, President Cárdenas proclaimed that it would be converted into a new revolutionary party. The Communists seized upon this announcement as their salvation. Although they had claimed that a Popular Front existed in one form or another, the following statement shows that they knew that they had failed to form such a broad movement. The article was entitled "President Cárdenas Lays Foundation for People's Front": "In a history-making manifesto, addressed to 'the Mexican Nation,' President Lázaro Cárdenas has announced the transformation of the National Revolutionary Party (PNR) into 'the Party of the Workers, Peasants, and Soldiers' to fight 'against despotism and oppression,' thereby definitely establishing the basis for the immediate formation of the Popular Front of Mexico." [22]

The new official government party, the Party of the Mexican Revolution or PRM, was organized into four sectors—peasants, labor, military, popular, each of which unanimously rejected the Communist party.[23] This rejection did not prevent individual Communists from working within the PRM, and, furthermore, as far as the Communists were concerned, the new official government party was synonymous with the Popular Front: "The Party of the Mexican Revolution has been set up as the special form of the People's Front in Mexico . . . The Party of the Mexican Revolution represents a bloc of all the organizations of the people, with one million workers and employees, 1½ million peasants, and a great number of groups of women, youth, intellectuals, and the whole army. The Communists belong to the Party of (the Mexican) Revolution through the workers' and peasants' organizations in which they are working. . ." [24]

Throughout the remainder of the Popular Front era, the Communists called upon their followers to support the official government party: "ALL UNITED IN THE PRM" [25] was a typical headline in the periodical of the Communist party, *La Voz de México*. The Communists insisted that the PRM had to be strengthened in order to carry on the struggle against Fascism and to realize the goals of the Mexican Revolution.[26]

Although the Communist party as such never joined one of the sectors of the official government party, individual Communists and Marxists who supported Soviet foreign policy were very active in the PRM. As we shall soon see, the labor sector was dominated by the CTM which, in turn, was heavily infiltrated with Communists and others who closely adhered to the policies of the Comintern.

How successful were the Communists in realizing a Popular Front in Mexico? If one thinks of a Popular Front in terms of France and Chile in the 1930's where several political parties and groups worked in common to support candidates and programs, then a Popular Front did not exist in Mexico. One Latin American specialist believes there were several reasons why a "real" Popular Front did not become a reality: the rejection by the army and of any coalition including the Communists and the presence of Leon Trotsky, which split the leftists (a factor analyzed in the next chapter):

"Most important of all the concept of a Popular Front simply did not fit the needs of Mexican political conditions. It had developed as a political device in countries where an institutionalized multiparty system already existed. Rather than a device of this sort, which would turn interest groups into competitive, hard-core class parties. . . Mexico required some sort of political mechanism that could channel the activities of the developing specialized interests into a constructive and integrated political system.

"As a consequence, President Cárdenas gave the projected Popular Front the 'finishing stroke' when, in December, 1937, he called for dissolution of the PNR and formation of a new revolutionary party." [27]

The writer agrees with this interpretation. Although a Popular Front, in the strict sense of the term, did not exist in Mexico, the mystique of the Popular Front did. The willingness of many anti-Fascist groups to accept the cooperation of the Communists facilitated their efforts to move into positions of strength in the labor movement (particularly in the CTM) and to participate in the labor organization which was the main factor in the labor section of the newly formed PRM. The Communists thus received the benefits of a Popular Front even though there wasn't a Front as originally envisaged by the leaders of the Comintern. The Communist party was legal; its members were influential in the organs of the official government party (and in the government itself); and the Communists were identified with other popular forces opposed to Fascism. The Communists, on their part, gave almost unqualified support to the Cárdenas government.

The Communists and the Cárdenas Administration

The Communists supported the Cárdenas government, for the most part, during the life of the administration. However, as Laborde stated in January of 1936 the Communists were being realistic in supporting such a government: "It is said that this is an engagement or an alliance of the proletariat with a class foreign to it and it is true: It is an engagement, but it is one of those engagements which Lenin considered not only admissible, but necessary . . . But, Comrades, this does not mean that we are Cardenistas: We are Communists . . . We support Cárdenas as conscientious allies, because we have certain common immediate objectives . . ." [28]

The Communists generally backed the administration's strongly anti-Facist foreign policy. Cárdenas personally attended the CTM's "Congress Against Fascism and War," opposed the forces of Franco in Spain, and welcomed the Spanish refugees to the country. In the League of Nations, Mexico voted for the application of sanctions against Fascist Italy for its colonial exploits. Since all of these policies were in accord with the foreign policy of the Soviet Union during the period, the Communists did not find it difficult to applaud most of the proclamations and actions of the government. [29]

The domestic policies of President Cárdenas were generally well received by the Communists. They especially praised the land distribution policy of the government: "Cárdenas follows a definite national revolutionary policy. He is engaging in agrarian reform and in anti-imperialist measures of the widest consequence. Cárdenas is granting land to peasants who were outside of the scope of the agrarian laws. He has established collectivization of land besides establishing collective ownership." [30]

However, when the government nationalized the railroads and the petroleum industry in the spring of 1938, the Communists reacted somewhat strangely at first. They called a strike in support of the expropriation of the petroleum industry, but it was at best a token strike. The Soviet Union opposed the government's action. One close observer believed that the Mexican Communists also opposed the expropriation.[31] If he is correct, it is not easy to figure out what the Communists were up to. Perhaps they felt that the more success the non-Communist government had with such programs, the less would be the attraction of Communism for the mass of the people. In time, however, the Communists joined other non-Communist groups within the country in support of the nationalization policies of the government.

The Communists supported President Cárdenas when he placed the administration of the railroads and the petroleum industries in the hands of their respective trade unions. When, however, the government officials assumed control of those industries on grounds of efficiency, the Communists approved of that too by the following resolution issued by the Central Committee of the Communist party in October of 1938: "In general terms, the direct administration of the industries by the trade unions is not advisable, since it places in danger the independence and the liberty of action of the trade unions in the realization of their true functions . . . The administration of the large nationalized industries should remain under the direction of the state, with the cooperation of the trade unions and with a system of workers' control." [32]

A few months later, January 28-February 3, 1939, during the Seventh Congress of the Communist party, Laborde elaborated the theme: "it becomes at the same time, defender of the workers and administrator, that is, defender of the industry. Inevitably, one function enters into conflict with the other, and the trade union has to choose between the industry and the workers. And it is very probable that it will abandon the interests of the workers, trying very hard to make the administration triumph . . . the workers' administration decentralizes and disperses the economy, instead of centralizing and organizing it." [33]

It should be pointed out that the Communist opposition to workers'

control of petroleum and railroads was consistent with Marxism-Leninism and that not since the period of War Communism in the Soviet
Union had Syndicalism or Guild Socialism (direct workers control)
been urged.

The Communists continued to support the government against internal revolts such as that caused by General Saturnino Cedillo, who
was easily crushed when he raised a private army to oppose the
government after Cárdenas dismissed him as Minister of Agriculture.
In fact, the Communists identified the rebels with a variety of "evil"
forces.[34]

The Communists also backed candidates of the PRM in various
elections. This policy began in the summer of 1937, before the government party was reorganized, when Laborde withdrew as the Communist candidate (from the Federal District in an election for the
Chamber of Deputies) in favor of the government candidates. At the
Seventh Congress of the Communist party, Laborde proclaimed his
famous slogan: "United Behind a Single Candidate" (Unidos Tras
un Solo Candidato). It signified that the Communists would support
the candidate of the PRM as a successor to President Cárdenas:
"United behind a single candidate in order to conquer reaction in the
elections . . . United in order to continue the revolutionary work of
Cárdenas." [35]

However, the support for the Cárdenas government was not unqualified. The government interference with a strike of the railroad
workers was rebuked by the Communists, [36] and the President was
criticized when his activities were contrary to the interests of the
Soviet Union: "The only inconsistency exhibited by Cárdenas in this
field (international relations) is his inexplicable backwardness in failing to renew diplomatic relations with the USSR and his lamentable
hospitality to Trotsky." [37]

Growth of Communist Movement During Cárdenas Administration

Two methods of measuring the growth of a Communist movement
under a non-Communist government are: 1) to analyze Communist
strength in specific organizations—the Communist party, labor and
agrarian organizations, and institutions of the government; 2) the other
method, to be discussed later, involves a consideration of whether
the non-Communist government's ideological position has contributed
to or hindered the growth of Communism.

During the administration of Lázaro Cárdenas, the Communists were very strong in the CTM, the dominant labor organization in the country. (The CTM and the role of the Communists will be discussed in detail when we analyze the labor movement later in this chapter). Since the main strength of the President was with labor, the more influential the Communists could become in the labor movement, particularly within the CTM, the greater would be their influence during the Cárdenas administration.

The use of both Communist and non-Communist sources provides us with a general view of Communist party growth during that period. In the summer of 1937 Laborde spoke of the rapid growth in Communist party membership since the latter part of 1935. Total membership was placed at 17,000 by the party newspaper.[38] In 1938 the Communist party claimed a larger number: "Before the VII Congress of the CI, the CPM numbered 2,000 members. By July 1938 it had more than 27,000 members."[39] Less than one year later, the Communists reported 33,000.[40] Although the above figures may not be accurate, it is almost certain that the Communist party grew in numbers during the Popular Front era under the administration of Lázaro Cárdenas. Credibility is lent to the figures given by the Communists in that they admitted to a sharp decline in party membership after World War II (the possible reasons for this decline will be discussed in the following chapter): "According to Dionisio Encina, secretary general of the Communist Party of Mexico, there are 13,000 members in the party. According to a key member of the Mexican cabinet, there are 8,000 at most."[41]

There are other factors to be considered in evaluating the development of the Communist movement. For example, the influence of the Communists grew with their activities in the labor movement and their support of the policies of the Cárdenas administration.[42] "The Party of the Mexican Revolution consists of the National Peasant Federation, the Confederation of Mexican Workers (Trade Union Federation), and many other people's organizations. The Communist Party of Mexico supports the present Government. As members of the trade unions the Communists also belong to the Party of the Mexican Revolution."[43]

The Communists were able to move into positions of influence on both a national and state level. The following quotation speaks of the broad level of Communist political activity during the Cárdenas administration: "The growing influence of the Mexican Communist Party can best be illustrated by part of the organizational report made before the Congress (i.e., Seventh Congress of the Party). According

to this report the membership of the Party includes the presidents of
73 municipalities, 23 syndicates, 178 aldermen, and 17 other city
officials. In the National Chamber of Deputies, the Party has two
members. Fourteen deputies of various state legislatures are also included in the ranks of the Party. The influence of the Party in important trade unions is strong and growing. The present development
leaves no doubt that the Mexican Communist Party has already become
a vital factor in the life of the nation." [44]

Miguel Aroche Parra, who rose in the Communist hierarchy to become a member of the Central Committee of the Communist party,
has written that the greatest number of militants in the history of the
Communist party were members from 1934-1940. According to Aroche
Parra, Communist elements participated in the following organizations: trade unions of Miners, Petroleum Workers, Electricians, Tram-
ways, Railroads, Textiles; trade unions of Workers at the Service of the
state, particularly the trade unions of Teachers, of Communications, of
the central department, in the leadership of the majority of the
Federations of Workers of the CTM in the states, in the Federations of
Workers at the Service of the state, in the CTM. In addition, members
of the Communist party "participated in the leadership of the ejidos,
cooperatives, societies of ejidal credit, Leagues of Agrarian Communities and Peasants Syndicates, in the most important student organizations, organizations of youth and women." [45]

Even though the Communists were espousing a popular cause by
opposing Fascism and, as a result, cooperating with various non-Communist groups within the country, their efforts could have been
hindered if the government in power had taken an anti-Communist
attitude. On the other hand, Communist influence within the country
at large would have been greater and the Communist dogma more
attractive if the ideological propensity of the government had been in
accord with Marxist doctrine.

Ideological Orientation of the Cárdenas Government

The revolutionaries made many promises in the Constitution of
1917 and the Six-Year Plan. President Cárdenas chose to emphasize
those concerning agrarian reform; labor and economic nationalism;
and education. We have aready dealt with the Communist reactions
to the agrarian reform (land distribution program) and economic
nationalism (expropriation of the railroads and petroleum industries);
a separate section will deal with the labor movement later in this

chapter. The present discussion will be confined to the government's attitude toward education.

When Lázaro Cárdenas was nominated by a PNR convention for the presidency, the party pledged itself to work for "the abolition of the lay school and the establishment of the Socialist school as the basis of education." Two weeks after the new President assumed office the Constitution was amended to provide: "The state shall impart Socialist education and, in addition to excluding all religious instruction, shall combat fanaticism and prejudice, so that the school . . . may imbue the youth with a rational and exact conception of the universe and social life." [46] This amendment stayed in force during the six years Lázaro Cárdenas was President of Mexico. Six years later Avila Camacho, who succeeded President Cárdenas, shifted the emphasis away from "Socialist education" and stressed democracy, nationalism, humanism, and the economic independence of Mexico.

Various political leaders had used the word "Socialism" throughout the Revolution. To some it signified an aggressive economic nationalism; others thought in terms of a vaguely conceived social justice; however, the group which identified "Socialism" with the Marxist idea of a classless society was very influential in the Secretariat of Education during the Cárdenas administration.

Many Communists were officials within the Secretariat of Education. In 1939 José Mancisidor, a member of the Communist party, became Chief of the Department of Secondary Schools (Departmento de Secundarias). Marco Arturo Montero, the former Secretary General of the Anti-Imperialist League and member of the Communist party, became Chief of the Radio Section. Roberto Reyes Pérez, also a member of the Communist party, directed the "España-México" School.[47] In addition, many other lesser Communist officials were employed by the Secretariat.

In 1938, the Secretary of Education, Gonzalo Vásquez Vela, declared that dialetical materialism was the philosophic groundwork of Mexican education.[48] This decision was soon reflected in the hundreds of thousands of low-cost pamphlet texts which were published through the Secretariat of Education and distributed througout the country. The writings of Marx, Lenin, and Stalin reached the hands of the rural population. Virtually every phase of Mexican social life was written from a Marxist viewpoint.

It is informative to evaluate one of the important publications of the period: *Detalles de la Educación Socialista Implantables en México* (Feasible Details of Socialist Education in Mexico). Luis G. Monzón, at one time a Communist senator, and a member of the Communist party, was a functionary of the Secretariat of Education when he wrote the book.

It states that Capitalism has produced the class struggle: the people (the exploited class) must fight to free themselves from the miserable existence in which Capitalism has placed them.[49] Furthermore, it is the duty of the Polytechnic Schools to join the proletariat against the Capitalists. The future will be as Marx envisaged: "Which are the goals of the Polytechnic Schools? To cooperate with Labor organized on the principle of the class struggle in order to procure the emancipation of the working classes from the yoke of capitalist exploitation, causing the caste of the privileged ones to disappear, and, as a corollary of this function, that the men who work and produce, in the center of a society without classes, place power in their hands, implanting their own dictatorship in order that the extinction of the enemy may be a real and positive fact."[50]

The new imperialist war, dooming Capitalism, can only have one conclusion: a classless society. "We are facing the danger of a new world conflict (October of 1935). The great thieves, the lords of monopoly capitalism have realized that if the planned conflagration breaks out and they send the great masses of workers to the fields of battle, as it would have to happen, the latter would turn their arms against their tryants, in order to convert the imperialist war into a world socialist revolution, which would end once and for all the corrupt regime of capitalist exploitation, that is, that it could end the shameful period of the Salary, in order to open the doors to the New Era, in which humanity may constitute a society without classes, composed only of the men who work and produce." [51]

Imperialistic Capitalist wars and Fascism are linked in Monzón's book with Mexico's enemy: the Anglo-Americans.[52]

The progress of the Soviet Union stands in contrast to the evils of Capitalism and Fascism, guiding Mexico with shining examples of Soviet education[53] and the way to a classless society: "In the world there should not exist exploiters and exploited, but only men of work, absolute owners of their own destinies, who labor for the benefit of the proletarian communities, such as is happening in the exemplary territories of the USSR." [54]

According to Monzón, Socialism cannot be separated from Communism. When one speaks of Socialism, he is speaking of a single process, or system, which inexorably moves toward a culmination in Communism. Thus, "Socialist education" does not differ significantly from "Communist education": "It is said that Socialism is one system and Communism is another, but that Socialism is a period of transition which the workers need to go through in order to enter . . . the field of Communism. We differ very slightly with such an opinion, since we believe that Socialism is a sole system, although divided into two periods: Socialism and Communist Socialism . . ." [55]

The process of "Socialist education" also involves the primary symbol of the hammer and sickle, the primary slogan calling for the workers to unite, and the hymn of combat: *The Internationale.*[56] But the main battle cry is familiar to all Communists: "The proletariat cannot wtihdraw from the last imperialist conflict, which will mark the cessation of the exploitation of man by man, by means of which their tyrants and hangmen will lose all, including their lives, and in which the proletariat cannot lose more than their chains, having, on the hand, a world to win." [57]

Reference is also made to the Comintern, considered to be the basis of the national and international United Front. It should include workers, peasants, school teachers, office workers grouped into the Workers' and Peasants' United Front of the Third International.[58]

At the conclusion the importance of the CTM, in relation to the Comintern, is brought into clear focus: "The CTM cannot be with the First International, less with the Second and much less with Fascism which longs to constitute the Fourth. Then, ideologically, it is with the Third International, and it will be with it frankly and formally, when it consolidates its structure, incorporating also in its center the strong, the dense, the formidable mass of the national peasantry and joins its action with that of the rest of the organized sections of the same tendency and by organizing in all the regions of the planet." [59]

It is quite obvious that the Communists could only benefit by the ideological orientation of certain officials of the Cárdenas administration in the field of education. It would be impossible to measure how many people in the rural areas where attracted to Communism because of the government's educational program. How many intellectuals looked to Communism because they believed this was the "natural inclination" of the masses?

The last CTM quotation cited above is especially germane to the next section to be considered. Because Communists and Marxists of all hues were very active in the labor movement (particularly the CTM) during the Popular Front era and the Cárdenas administration, an analysis of the labor movement is important to an understanding of Communist influence during the Popular Front era.

The Labor Movement

One of the most important tactical decisions during the Seventh Congress of the Comintern was to stop Communist trade unions from opposing "reformist" labor organizations in their efforts to bring about trade-union unity. In his speech to the Comintern Congress, Laborde called for trade union unity as the basis of the Popular Front in Mexico.[60]

The change in Communist tactics toward the Cárdenas administration, reflecting the transition from the Third Period to the Popular Front era, was first noticed in the labor movement. In 1935, Communist and non-Communist labor officials formed a National Committee of Proletarian Defense (Comité Nacional de Defensa Proletaria). The Committee produced a "Pact of Solidarity" which was signed on June 15, 1935 by various labor officials including Fernando Amilpa of the Marxist-oriented CGOCM and Valentín Campa of the Communist-controlled CSUM. During the meeting, preparations were begun for the calling of a national Workers' and Peasants' Congress, which would establish one central labor organization.[61]

The Mexican Confederation of Workers

From the National Congress, held February, 1936, and sponsored by the National Committee of Proletarian Defense, emerged the Mexican Confederation of Workers (CTM). Lombardo Toledano was elected Secretary General and two Communists were placed on the Executive Committee.

An analysis of the reasons behind the formation of the CTM can shed more light on the tactics of the Communsts in the labor movement during the Popular Front era. Most writers agree that President Cárdenas encouraged the formation of the new labor organization in order to obtain unified labor support for his government during the power struggles with Calles. However, it must also be kept in mind that the CTM came into being approximately six months after the termination of the Seventh Congress of the Comintern and the proclamation of the "line" of the Popular Front. One of the organizers of the CTM, Fidel Velázquez, told the writer that neither the Seventh Congress of the Comintern nor President Cárdenas influenced the formation of the labor organization. He stated that various labor leaders and groups representing Communists, Anarchists, Syndicalists, and so forth, merely came together to form a new trade union, each with its own ideas.[62]

Lombardo Toledano generally agreed with Fidel Velázquez that the Seventh Congress of the Comintern was not an influence. According to Lombardo, he wished to help form the CTM to bring all the elements of the working class into one labor organization, regardless of their ideological position. He also stated that he wanted to give all types of workers a political education and a political party so that they not only could help themselves, but could also become a vanguard to solve the problems of the rest of the country.[63]

Although one cannot prove that Lombardo Toledano or Fidel Velázquez were influenced by the Seventh Congress of the Comintern, their interpretations can be challenged on several grounds. The view of Fidel Velázquez, that neither President Cárdenas nor the Comintern influenced the formation of the CTM, requires little comment. Cárdenas did need labor support and it is true that no major labor organization has ever been formed in the country without government encouragement and support. Furthermore, the formation of the CTM followed very closely on the heels of the Seventh Congress of the Comintern and the "line" of the Popular Front. It is hard to deny that the proclamation of the Popular Front was an influence in the establishment of the CTM in light of the active role played by the Mexican Communists when it was created.

During this period, Lombardo Toledano made a trip to the Soviet Union, ostensibly to study. Upon his return, the Communists welcomed him with open arms thinking he had been won over to the cause of Communism. Lombardo stated emphatically that the Communists had been incorrect in this assumption.[64] Be that as it may, Lombardo Toledano wrote from Moscow in September, 1935, that he had been in contact with Losovsky.[65] He also wrote of his intention to speak to Stalin and the leaders of the Comintern. The letter concluded that he was so impressed with the Soviet Union that he would "redouble work in favor of the proletarian revolution." [66] Shortly after his return, he became very active in the formation of the CTM.

In addition, Lombardo's explanation that he wished to create a party for the workers is a little lame since the PNR (the official government party) already existed, and when the CTM was formed, it affiliated with the PNR. It is more plausible that Lombardo Toledano wanted to bring the workers into an organization which he could mold to his own ideological beliefs.

It is the writer's contention that the CTM was the product of the coincidence of political reality as interpreted by President Cárdenas and the "line" of the Popular Front as handed down by the Comintern. Communists, Marxists, and non-Communists came together, for diverse reasons, to create a new labor organization which was to receive the encouragement and support of both the government and the Comintern leaders.

At the outset, the CTM was very close to the orientation of the Comintern.[67] It supported the policies of President Cárdenas and declared itself in favor of the Popular Front.[68] In addition, the leaders of the new labor organization declared that "the Committee has tried to base its activities in all cases on the principle of recognizing the contradiction which exists between the interests of the proletarian class and those of the exploiting class, between which, therefore, there is no possible collaboration." [69]

As indicated previously, the period of the Popular Front witnessed Communist support for the loyalists of Spain during the Spanish Civil War. There also were many examples in CTM publications of support for the "Spanish people." [70]

In February of 1937, an article appeared in *Inprecorr*, the Comintern journal, which criticized the leadership of the CTM: "The Mexican Confederation of Workers (CTM), a national trade union center, the majority of the organized workers having approved at its organizational Congress participation in the Popular Front, has not had a consistent popular front policy, and the left elements of its leadership have yielded to the pressure exerted by the reactionary trade union leaders who still are in the leadership of the CTM and in opposition to the well-known position of the President." [71]

Approximately two months later, in April of 1937, a split occurred within the ranks of the CTM. The Communists and the trade unions under their influence walked out of the organization.

The reasons behind the split stemmed from a struggle for power between the Communist party and Lombardo Toledano. Ideological factors were not involved here, as Lombardo himself later admitted.[72] Further evidence of the lack of any ideological dispute is indicated by the fact that some of the conservative groups, e.g. the railroad and electrical unions, supported the Communists because they were opposed to Lombardo.

Friction originally developed when the Communist party tried to use its influence in the Ministries of Communications and Education and when they tried to organize unions of government employees under Communist control and introduce them into the CTM. In addition, the Communists presented their own candidates for election to the Chamber of Deputies. The majority of the CTM leadership, however, supported the candidates of the PNR.

The showdown came during the Fourth National Council of the CTM, when a majority of the council refused to seat representatives of the Communist-controlled teachers' union and other Communist delegates. As a result, the two Communist members of the Executive Committee, Jorge Fernández and Valentín Campa, along with their followers and some conservative allies, walked out of the council. However, they represented a minority, 160,000 to 175,000 members out of a total of approximately 700,000.[73]

At the time of the split, the anti-Communists within the CTM came together under the leadership of three CTM officials: Rodolfo Piña Soria, Benjamín Tobón, and Rodrigo García Treviño. The group soon began to edit the magazine *Acción Social* in order to express its anti-Communist views. At the beginning, Lombardo Toledano reluctantly consented to the formation of such a group which would struggle against the Communists within the CTM. He feared that by walking out of the CTM, the Communists and their followers were trying to have him removed as Secretary General of the organization. A short time later, the anti-Communist group had a falling out with Lombardo because its leaders felt that he had moved into the Communist camp after the original split was reconciled. The anti-Communists then became known as the Socialist Groups of the Mexican Republic (Grupos Socialistas de la República Mexicana) and fought against the "Russophiles."[74]

Lombardo Toledano denounced the Communists for walking out of the CTM. He stated that he had originally wanted the Communists in the CTM so that all the workers would be included in the class struggle to defeat the Capitalist system. However, he accused the Communists of acting against the Comintern by leaving the CTM. Their action made the realization of the Popular Front impossible. Furthermore, the labor leader criticized the Communists for losing their reason and becoming a counter-revolutionary faction which would provoke anti-Communist movements and revulsion against the Soviet Union.[75]

The Comintern took a direct hand in sealing the breach and bringing the Communists back into the CTM. The Comintern leaders agreed with Lombardo Toledano that the action of the Mexican Communists in the CTM was contrary to the purposes of the Popular Front. As a result, Earl Browder, Secretary General of the Communist Party of the United States and a Comintern official, talked to Lombardo and the Communist leaders who recognized the importance of his efforts: "The Mexican Communists were aided by the advice and support of the General Secretary of the Communist Party, USA, Earl Browder, who cited many examples from the history of the American labor movement to justify such an action as Laborde . . . and the Mexican Communist leaders contemplated." As a result of Browder's activities, "The CP of Mexico came out with a declaration for unity, called all the split-off sections of the CTM to return, declared definitely against any attempt to 'take over' the CTM, and definitely withdrew (indeed, had already begun to withdraw) all opposition candidates to those of the CTM in the national elections." [76]

During a Plenum of the Central Committee of the Communist party, held June 26-30, 1937, the major report delivered by Laborde pointed out that the split within the CTM had weakened efforts to form a Popular Front, had weakened the position of CTM vis-à-vis the official government party (PNR), and had weakened the struggle against Fascism and war.[77] Furthermore, it had been a mistake to abandon the Fourth Council of the CTM. With this action, the Communist party took responsibility for the split and recanted its position.

Laborde chided the Communists on the Executive Committee of the CTM for promoting the interests of the party before those of the labor organization, for placing their own candidates for election in opposition to the representatives of the PNR, and finally, for concerning themselves with immediate popular struggles, when they should have supported Lombardo Toledano's efforts to prepare the congress of the Popular Front (i.e., the congress which established the CTM).

Laborde called upon the Communists to do everything in their power to re-establish unity within the CTM, and tried to convince them that unity was necessary in an ideological sense: "We did not comprehend that the unity of the CTM in itself has an indisputable revolutionary value, from the national and international point of view . . ." [78] Therefore, there must be "unity at all costs": "the Communist party must struggle with all its forces for the re-establishment of the unity of the CTM and be disposed to make all concessions and make all sacrifices necessary to attain unity." [79]

Since the split within the CTM occurred less than one year after the Seventh Congress of the Comintern, it is a fair assumption that many of the Communists were still under the influence of the policies of the Third Period, even though the CTM was formed in accordance with the tactics of the Popular Front era. One author, a member of the Central Committee of the Communist party at the time of the split, emphasized the near-fatal blow the Communists inflicted upon themselves: "The break from the CTM constituted for the Communist Party the most tremendous blow it received . . . the circumstances of this blow to its directing possibilities, to its organic force, to its prestige, was not delivered by any enemy, but resulted from the application of an incorrect tactic, a result, more than its ignorance, of the vanity of its direction, of the stubborn insistence on applying its sectarian conceptions . . ." [80]

The reconciliation of the split also resulted in greater power for Lombardo Toledano, who was now assured of the support of the Communist party. On the other hand, it is also possible that the position of Fidel Velázquez and his followers within the CTM was strengthened as a result of the Communist splitting tactics. Many might have turned from Lombardo and the Communists in disgust, in the hope of finding an alternative leadership for the CTM.

There is strong evidence that Lombardo Toledano worked closely with the Communists after they re-entered the CTM. *Acción Social* reproduced a photostat of a letter written by Lombardo on May 16, 1939, to the Federation of Workers of the state of Oaxaca, asking their leaders to cooperate with and expressing confidence in a representative of the Communist party, Graciano G. Benitez, in his organizing efforts in Oaxaca. Lombardo signed the letter as Secretary General of the CTM.[81]

The CTM expanded during the Popular Front era. The Workers University (Universidad Obrera), established with financial support from the government, became the cultural center of the CTM, offering courses in Marxism and publishing a variety of material. The periodical, *El Popular*, was established as the official organ of the CTM, also with governmental financial aid. Lombardo Toledano was the nominal director, but he was out of the country when it was founded by several anti-Communist leaders within the CTM. Rodolfo Piña Soria, Benjamín Tobón, Manrique Páramo, and Rodrigo García Treviño. At first, *El Popular* reflected the political orientation of its founders and was anti-Communist, though somewhat modified by the influence of the Popular Front environment of the labor movement. A short time later, when the anti-Communist group and Lombardo were in opposing camps, *El Popular* came under the strict control of Lombardo and was usually in accord with the Comintern "lines"

(We shall consider examples from *El Popular* at subsequent points in this study).[82]

Tactics of the CTM Leaders

Lombardo Toledano and the CTM leaders organized several peasant groups and brought them into the CTM. At the same time, however, President Cárdenas instructed the president of the PNR, Portes Gil, to organize the peasants on a local and national basis under the control of the official government party. The national organization became known as the National Peasants' Federation (Confederación Nacional de Campesinos or CNC).

The President let it be known to the CTM officials that their activities with the peasants were contrary to the wishes of the government. President Cárdenas convinced Lombardo Toledano that he should give up the peasant groups he had helped to organize—with the understanding that the members of the CNC Peasant Leagues would be able to consult with the CTM on matters of mutual interest. The CTM officials, in turn, told their followers that by giving up the peasants, the CTM had contributed to the formation of a "true" United Front and the development of the Revolution.[83]

The organization of the peasants by the government confirmed what had occurred during the Third Period: the Communists had failed to win over the peasants. If the CTM had been able to secure the allegiance of the peasants, the Communists, through their positions of influence in the CTM, would have been able to reach a majority of them. But, as matters stood, the peasants were loyal to the government, not to any Communist-controlled peasants' league or Communist-infiltrated labor organization.

Although the CTM lost the majority of the peasants, the organization was still very powerful during the administration of Lázaro Cárdenas. When the Party of the Mexican Revolution (PRM) came into being in 1938, it was divided into four sectors: peasants, labor, military, and popular. The CTM was the dominant group in the labor sector, much stronger than the CGT or the fractured CROM. It continued as the dominant group in the labor sector of the official government party when the party was again reorganized in 1941. At that time the military sector was dissolved and incorporated into the popular sector under the Avila Camacho administration.

When the CTM became part of the official party and a strong asset for President Cárdenas, the Communists were very optimistic. They were now back in the good graces of the CTM and were working closely with the Secretary General, Lombardo Toledano. Furthermore, the Communists viewed the new official party, the PRM, as the Popular Front peculiar to Mexico, and the CTM as the bedrock of the Popular Front policy.[84] As the CTM became more influential in government circles and the country at large, the Communists, already a powerful force within the CTM, increased their influence within the labor movement.

According to the tactics of the Popular Front, complete backing was given to the government against the threats of revolt. As a result, the CTM gave its full support to the government's crushing of a revolt led by General Saturnino Cedillo. An interesting article in *El Popular* explained the defeat of the fallen general in Marxist terms: "It may perhaps be said that the punishment meted out to Cedillo—exposure to the finger of ridicule—is even worse (than execution). Cárdenas was able to use the weapons of dialectic because history is with him. Heroes triumph when they know how to interpret history, when they recognize the historic moment; but when they forget this, they fall with a resounding crash, never to rise again. In Mexico, we have just had an example of this fact." [85]

Toward the latter part of President Cárdenas' term of office, the President received almost unqualified support from the CTM and Lombardo Toledano: "President Cárdenas realizes a revolutionary program which is the same as that of the CTM . . . The CTM is the enemy of those who do not follow the program of President Cárdenas."[86] In another instance, Lombardo described President Cárdenas as one of the great men of the country: "Cárdenas has done the most that a man can do in life, the only thing to which a man can aspire; Cárdenas has accelerated the historic destiny of Mexico; therefore he is great; therefore he will be imperishable." [87]

The leaders of the labor organization strongly supported a Popular Front. They hoped that the CNC, the CROM, the CGT, the CTM, the Communist party, and the official government party might be brought into one broad organization. A formal invitation was actually sent by the CTM to the Communist party to form a Popular Front[88] approximately one year before the PRM was created as the "Mexican form of the Popular Front."

Lombardo Toledano was a strong advocate of the Popular Front, as indicated by his report to the Fourth National Council of the CTM in 1939. His views were similar to those of Hernán Laborde, expressed to the Seventh Congress of the Comintern: "What is the program of

International Communism at present? The program of the Popular Front is the program of the petitions of those who agree with all the sectors of the people, including those sectors not proletarian, like the middle class and the sector of the petty bourgeoisie. The Popular Front is not, therefore, a tactic or retrogression nor counter-revolution, because the working class, at the moment, and inclusive of breaking with its circumstantial allies, can go to the true revolution and transform the bourgeois regime." [89]

The CTM and labor groups almost everywhere supported the forces opposed to General Franco in the Spanish Civil War. It was not just propaganda: When the Cárdenas government took a strong stand in favor of Republican Spain, the CTM held pro-Loyalist demonstrations all over the country. The workers within the labor organization also pledged to work without pay to send munitions to the Loyalists.

The CTM also strongly supported President Cárdenas when he welcomed Spanish refugees into the country. Many refugees joined the trade unions of the CTM and found positions with Lombardo Toledano's Workers University. Aiding the Spanish refugees was a popular cause, and the Communists within the CTM were able to bask in the light of this favorable propaganda.

The Latin American Federation of Labor

In the fall of 1938, the CTM was the main force in bringing a Congress to Mexico City, September 5-8, which was attended by representatives from thirteen Latin American countries plus delegates from France, Spain, India, Switzerland, Sweden, and Trinidad. One result of this meeting was the formation of the Latin American Federation of Labor (Confederación de Trabajadores de América Latina or CTAL) with Lombardo Toledano as Secretary General. The new organization had headquarters in Mexico City.

During the Popular Front era, the CTAL was a true "Popular Front" group, with Aprista, Communist, and Socialist national affiliates. Although the CTAL did not become Communist-controlled until the second World War, Communists were in official positions before that and the organization was very close to the position of the Communist Party of Mexico and the Comintern.

The CTAL joined other groups in Latin America in declaring its opposition to Fascism: "The manual and intellectual workers of Latin America declare that Fascism is contrary to the means and objectives of the proletariat, to the progress of peoples, and to the development of culture, for it should be combated in all its forms. . ." [90] The organization also took the same position as the Comintern in regard to events in Spain: "The Congress agrees that all and each one of the delegates present acquire the solemn obligation of developing an intense campaign of solidarity in favor of the Spanish people, in conformity with the guide lines marked by the Executive Committee. . ." [91]

There were several Communists on the Executive Committee of the CTAL, but not yet a majority. Only one national central organization from each country, the one which represented a majority of the organized workers, was admitted as a member. Mexico was represented by the CTM. Thus, by infiltrating both the CTM and the CTAL, the Communists were in a very strong position. Furthermore, Lombardo Toledano, as Secretary General of the CTM and of the CTAL, "became the most important Communist-oriented trade union leader in the hemisphere." [92]

Refugees, Agents, and Slogans

During the Spanish Civil War the Mexican Communists were unrelenting: "Let us organize the collection of funds to send food, clothes, medicines, machine guns, and airplanes to Spain." [93] The Communists did more than just print exhortations for the Republican forces of Spain; they collected funds, and through the efforts of a Communist party member, Rosendo Gómez Lorenzo, they recruited many young Mexicans to fight in the Spanish Civil War.[94] Several members of the Communist party fought in Spain, including David Alfaro Siqueiros.[95]

The Mexican Communists received a great deal of favorable publicity in supporting the Republican forces of Spain, but their activities with some Communist Spanish refugees cast them in an unfavorable light.[96] The newspaper *Ultimas Noticias*, June 8, 1939 reproduced a letter ostensibly sent by the Spanish Communist, Magarita Nelken, to the Communist Party of Mexico. It stated that Negrín y Alvarez del Vayo (actually a Communist sympathizer) had made arrangements for Communist Spanish refugees to go to Mexico with the help of the well-known Spanish Communist "La Pasionaria" (Delores Ibarruri). Inasmuch as the Communist party had the confidence of the Mexican government, the Spanish refugees could be placed in public positions. The Mexican Communists denied that any such letter had been

written. Laborde stated the official Communist position in a report to
the Executive Committee of the party: "The [attitude] of a part of
the Sections of the Railroad Union against help for the Spanish
refugees, taking this question as a pretext to try for the division of the
CTM, is a shameful fact for the proletariat of Mexico, which only is explained by the poisonous labor of the reactionary press. It is the fruit
of the 'letter of Margarita Nelken,' of constant lies and calumnies, of
all of a systematic propaganda, tending to infuse diffidence and hate
among the masses of the people toward the refugees." [97]

But in an article in the newspaper *Excelsior*, September 14, 1939,
Diego Rivera named several foreign Communists who had arrived in
the country: Marcel Rosenberg, former Soviet Ambassador in Valencia
during the Spanish Civil War; Enea Sormenti; and an individual
called "Ross." In writing about various foreign agents who appeared,
García Treviño referred to an Arturo Ramírez. He had been Secretary of Organization of the Central Committee of the Communist
party during the Cárdenas administration. According to this account,
he entered the country around 1927 as a Lithuanian political exile with
a passport in the name of J. Chimbaum or Scheibaum. But his
real name was not Ramírez or Scheibaum; he was a Russian called
Rudi Brusilovski.[98]

The over-riding issue which was to determine all Communist activities (e.g., trade union unity, cooperation with non-Communist elements, etc.) throughout the Popular Front era was the Comintern
theme: Fascism is *the* danger.[99]

The Communist attitude toward the United States was also determined by the Popular Front "line" and the fear of the Fascist
danger. There were the usual references to "Yankee imperialism" in
Communist (and non-Communist) publications. Nevertheless, efforts
were made to have the United States support the collective security
efforts of the Soviet Union. The Mexican Communists (in sharp contrast to the subsequent period of the Nazi-Soviet Pact) frequently
joined other Latin American Communists in professing friendship for
the United States: "The democratic Congress of Latin America, which
was held in Montevideo, the capital of Uruguay, and was attended by
numerous delegations from the democratic parties of the American
continent, has ended its work. At this Congress, which was remarkable
for many reasons, a resolution in favor of an alliance of the two
American continents for the defense of democracy, peace, and liberty
of the peoples in view of the growing fascist barbarism, was adopted.

At the same time the Congress expressed its support of President Roosevelt and sent him a telegram of greeting." [100]

The Communists and their Marxist allies also waged a relentless attack on Leon Trotsky. The campaign in Mexico against the Russian revolutionary was more vicious than any other with the possible exception of the one in the Soviet Union. Trotsky's presence in Mexico calls forth several questions which must be answered in order to allow a better understanding of the Communist movement: What were the possible motives of President Cárdenas in allowing him to reside in the country? What effect did Trotsky's presence have on the Communist movement there? What was the role of the Communists (if any) in his death?

CHAPTER VII

FROM THE NAZI-SOVIET PACT TO WORLD WAR II

Leon Trotsky arrived in Mexico in early 1937 and was assassinated on August 20, 1940. Thus he lived in the country during a substantial part of both the Popular Front era and the Nazi-Soviet Pact. However, his activities in Mexico and his death were not a result of a change of "line" by the leaders of the Comintern, nor do the effects this had on the Communist movement fit into any one category; Leon Trotsky in Mexico was a special case, the importance of which transcended any given time period,

When President Cárdenas agreed with Diego Rivera, a leading Trotskyite, to give Trotsky refuge in the country, many people were surprised[1] and questioned the possible motives of allowing such a controversial person to enter Mexico and make his home there. The answer to this question cannot be easily documented. Nevertheless, the writer presented the question to three well-known persons who were in Mexico at the same time Trotsky was in the country.

Fidel Velázquez professes to feel that no outside influence affected the President's decision, that Lázaro Cárdenas allowed Trotsky to enter and remain in the country simply because it was the President's policy to give political asylum to all.[2]

Two other observers believe differently. Lombardo Toledano believed that President Cárdenas used Trotsky to show the world, particularly the United States, that the President was not a Communist and that he did not take orders from Moscow.[3] García Treviño, certainly of a different political orientation than Lombardo Toledano, shares his interpretation of the President's motives.[4]

If their interpretation is closer to the truth, then the Mexican Communists, who supported the policies of Stalin and the Comintern, were given a setback. A very influential enemy was placed in their midst, and President Cárdenas displayed a strong independent policy which portended difficulty for the Stalinists of the Communist Party of Mexico if they threatened the safety of Trotsky and, as a result, stained the prestige of the country and its President.

Trotsky's presence affected the Communist movement in two ways. In the first place, the split between the Communist Party of Mexico and its allies in the CTM on one side and Trotsky, some Communist

dissidents, and anti-Stalinist Marxists on the other was aggravated
further. It is quite possible, too, that the purge in the Communist
party, which preceded Trotsky's death by a few months, was directly
related to his presence in the country and the plans Stalin and the
Soviet leaders had for him. (We shall analyze the purge later in this
chapter). In the second place, the setback to Mexican Communism
during the Nazi-Soviet Pact was compounded by the reaction of President Cárdenas to Trotsky's death.

The split in the left, caused by the presence of Trotsky, was evident
in the propaganda barrage issued by the Communists (i.e., Stalinists)
and their allies in the CTM and the publications which came forth
from the Trotskyites. The Communists accused Trotsky of splitting
the forces of the proletariat and playing into the hands of their
enemies.[5] They also accused him of being in league with the forces of
reaction, within and without the country: "It should be kept in mind,
furthermore, that Trotsky sill lies in ambush in Coyoacán, ready to
meddle to the full, in keeping with his role of provocateur and
splitter, allied to Mexican reaction as he is allied to world reaction.
In this role he has begun to link himself with the reactionary leaders
of the so-called Social-Democratic Party, such as General Antonio
I. Villareal and others. Therefore, the Communist Party must persist
in the struggle for consolidation of the CTM, for complete unity of
the proletariat, against the activities of Tortsky, and for political
liquidation of the little 'Fourth International' group." [6]

During the Popular Front era, as we have seen, the main theme of
the Communists was the struggle against the Fascist danger. The
Mexican Communists used the anti-Fascist slogan to identify Trotsky
with the Nazis[7] and continued the Fascist charge throughout the
Popular Front era: "It is evident that Trotsky is not just scratching
his beard in Mexico City. He has definite plans concerning his usefulness to the Fascists in relation to Mexico as well as Latin America.
Undoubtedly hidden Trotskites in the labor movement and in the mass
organizations will endeavor to raise slogans calling for more hasty
nationalization measures instead of broadening the National Front
for its struggle against Fascism. Such a policy would narrow it and
create inner struggles that will play into the hands of the Fascists . . ." [8]

The CTM and its leaders leaders closely followed the line of attack
used by the Communist party. Lombardo Toledano repeated the
charge of Fascism and division among the people.[9] The Secretary
General of the CTM pointed out, and correctly so, that the orientation of Trotskyism was contrary to the tactics of the Popular Front:

"Trotskyism commends publicly a tactic of struggle opposed to the line of the Popular Front. He considers that the proletariat ought to be sufficient in itself and should not have any alliance, although it may be transitory, with any government, nor with governments of a democratic or progressive character, because that is collaboration and reinforcement of the power of the exploitative bourgeoisie." [10]

In a formal resolution, the Executive Committee of the CTM denounced Trotsky, accusing him of aiding the development of world Fascism.[11] In 1938, the First National Congress of the CTM passed a lengthy resolution pertaining to Trotsky. Proposed by Lombardo Toledano, the document contained five principle charges against Trotsky:

"1. Leon Trotsky and his followers falsify facts when they assert that Trotsky is the continuator of Leninist theory. Trotsky never was a genuine Marxist-Leninist.

"2. Trotsky acts, at least objectively, in complicity with international fascism.

"3. Trotsky is an enemy of the People's Fronts, and particularly of the peoples of Spain and China who are fighting at this time against fascism.

"4. Trotsky participates in the internal problems of Mexico as an enemy of the unity of the working class.

"5. Trotsky, by all his activity regarding the fundamental problems of the historic period, has revealed himself as an enemy of the working class of the world." [12]

For their part, Leon Trotsky and his followers were extremely critical of the Communist Party of Mexico, the Communist leaders, and Lombardo Toledano. A Mexican branch of the Fourth International was established, and it soon began to publish a periodical called *Clave*, to which Diego Rivera and Leon Trotsky contributed. One of *Clave's* themes was an attack on the Soviet Union. The internal wokings of the Soviet state and the CPU were rebuked: "Reactionary bureaucracy has established in the USSR a hateful totalitarian state, thanks to a bloody regime of continuous terror, complementing with the attacks of gangsters against foreign revolutionaries and with corruption of the workers and intellectual movement." [13] In addition, the interpretation given to the slogan of "defense of the USSR" by the Stalinists and their allies drew sharp criticisms from the Trotskyites. In one of his articles, Leon Trotsky wrote that the defense of the Soviet Union must be placed in its proper perspective: "In the USSR the overthrow of the bureaucracy is necessary in order to maintain the property of the state. It is only in that sense that we are for the defense of the USSR." [14] Trotsky also called for the defense of the Soviet Union if it was in conjunction with defense of the world revolution.[15]

The issue of defense of the Soviet Union exemplifies the sharp contrast between the Mexican Communist Party (i.e., the Stalinists) and the Trotskyites. As we have seen, when the leaders of the Communist party spoke of defending the Soviet Union, they were thinking in terms of defending the Soviet Union against an "imperialist" attack. This was Russian nationalism speaking through the Mexican Communists, not a Marxist movement which transcended the state, such as Trotsky and his very articulate followers were attempting to create.

Another of the main themes in the Trotskyite propaganda was the sharp attack against the tactics and leaders of the Mexican Communist party. An interesting criticism of the Communist party was the accusation that it was really a party of the petty bourgeoisie (a fact which Dionisio Encina once admitted at a party congress): "The so-called 'Communist' Party of Mexico suffers the same disintegration as all the sections of the Comintern. From a party of the proletarian vanguard it has definitely been transformed into a party of the conservative small bourgeoisie. A party of the small bourgeoisie, as it is known, hopes for the health of the Pope of Rome; another part, more adventurous, hopes for the (health) of the Fuhrer of Moscow." [16]

Hernán Laborde was the object of personal attack by Trotsky. Both he and the Comunist Party of Mexico were included: "The other Mexican agent of the GPU, Laborde, leader of the so-called Communist Party (who would believe it?), declared in the fall of last year, in a solemn meeting, before a numerous public and and before the President of the Republic, that I was secretly allied (I beg you to take notice!) with General Cedillo and with Vasconcelos; obviously in order to realize a fascist coup d'état. Compromising himself and dishonoring his party, Laborde resolved to launch such an idiotic accusation, only because, as well as (Lombardo) Toledano, he had received orders in that sense, from Moscow, where for a long time the measure not only of morality but also of logic and psychology have been lost. The student cannot be higher than his teacher. The agent of the GPU is not free to do what he may wish, he is obligated to fulfill the orders of the patron. If this were not done, the party of Laborde would have been cut off, immediately, from the subsidy of Moscow and would have been toppled like a castle of cards." [17]

The Trotskyites criticized both the tactics of the Popular Front and the Nazi-Soviet Pact. They believed that the Popular Front era, with its general policy of cooperation with the government and non-Communist groups, would only undermine the working class and leave the way open to Fascism.[18] The Nazi-Soviet Pact was considered by the Trotskyites to be the symbol of Stalin's betrayal to the cause of world revolution.[19] Trotsky identified the Pact with the Soviet bureaucracy: "In reality the signing of the treaty with Hitler only serves to measure once again the degree of decomposition of the Soviet bureaucracy and its disregard of the world working class, including the Comintern. . ." [20]

Trotsky continued his attack against the Mexican Communists. The party and its Secretary General, Hernán Laborde, were attacked for blindly following the Comintern through the twists and turns of the Popular Front tactics and the Nazi-Soviet Pact in accordance with the dictates of Moscow.[21] Lombardo Toledano, the Secretary General of the CTM, was called a "lackey of Stalin and agent of the CPU": "One of the most jealous and shameless of the bureaucracy of Moscow is the Secretary General of the CTM, (Confederación de Trabajadores de México), Lombardo Toledano. His unworthy activity is developing before the eyes of all. He defends Stalin, his violences, his treasons, his provocations and executions. He does not have any astonishment that he may be the worst enemy of Trotskyism. . ." [22]

Trotsky also vigorously criticized the resolution of the 1938 CTM Congress which pertained to him because, as he claimed, it was drafted in Moscow and executed by Stalin's agent, Lombardo Toledano.[23]

There is very strong evidence that several of the Mexican Communists were involved in the first attempt on Leon Trotsky's life on May 24, 1940. The Chief of the Secret Service of the Mexican Police in charge of investigating the two assaults was Leandro A. Sánchez Salazar. As co-author of a book analyzing the events surrounding the death of Trotsky, he presented a very strong case demonstrating the complicity of the Mexican Communists. According to the results of the police investigation, it was David Alfaro Siqueiros who led the first assault into the home of Trotsky. Armed and dressed as policemen, approximately twenty Mexican Communists took part, including David Serrano Andonegui, a member of the Central Committee of the Communist Party of Mexico.[25] The investigation also indicated that Siqueiros planned the attack with several foreign Communists who were in the country.[26] Trotsky was assassinated in the second attack by a man who went by several names, including Jacques Mornard.

After the first attack a Trotskyite, Robert Sheldon Hart, one of Trotsky's body guards, was found dead a short time later. The police concluded that he was killed by the brothers-in-law of Siqueiros, Luis and Leopoldo Arenal. Although Trotsky vouched for the assassinated man's loyalty, the Chief of the Secret Police felt he was an agent of the GPU and killed because he knew too much.[27] It was Robert Sheldon Hart, according to the investigation, who let the armed men into the home of Trotsky.

In a document sent to Sánchez Salazar, Trotsky wrote that the GPU had prepared the public for the attack[28] in the following periodicals: *El Machete, La Voz de México, El Popular,* and *Futuro.* Trotsky particularly criticized Lombardo Toledano in this document. He asked why he was so critical of him when he arrived in the country if he had not known him before. Trotsky answered his own question: Lombardo must be under the orders of Stalin. He claimed, too, that the Secretary General of the CTM was a paticipant in the "moral preparation of the terrorist act," through his anti-Trotsky propaganda. He concluded by advising the police to question Siqueiros as well as the present and former leaders of the Communist Party of Mexico.

The Communists were criticized by non-Communists of the left for their part in the first assault on Trotsky. *Accón Social,* under the editorship of Rodrigo García Treviño and others, stated: "the fact is that with all the energy we express our most severe condemnation of the activities of the terrorists who assaulted Trotsky and of the Communist Party of Mexico, which at the same time that it condemns these criminals in words, has defended them in fact." [29]

The Communist Party of Mexico denied that any of its members participated in the assault. In a statement signed by Dionisio Encina, the official position of the party was that it had no contact with the indigenous elements and other "agents" who were responsible for the attack.[30] Another article singled out particular individuals who were involved and denied that they were members of the party: "David Alfaro Siqueiros, who appears to be responsible for the assault, is not a member of the Communist Party of Mexico. Neither are

Antonio Pujol, nor Luis, nor Leopoldo Arenal members of the Party." [31]
It might be pointed out that Siqueiros had been one of the most
prominent militants of the party for years and that he had not been
involved in the purge which preceded Trotsky's death. Whether or
not he happened to have his party card in his pocket at the time of the
assault was beside the point.

Approximately three months after the first assault, Leon Trotsky
was assassinated by the individual called Jacques Mornard.[32] It is
generally agreed that no Mexicans were directly involved in the
assassination.

Reactions to Trotsky's death were heard throughout the world.
Lombardo Toledano and the officials of the CTM "deplored the
violence under the direction of foreign forces." [33] In contrast to such
mild phrases was the statement of the periodical Acción Social: "On
the other hand, if the consistent fault of being a blind and cold instrument of the orders and directives which it receives from a foreign
power can be attributed to some sector, it is to the Communists . . .
the Mexican Communists are nothing more than blind and con-
ditioned agents of Moscow." [34]

More important for the Communist movement was the reaction of
President Cárdenas: "In the case of the Communists we want to
point out that if they have considered it useful to their interests
to abandon the field of cooperation with the organized workers of
Mexico for their progressive improvement and syndical defense and
have allied themselves with a foreign power which represents an
aggression to the sovereignty of the country, organizing armed assaults
in union with Mexican and foreign elements and realizing prudently
that they dishonor civilization and that they place in doubt the
capacity of the government and the people of Mexico to maintain in
the Capital of the Republic a state of security and of tranquility for
the citizens who reside in it, these elements have committed the
crime of treason to the country, they have prostituted their doctrines
of redemption and of proletarian progress, they have damaged their
country, making it conspicious, committing a crime which history will
censure as dishonorable for whomever may have inspired it and as
ominous for those who consummated it and cooperated in its effectiveness." [35]

President Cárdenas reacted to the assassination in deeds as well as
words: he tried to remove the Communists from all positions of influence in the PRM.[36]

The Nazi-Soviet Pact

The Nazi-Soviet Pact which began at the end of August, 1939, a month before World War II broke out, and lasted until June, 1941, when Germany invaded the Soviet Union, caused a radical change in policy by the Comintern.[37] The new "line" indicated that the war between opposing imperialist forces made it necessary for the Communists to change their tactics. They were directed by the Comintern to support the peace policies of the Soviet Union, including the Nazi-Soviet Pact and efforts to bring the war to an end as soon as possible. Communists also were called upon to support the territorial gains of the Soviet Union (made at the expense of Finland and Poland, Rumania, and the three Baltic republics, Estonia, Latvia and Lithuania, which completely disappeared). They were instructed, as well, to break their relations with the Socialist leaders and non-Communist trade union officials and make efforts to form the "United Front from below."

The Communists and their allies in the CTM and CTAL followed very closely the new "line" and tactics of the period of the Nazi-Soviet Pact. Almost immediately after the Non-Aggression Treaty between Germany and the Soviet Union was signed, the periodical of the Communist Party of Mexico proclaimed its support for the treaty and the "policy of peace of the USSR." [38] Ths following month, in a report to the Central Committee, Laborde defended the action of the Soviet Union: "The Soviet Government had to sign the pact of non-aggression with Germany in order to frustrate the anti-Soviet and imperialist works of Chamberlain and to impede a coalition of the imperialists against the USSR." [39]

Lombardo Toledano supported the Nazi-Soviet Pact and defended the desire of the Soviet leaders to stay out of war:[40] "For many years the USSR manifested its unmistakable desires of arranging a general pact of collective security in Europe. Its pacifist policy cannot be placed in doubt. What now occurs is that Moscow does not want to continue fulfilling the role of peon in the fierce works of the Chamberlain-Daladier pair and has arranged a treaty of non-aggression with Germany—not of armed collaboration as some bourgeois journalists have absurdly insinuated—it has assured its frontiers, it has destroyed the Berlin-Tokyo Axis, leaving Japan abandoned to its own forces, and it withdraws from international intrigues, turning its back on all the interested powers, in order that they may settle their differences among themselves as best they can." [41]

Encina, in his report to the First Extraordinary Congress of the Communist party, March 19-24, 1940, followed the Comintern line in stating that since both sides were struggling to preserve and increase their imperialist domains, the responsibility for the war rested with the bourgeoisie of each country and their imperialist policies.[42]

Another Communist tactic was to attempt to weaken the democratic governments. They called for efforts to bring the war to a speedy conclusion, but they missed no opportunity to weaken, and even destroy, the democratic governments. Encina prodded his followers to turn the conflagration into a civil war against the bourgeoisie to bring about the dictatorship of the proletariat.[43]

The Communists continued to hammer away at the theme of the imperialist war. A headline of *La Voz de México* declared "TO STRUGGLE AGAINST THE IMPERIALIST WAR IS TO DEFEND THE SOVEREIGNTY OF THE COUNTRY." [44] The Central Committee of the Communist party, March 10, 1941, issued a manifesto similar to Encina's declaration the previous year and, incidentally, Lenin's analysis of World War I: "The present war, it must be reiterated time and time again, is the armed clash of two groups of equally imperialistic powers, which are fighting for the right to dominate and exploit the world. While the totalitarian powers wish to enlarge their colonial empires by snatching away from their rivals their domination over the backward peoples, the so-called 'democratic' powers are trying to maintain their vast colonial empires and their sway over the markets which they conquered through predatory wars and the subjugation of free peoples." [45]

The leaders of the labor movement echoed the same theme. Lombardo Toledano referred to the struggle as an "inter-imperialist war." [46] The Executive Committee of the CTAL, in a meeting June 10-15, 1940, passed a resolution declaring that only the workers suffer in this war between Capitalist forces.[47]

The Comintern line of neutrality in an imperialist war was emphasized by Encina in his speech to the First Extraordinary Congress of the Communist party.[48] The Manifesto of the Central Committee of the Communist party made clear one reason for neutrality: "In such a war, absolutely alien to the interests of the people of Mexico, there is no reason for linking our Fatherland to either of the imperialist camps. . . . The Mexican Revolution is part of the struggle of all oppressed peoples on earth to shake off imperialist domination and has nothing in common which the interests of Hitler's imperialism; for, whichever group of imperialists is victorious in this war, the chains of slavery and exploitation of weaker nations will be fastened more tightly." [49]

Lombardo Toledano and most officials of the CTM took the same position: "Mexico should maintain its independence, its autonomy, its neutrality; the war is the enemy of the Mexican Revolution. . ." [50] The CTM passed a similar resolution: "the XII National Council considers it more necessary than ever to keep the war outside of the frontiers of our country and of the American Continent. . ." [51]

Although the Mexican Communists and their compatriots adopted a neutral position between the Allies and the Axis during the period of the Nazi-Pact, their "neutrality" renewed the vehement anti-American position which had been somewhat modified during the Popular Front era. Slogans referring to the menace of "Yankee imperialism" appeared more frequently in Communist publications.[52] Communist opposition to the proposed establishment of U. S. military bases in the country produced a clever appeal to economic nationalism and the theme of American economic imperialism: "Mexico cannot make the copious expenditures that are required for the construction of naval and air bases, except in exchange from a tremendous aggravation of the economic condition of the country and the people. And as to loans from the United States for this purpose, to accept them would be equivalent to mortgaging the sovereignty and the independence of our fatherland." [53]

The relative friendless toward Franklin D. Roosevelt during the Popular Front era was replaced by bitter denunciations during the period of the Nazi-Soviet Pact. The Communist press often referred to him as a dictator type allied with Wall Street.[54] This theme was repeated in the periodicals under Lombardo Toledano's direction: "President Roosevelt, having already abandoned in a definite manner the policy of the New Deal, seems to have arrived at a friendly understanding with the sectors of Wall Street, which signifies his ties with the most reactionary circles of North American finance capital." [55]

One of the sharpest critics of the United States, Dionisio Encina, elected Secretary General of the Communist party in 1940, gave his interpretation of the role of the United States in relation to the war at the First Extraordinary Congress of the party. "The United States has an interest in prolonging the war in order to obtain a threefold objective: First, to make possible the realignment of forces susceptible of being launched against the Country of Socialism (USSR); second, to weaken the rival imperialists, in order to be able to extend its hegemony and sphere of influence to the dependent and colonial countries and to establish itself in monopolistic form in Latin America; third, to make a great deal of business with the war while the blood of other people flows. The United States follows the same tactic today which it followed in 1914: While the rest of the people bleed, to draw out the maximum benefits from the war." [56] This statement is ironic in view of the policy of the Soviet Union.

The Communists were strong supporters of the foreign policy of the Soviet Union. When the Soviet leaders thought it was in their best interests to proclaim the cause of peace, the Communists were quick to pick up the theme. At the Eighth Congress of the party, a resolution was passed which fully supported the "peace efforts" of the Soviet Union.[57]

The Soviet Union also found staunch defenders of its territorial ambitions. Victor Manuel Villaseñor, writing in *Futuro,* criticized the "capitalist press" for its slanderous reporting of the policies of the Soviet Union. In an article entitled "The USSR Against Imperialism," he described some of the policies and territorial gains of the Soviet Union: "The accord of the German-Soviet Pact of Non-Aggression, the occupation of Byelorussia and of the Western Ukraine by the Red Army, and more recently the initiation of the Russo-Finnish War, are facts which have served as a pretext in order that the capitalist press of all the countries develop the abominable campaign of injuries and calumnies against the USSR, which until now has been presented with the preconceived end of sowing confusion and procurring the division of the progressive sectors of the world." [58]

During the period of the Nazi-Soviet pact, Soviet expansion at the expense of Poland and Finland was supported by the Communists and their allies. Laborde defended Soviet incorporation of Polish territories as saving the people from the Nazis and reclaiming lost Soviet territories.[59] The periodical of the CTM, *El Popular,* stated that the Soviet Army moved into Poland to establish peace.[60]

In his report to the First Extraordinary Congress of the party, Encina defended at length the Soviet actions during the Soviet-Finnish War.[61] He stated that it was primarily a defensive action to prevent and protect the Soviet Union from aggressive designs encouraged by the United States.[62] It would be necessary, he said, for the Communists to increase their propaganda so that the real nature of the struggle in Finland (i.e., the Soviet interpretation) would be understood by the government and the people who did not know the defensive character of the war and how the Soviet forces had "liberated" the Finnish people.[63] And finally, Encina branded as ridiculous the thought that the Soviet Union could have imperialist aims in Finland: "In fact, what has happened with the Finnish conflict? As the Soviet Union did not have, nor can it have imperialist aims, because it struggles to free and not to dominate and to enslave the people, after having given a hard lesson to the general Finnish reactionaries who allowed themselves to instigate war against the Soviet Union, the latter, after occupying strategic points which are necessary for its defense, in spite of having before it a defeated army, offers Finland an honorable peace, which does nothing to affect its independence, and furthermore proposes a treaty of friendship and the establishment of commercial relations advantageous for that country. . ." [64]

In their publications and speeches, the Communists and their allies did not mention the fact that the Soviet Union collaborated with the Nazis during the period of the Nazi-Soviet Pact. The Pact thus posed no dilemma for the Mexicans who read it as a statement of neutrality and defense of the Soviet Union against the Nazis. Nevertheless, many left the ranks of the Communist party as a direct result of the Pact.

Agents and Purges

In the spring of 1940, several foreign agents arrived in the country: Dimitri Manuilsky, former president of the Comintern who was traveling under the assumed name of "Kalowsky"; Leon Haikiss, former Soviet Ambassador to Spain and in 1940 Secretary of Organization of the Comintern, who was traveling under the assumed name of "Leon Jacome;" and James W. Ford, Secretary of the Executive Committee of the Communist Party of the United States. Others included representatives of the Communist parties of the United States, England, Germany, Spain, Catalonia, and Italy.[65] Also in the country at the time was Victoria Codovilla, leader of the Communist Party of Argentina and one of the Comintern's principal Latin American agents.

The appearance of the foreign agents coincided with a major purge of the Communist party. In February, Vicente Guerra, Arturo Ramírez (Rudi Brusilovski), and Manuel Lobato were the victims.[66] The following month the removal of Hernán Laborde, Secretary General of the Communist party, and Valentín Campa, an expert in trade union matters, was announced.[67]

The Central Committee of the party passed a resolution accusing the Guerra-Ramírez-Lobato faction of several crimes—Trotskyism, opposition to the United Front, and so forth, as well as not being critical enough of the policies of the government.[68] The latter point indicates that the Communists were somewhat more critical of the administration during the period of the Nazi-Soviet Pact than during the Popular Front era. What shall presently see how their ardent support for Lázaro Cárdenas cooled somewhat.

Two weeks after Laborde and Campa were removed, the first Extraordinary Congress of the Communist party was held. Preparation for the Congress was under a "Purifying Commission" headed by Victorio Codovilla. His main purpose, according to a member of the Central Committee who voted for the Laborde-Campa expulsion, was to purge Laborde, Campa, and their followers within the party.[69]

The Laborde-Campa leadership was attacked during the Congress, particularly in a speech by Andrés García Salgado, described by the *Daily Worker* of March 24, 1940. Before the Congress terminated, a resolution was passed condemning those who were purged:

"The Congress approves unanimously the cleansing of the traitorous group from the heart of the party, and considers that the responsibility of the old direction as well as the state of things which existed are established. The most serious acts were those of Hernán Laborde and Valentín S. Campa, by their falsifying of the political line, and by having handed over the practical direction of it into the hands of the traitorous Guerra-Ramírez-Lobato group, and covering their criminal activity." [70] As one reads the denunciations of former Communist leaders, two principal questions come to mind: Why did the purges accur when they did? What was the role of the Comintern agents who appeard in the country?

Putting aside the denunciations issued by the new Communist leadership under Dionisio Encina—"Trotskyites," "opportunists," "saboteurs," and so forth—we can address ourselves to three main considerations. In the first place, the purges occurred during the period of the Nazi-Soviet Pact. It is possible that several members of the Communist party did not want to support the new Comintern policy and what it entailed. A *New York Times* article of January 26, 1940, stated that the dissidents under Vicente Guerra, Arturo Ramírez, and Manuel Lobato were opposed to Soviet actions in Finland and Poland.

A second consideration is that the purges occurred a few months before the first attack on the home of Leon Trotsky and the subsequent events which led to his death. We have seen how some of the Mexican Communists were involved in these events. It is also known that Comintern agents arrived during that period. In this regard there is a good possibility that Laborde, Campa, and the others who were purged from the Comunist party, opposed the assassination of Trotsky. It is quite possible they did not want to diminish the influence of the party within the country, particularly since President Cárdenas had given asylum to Trotsky. Furthermore, they might not have wanted to jeopardize the subsidies they were receiving from the Cárdenas government.[71]

In the third place, we have the account of the Peruvian ex-Communist Eudocio Ravines, who was sent by the Comintern to organize the Popular Front in Chile. According to this interpretation, there was tension between Laborde and his followers and Lombardo Toledano which led to the purge. Ravines stated that he had a conversation with Codovilla, in which the latter related the following: "We came from Mexico and we have directed the cleaning out of the party there; it has been a thorough purge; we have expelled Hernán Laborde, Campa, and a useless nucleus. We had Dionisio Encina elected, a type I believe can be trusted. Laborde and Campa had foolish ideas in their heads, like criticizing Lombardo Toledano. The House (the Comintern) had to commission Comrade Browder to go to Mexico and prevent the Party from creating frictions with Lombardo; you know the point of view of The House about this particular: Lombardo's group interests us more than that of the Party. Now a directed group remains to which it will never occur, never in its life, to confront Lombardo Toledano nor to cause him the least bother." [72]

In the writer's view, although this is admittedly conjecture, the second interpretation seems the most logical. It is possible that some Communists were opposed to Soviet tactics during the period of the Nazi-Soviet Pact, particularly in Finland and Poland. But certainly this was not shocking to such militants as Laborde and Campa who had learned to live with the twists and turns of Comintern and Soviet policies. As we have seen, Laborde supported the signing of the Nazi-Soviet Pact and subsequent Soviet operations in Poland. Furthermore, the differences between the Communists and Lombardo Toledano, which led to a temporary split of the CTM in 1937, did not result in any purges. There is no reason to believe that further differences would have led to a purge three years later.

But a major operation, such as the organized assassination of Trotsky, was another matter. It is very possible that Laborde and Campa believed all their gains under the Cárdenas administration would be lost, and the assassination of Trotsky was not worth the price. Under the circumstances, it is quite possible they refused to follow the dictates of Soviet (i.e., Stalin's) foreign policy. The appearance of important Comintern agents, and the timing of Trotsky's death a few months after the major purge make this, in the writer's view, the most logical of the three interpretations.

Not long after their expulsion, Laborde, Campa and their followers formed their own Party of Workers and Peasants of Mexico (Partido de Obreros y Campesinos de México, or POCM).[73] Although the new party followed the policies of the Comintern and Soviet leaders, it was seen by the Communist party leaders as a group of "revisionists," and "anti-Marxists." Thus, it might be said that not only the life, but the death of Leon Trotsky in Mexico contributed to the splitting of the left.

The reverberation of the Laborde-Campa purge was felt in the Communist party for some time afterward. Many militants left the party after the 1940 Extraordinary Congress, among them Andrés García Salgado (who denounced the Laborde-Campa faction during the Congress), Rafael Carrillo, and Mario Pavón Flores. In 1943 the apparent unity of the party was disrupted again. After heated debates, the Plenum of the Central Committee, in March, 1943, expelled another group of militants—Enrique Ramírez y Ramírez, Miguel Velasco, Angel Olivo, Luis Torres, Genaro Carnero Checa, Juan Ortega, and José Revueltas.[74]

A Change in the Leadership of the CTM

A few months after the major purges, the CTM witnesesd a change in its leadership. In September, 1940, Fidel Velázquez replaced Lombardo Toledano as the new Secretary General. Both Velázquez and Lombardo professed there was nothing unusual about this change. Velázquez told the writer that the term of office of Lombardo had expired and that he (Fidel Velázquez) received a majority of votes for Secretary General in an election shortly thereafter.[75] Subsequently Lombardo Toledano wrote that he gave up the position as Secretary General of the CTM, before the Second National Congress in February of 1941, in order to be able to take on the duties of President of the CTAL, "at the petition of the trade union organizations of all the Hemisphere in a dangerous period for our world." [76]

With all respect to these gentlemen, it seems that there was more involved in the change of leadership in the most important labor organization of the country. The election which Velázquez referred to took place during the period of the Nazi-Soviet Pact. Lombardo Toledano, pro-Communist in orientation and a supporter of Comintern and Soviet policies, was replaced by Fidel Velázquez, a non-Communist who subsequently became anti-Communist. (It is true, though, that Velázquez followed Lombardo's lead in international affairs up to the end of World War II).

Furthermore, Lombardo's stated reason for leaving the position of Secretary General of the CTM may be questioned. He became Secretary General of the CTAL when it was formed in 1938. For all practical purposes, he directed the continent-wide labor organization from its inception. There might have been a change in title from Secretary General to President of the Executive Committee, but the seat of power did not change hands. In addition, the world war started in September of 1939 and there was no appreciable change in international relations for the Communists and their allies until the Soviet Union entered the war in June of 1941. The world situation was not any more "dangerous" for the Communists, and their sympathizers, in February of 1941 than it had been in September of 1939.

Several possible reasons can be considered in regard to the change in leadership in the CTM. Cárdenas might have been fed up with the Nazi-Soviet Pact and the death of Trotsky and withdrew his support of Lombardo Toledano, which resulted in the latter's removal as Secretary General of the CTM. A second interpretation involves Avila Camacho who had just been elected President. He was not as sympathetic to the views of Lombardo as President Cárdenas had been, and he might have insisted that Fidel Velázquez take over the leadership of the CTM. The second interpretation is the more logical, since each President had his own favorite labor leader.

It is the writer's contention that the change in the leadership of the CTM was a direct result of the repercussions of the period of the Nazi-Soviet Pact. We have seen how Lombardo supported the Pact, referred to the war as an "inter-imperialist war," declared that Mexico should remain neutral, and through the periodicals under his direction, attacked President Roosevelt and supported the territorial gains of the Soviet Union. The Communists were very strong in the CTM, but they never had a majority of the membership under their control. It is quite possible that Velázquez's hand was strengthened as a result of the split within the ranks of the CTM between Lombardo and the Communists in 1937. He made his bid for power during the period of the Nazi-Soviet Pact, and as a result of Lombardo's espousal of the policies of the Comintern and Soviet leaders, the majority of the members of the CTM voted to oust him as their Secretary General and turned to Velázquez.

In short, the period of the Nazi-Soviet Pact was anything but good for the Communist movement. Government support all but ceased. Many of the former militants were purged from the party; a new "Workers and Peasants Party" came into being shortly thereafter, splitting the Communist forces further. A non-Communist (who later became an anti-Communist) emerged as the new head of the CTM. As was true in many places, the local Communist movement suffered as a result of Soviet foreign policy of the Nazi-Soviet Pact period.

Tactics During the Nazi-Soviet Pact

The Communists continued in their efforts to strengthen their ties with the CTM and Lombardo Toledano. Although he gave up the position of Secretary General, there is no doubt that Lombardo continued to be a power within the organization, and, through his positions as President of the CTAL, in the Latin American labor movement as a whole. The high regard in which the Communists held Lombardo was emphasized by Encina: "We shall work also in fraternal union with all the revolutionary elements which exist in the . . . unions and in the direction of the CTM, in order to consolidate and develop the great syndical organization of the proletariat. We shall work with fraternal · spirit with our great friend, Comrade Vicente Lombardo Toledano, that famous figure of the Mexican Revolution, who is the victim of the most despicable and vile attacks on the part of the Mexican reaction because the latter knows that he is of those who do not submit nor do they sell themselves, because he represents the revolutionary tradition of the Mexican workers' movement." [77]

The importance of the CTM to the Communist movement was recognized by the Comintern leaders. In a letter from Georgi Dimitrov, president of the Comintern, to the Communist leaders on commemoration of the First Extraordinary Congress of the party, in March, 1940, Dimitrov stressed the importance of a close working relationship between the CTM and the Communist ptarty.[78]

An interesting point was brought out during the Congress. When the Red Trade Union International was dissolved in 1934, during the Popular Front era, the Comintern and Soviet leaders instructed the labor organizations formerly affiliated with the Profintern to seek admission to the Socialist-controlled International Federation of Trade Unions (IFTU) located in Amsterdam. Shortly after it was formed in 1936, the CTM joined the Amsterdam International. During the First Extraordinary Congress, however, the Communist Party of Mexico passed a resolution calling upon the CTM to leave the IFTU[79] (which they subsequently did). Probably the major cause of this action was that the IFTU backed the Allies from the outbreak of World War II, whereas the CTM was "neutral in favor of Germany" until Germany attacked the Soviet Union in June of 1941.

The Communists became more critical of the government in comparsion to the Popular Front era. During the First Extraordinary Congress, the government was reprimanded for its attitude toward some of the striking workers (i.e., breaking strikes).[80] The government was also criticized when the land distribution program slowed down (discussed in Chapter II) and when it criticized the Soviet invasion of Finland.[81]

The Communist view of the Mexican Revolution was consistent with the orientation of the period of the Nazi-Soviet Pact. As mentioned previously, the Communist goal had always been the same: transformation of the Revolution of 1910 into a Socialist (i.e., Communist) Revolution which would make possible the dictatorship of the proletariat. This slogan was emphasized in the Third Period. During the Popular Front era, however, it was played down, and Communist periodicals gave greater stress to the development of a Popular Front "to realize the goals of the Revolution." But once the Popular Front era gave way to the period of the Nazi-Soviet Pact, the old slogan returned: "The Party, the Extraordinary Congress terminated, should set itself the task to apply its resolutions with enthusiasm and with faith, conscious of its historic responsibility and of the fact that it is the decisive factor in order that the democratic agrarian and anti-imperialist revolution can be developed toward its ultimate consequences and be transformed into a Socialist revolution." [82]

Usually, when the Comintern proclaimed a new "line" which brought about a more militant shift to the left, the Communist party would issue resolutions of a self-critical nature. The period of the Nazi-Soviet Pact was no exception. A rather startling confession came out of the First Extraordinary Congress, startling in the sense that it was admitted by such a high functionary as Encina: "More than a proletarian party we have been until now a small bourgeois party which has essentially been preoccupied with electoral problems." [83]

The Soviet Union Enters the War

The period of the Nazi-Soviet Pact came to an end when Germany invaded the Soviet Union on June 22, 1941.[84] According to the Communists, the "inter-imperialist" phase of the war had ended; the "people's war" or "great patriotic war" had begun. During the period through 1945, no effort was to be spared to bring the war to a victorious conclusion for the Allies. Strikes were discouraged as being a hindrance to the war effort. The Soviet and Comintern leaders called for a second front in Europe to relieve the pressure of the German armies on the Soviet Union. And as a final gesture of Soviet good faith in the Allied war effort, the Comintern was dissolved.

The Mexican Communists followed the lead of the Soviet and Comintern leaders by declaring that the nature of the war had now changed. Their position was presented by Encina: "The first of August finds us before fundamental changes in the character of the second world war initiated in 1939. The war was until June 22 an imperialist war, but as a consequence of the aggression of the Hitler hordes against the Soviet Union, the war has been transformed into a common war against the fascist aggressor." [85]

The attitude of Lombardo was very similar to that of Encina. In an article entitled "Barbarity Against Civilization," he explained his interpretation of the war: "The aggression against the USSR has changed the ends and the destiny of the war totally. The participation of the Socialist power has transformed the conflict into a struggle of all the countries of the world, dividing it into two groups: Nazi-fascist and anti-Nazi-fascist. The inter-imperialist character which it had in its beginnings necessarily disappears with the intervention of the Soviet Union. . ." [86]

Those Mexican and Latin American labor organizations which were strongly influenced by the Communists were completely in accord with the Communist position. The CTM passed a resolution calling upon all Latin American countries to participate in the war effort. No sacrifice would be too great now that the Soviet Union had entered the war.[87]

The resolutions passed by the CTAL were very similar. In November of 1941, during the First General Congress, a resolution was passed which emphasized the importance of the war to all the people of Latin

America. This particular resolution reflected the thinking of the Comunist leaders that, now that the Soviet Union was attacked, the war had become a "people's war": "The CTAL declares, in its First Ordinary Congress, that the present war against the totalitarian regimes, is the war of the Latin American people in defense of their dearest interests, material and moral. It declares, likewise, that this struggle is vital for the future of all the free people of the world, and for them it makes today a call to men and women in order that they may be conscious of the fact that this is THEIR WAR, that they may be prepared to cooperate enthusiastically in the defense of the people who constitute, in this hour, the first entrenchment in this historic and world struggle against tyranny and violence." [88]

During the period of the Nazi-Soviet Pact, the Communists did not want the Mexican economy to contribute to the war effort. The attitude that neutrality during the "imperialist war" was to be both economic and political changed when the Soviet Union entered the war. The Communists encouraged the government to use all its resources against the Axis,[89] and encouraged all the countries to come into the struggle on the side of the Allies, Mexico included. They fully suported the war effort of the government.[90]

The attack against Capitalist "imperialism" was discarded when the "people's war" began. The slogan of "Yankee imperialism" was laid to rest for the duration of the war.[91]

Lombardo Toledano was even more explicit in burying the two imperialisms, American and British, as long as it was in the interest of the Soviet Union to receive a maximum amount of support from its allies: "Fortunately we are very far from the period in which Yankee imperialism was confused with the generous and great people of the United States, and British imperialism with the stupendous people of England. We are also very far from those romantic and sterile attitudes which used to carry us—which carried our fathers and grandfathers—to shout passionately against imperialism, without realizing concrete and decisive works for the definite liberation of our countries." [92]

The new era of friendliness also called for dropping the attacks against Franklin D. Roosevelt. As we have seen, during the period of the Nazi-Soviet Pact, the Communists and their allies accused the American President of wanting to establish "dictatorial governments on the continent." He also was identified with "reactionary circles of North America finance capital." But all this changed with the advent of the great "patriotic war." [93]

Lombardo Toledano also expressed friendship toward the American President: "We are sincere friends of the great President Franklin Delano Roosevelt . . . The policy of 'good neighbor' is a formulation of the present government of the United States, but it is also a policy which we sustain as our own." [94]

The anti-American theme of the period of the Nazi-Soviet Pact was now converted into pro-Americanism. Lombardo wrote that an alliance had always existed between Mexico and the United States. According to this interpretation, one might be led to believe that this phenomenon of anti-Americanism had never been a part of the Mexican environment. Th following quotation is interesting in that it shows the complete turnabout from the extreme anti-Americanism of the period of the Nazi-Soviet Pact:

"The desire of the present-day enemies of Mexico and the United States is to disrupt the unity and prevent the historical development of our two countries. This is what the Fifth Column is attempting to do. Its main aim is to pit the Mexican people against the American people.

". . . the alliance between our country and the United States . . . is not an accidental alliance. It is not an alliance just of today, but an alliance which began and developed from the genesis of our two nations.

"They who conspired against the alliance of our nation with the United States are Mexican traitors. They who work against the alliance of the American people with the people of Mexico are Yankee Traitors. I declare the sincere friendship of the workers and the people of Latin America with the great people of the United States." [95]

Because the Communists and pro-Soviet labor leaders supported the foreign policy of the Soviet Union and presented themselves as responsible proponents of the Allied war effort, they also benefited from the general sympathetic feeling for the Soviet Union which existed in the country. Such organizations as the Mexican Friends of the Soviet Union gained in popularity.[96]

Lombardo Toledano continued to make speeches and to write many articles praising the Soviet Union. One such speech was made to the First General Congress of the CTAL on November 22, 1941. He pointed out that support of the Soviet Union did not add to the danger of Communism. On the contrary, such support would strengthen the chances for Allied victory and make possible a world in which people would be able to determine the type of government under which they wanted to live.[97]

The Communists strongly backed Soviet efforts for a second front in Europe. In one of the articles in *La Voz de México,* they identified the need for a second front with the defense of Mexico.[98] A subsequent issue carried the headline: "NOW MORE THAN EVER THE SECOND FRONT!"[99]

The Communists and their supporters emphasized that the war could be shortened if a second front were opened in Europe. According to Lombardo Toledano: "If a second front is opened now, the war can be won in a few months. If not, the war may take several years. Latin American countries are very much interested to see a second front establishd now."[100] The CTAL, during its Congress in 1943, passed a similar resolution: "Upon defining its position facing the war, the Latin American Federation of Labor pronounced itself: for the immediate invasion of Europe and the establishment of a second European front in order to liquidate rapidly, with the combined power of the United Nations, Hitler Germany and to obtain victory in the shortest time and with the least loss of life and material goods. . ."[101]

Resumption of Diplomatic Relations with Soviet Russia

During the war, the Soviet and Comintern leaders took advantage of the sympathetic feeling toward the USSR in order to establish diplomatic relations with as many countries as possible. It would not have been wise politically for the Cárdenas government to resume diplomatic relations, particularly during the period of the Nazi-Soviet Pact when there was a great deal of antagonism toward the Soviet Union. But once the USSR joined the Allies, during the administration of Avila Camacho, the Communists pushed for the speedy resumption of diplomatic relations.

Until the resumption of diplomatic relations in late 1942, the Communists and their allies worked hard in their campaign to have the two countries establish normal relations again. In the First General Congress of the CTAL in November, 1941, a resolution was passed calling for the "establishment of resumption of commercial and diplomatic relations of the Latin American countries with the USSR."[102] The Communist Party of Mexico stressed the theme that normal relations would contribute to the war effort: "The resumption of relations with the USSR would prove that the thought which Mexico has maintained is just; that the difference of social systems of government cannot be an obstacle for the existence of normal relations between the people. The resumption of relations of our country with the USSR would reinforce the unity of the United Nations and contribute to the victory against barbarity." [103]

On November 19, 1942, diplomatic relations were formally re-established. The new Soviet Ambassador, Constantin Oumansky, arrived in June, 1943. He proceeded to build up a very large embassy staff, and, as reported in the *New York Times* of November 28, 1943, the Soviet Embassy was very popular both socially and politically. In a sense, the establishment of the Embassy filled a void for the Communists left by the dissolution of the Comintern on May 22, 1943.[104] One can conclude that the Communist Party of Mexico continued to receive guidance and support from Moscow, via the Soviet Embassy.

The Communists were not appreciably affected by the decision to dissolve the Comintern. Various articles appeared in Communist periodicals praising the role of the international Communist organization. The eulogy of Lombardo Toledano was particularly interesting in that it showed his attitude toward the Comintern and its activities: "Free men of all the earth — And among them, of a particular type, those who, like I, never were members of the Communist International nor of any of its affiliate parties—cannot greet less respectfully the historic resolution (i.e., announcement of the dissolution of the Comintern) of an organ which, without having succumbed through the most severe attacks of our time, inclines its banners before the supreme interest of reinforcing the unity of the people for the struggle to death against the most terrible enemy which humanity has known." [105]

Communist Strength Toward the End of World War II

There are two indicators of Communist strength which can be measured with some precision: the number of members in the Communist party, and Comunist influence in the labor movement.

As we have seen, the Communist party claimed a membership of 33,000 in the spring of 1939, during the Cárdenas administration. At the end of the war, in the fall of 1946, Encina stated there were only 13,000 members in the party. Several reasons lie behind this decrease. As mentioned previously, the Nazi-Soviet Pact was a factor (as it had been throughout Latin America). The membership was further depleted in 1940 when Leon Trotsky was assassinated and several Mexican Communists were implicated. In all probability, the size of the party was affected by the purges of the 1940's. Many who sympathized with the former Laborde-Campa leadership followed when they were expelled from the party. The exodus continued for a few years with the subsequent purges of other prominent Communists. A by-product was the formation of a rival Communist organization, the Party of Workers and Peasants of Mexico (POCM). This served as a further attraction for those who contemplated leaving the Communist party. Furthermore, although Avila Camacho stressed the theme of national unity throughout the war, he was not as sympathetic to the Communist cause as Lázaro Cárdenas had been (in condoning Communist influence in the Secretariat of Education and providing funds for the Communist party).

The second indicator of the strength of the Communists is to assess their influence in the labor movement. Although they received a setback when Lombardo Toledano ceased to be Secretary General of of the CTM, the position of the Communists in the CTM remained generally the same during World War II when Lombardo's policy of full support for the government and the Allied war effort was continued. Thus, the CTM leadership agreed not to call any strikes while Mexico was at war.[106] Some Communists might have been removed from positions of strong influence, but, generally, it might be said that Communist strength within the CTM changed but little through 1945.

The same cannot be said of Communist influence in the Latin American Federation of Labor (CTAL) to which the CTM was affiliated. Between the First General Congress, November, 1941, and the Second General Congress, December, 1944, the Communists increasingly took over important positions within the organization. The culmination was reached during the Second General Congress, held in Cali, Colombia. Of the twelve members elected to the new Executive Committee, seven were avowed members of the Communist parties in their respective countries. The five who were not members of a Communist party included Lombardo Toledano and two others who closely followed the Communist line. Only two members of the new Executive Committee, Juan Briones of Chile and Fidel Velázquez of Mexico, were definitely anti-Communist.[107] In addition, most of the Secretaries named at the Second General Congress were Communists. Of the four commissions established to prepare resolutions for submission to the plenary sessions of the Congress, three were headed by openly declared Communists.[108] Thus, from December, 1944, through the end of World War II, the Communists controlled the CTAL, the most powerful labor organization in the hemisphere.[109]

In 1945 pro-Communist and non-Communist labor representatives formed the World Federation of Trade Unions (WFTU). The Red International of Trade Unions (RILU) had been dissolved in 1934, and the IFTU officially went out of existence to pave the way for the WFTU. Lombardo Toledano attended the London conference which laid the basis for the establishment of the WFTU. He also was a delegate to the Paris conference which established the WFTU on October 3, 1945, and was one of the thirteen members of the Administrative Committee which was formed. Shortly thereafter, the CTAL adhered to the new trade union organization.[110]

To summarize: the Communists regained some of the losses they had suffered during the period of the Nazi-Soviet Pact and the strength of the Communist movement increased during the latter part of the war. The loss in the membership of the Communist party was offset somewhat by Communist gains in the CTAL. Their position in the CTM remained rather stationary as long as Mexico was a partticipant in the war, but Lombardo Toledano's removal as Secretary General portended further losses for the Communists once the war ended. Over-all, Communist strength was much greater before the Nazi-Soviet Pact, during the Popular Front era, than it was after the Pact was terminated, even including the period of the "people's war."

Communist Policy Toward the End of the War

For the remainder of the war, Communist policies were determined by one overriding objective: national unity to win the war. The Mexican Communists continually stressed this theme in their perodicals: "Our Program for this struggle is NATIONAL UNITY for the direct participation in the war to assure the fulfillment of the Atlantic Charter, militant and progressive unity of this nation of ours . . ."[111]

The Mexican supporters of Soviet foreign policy made every effort to strengthen national unity within the country. In the labor movement, they tried to encourage major labor and employer organizations to sign pacts for cooperation in the war effort. According to the *Daily Worker* of September 16, 1945, such an agreement was signed between the CTM and the Manufacturers Association of Mexico.

The Communists and their friends came to the conclusion that Soviet interests and the Allied war effort could best be promoted with a minimum of disruption within the various Latin American countries. Thus, all governments were to be supported, whether democratic or dictatorial. Lombardo Toledano, President of the CTAL and still a power in the CTM, often praised particular dictators. He once referred to Manuel Prado of Peru as a "native Stalin" and considered General Anastasio Somoza of Nicaragua to be the "paternal dictator."

As the war drew to a close, the Communist and pro-Soviet labor leaders continued to stress the theme of national uinty. Perhaps the words of Lombardo Toledano best depict how far this position was removed from such earlier slogans as "Socialist Revolution" and "dictatorship of the proletariat":

"In these moments in many countries of Latin America the impatient, the unprepared, those who play the game of the Axis powers without realizing it, raise the cry that national unity is impossible in those countries where there are no democratic governments and that it is necessary, before anything else, to take advantage of this war to make a revolution immediately with the object of overwhelming the dictator or president who is not loved by the people, and afterwards, only afterwards, to cooperate to win the war or help the United Nations to win it.

"This opinion, presented thus, in an intransigent form, is the opinion of the 'fifth column.' We have a different opinion: we believe that it is necessary to bring about national unity in all parts where the government is disposed to struggle against the Axis and that national unity can and ought to be realized with all sectors of the country. . ." [112]

CHAPTER VIII

CONCLUSIONS

What was the impact of the various foreign agents who came to the country to work with the Communist movement? How closely did the Communists and their allies follow the policies and tactics proclaimed by the leaders of international Communism? What factors are relevant to an analysis of "Communism in Mexico" through the end of the second world war?

A first conclusion is that the foreigners who appeared in the country were primarily concerned with the organizational problems of the formation and development of a Communist party and not with larger political questions. They were influential with the local Communist party as distinguished from other elements of the Communist movement. It is true the American Communist leader and Comintern official, Earl Browder, played an important part in bringing the Communists back into the CTM in 1937. This particular activity went beyond the Communist party to the labor movement. Generally, however, the Comintern and non-Comintern "agents" limited their endeavors to the Communist party.

The Comintern was opportunistic in contracting foreigners who were already in the country. There were several foreigners active in the Communist movement who certainly were not sent by the Comintern. This group included José Allen, Frank Seaman (Charles Francis Phillips), F. Mayer, M. Paley, and Linn A. E. Gale. The evidence the writer has obtained also indicates that M. N. Roy, the Indian nationalist turned Communist, was not a Comintern agent when he first appeared in the country. He was contacted by the International Communist organization while in Mexico and became an active Comintern agent only after he left the country. This tactic of international Communism can teach us a lesson in the present. For example, it is quite possible that China might develop an apparatus along the lines of the Comintern, if it has not done so already, in order to spread its influence through various parts of the world. A present day African, Asian, or Latin American nationalist could be susceptible to the overtures of Chinese Communism as were his predecessors of fifty-five years ago by the Soviet variety.

The first agents who were sent by the Comintern (Sen Katayama, Luis Fraina, Michael Borodin) were not very effective in influencing the Mexican Communists. The diplomatic representatives of the Soviet Union who replaced them in the latter part of the 1920's might have been more efficient in the handling of funds, but this was more than offset by the friction generated between them and local leaders and the government. Although there were Comintern agents active in the direction of the Communist party during that period, the first Comintern agent who radically changed the course of the Communist party was Dimitri Manuilsky.

The attempted insurrection of the Communists in 1929, a reflection of the tactics of the Third Period and the efforts of Manuilsky, ended in complete failure for the Communist party. The Communist movement was damaged by the subsequent government persecution, the break in diplomatic relations with the Soviet Union, the purge of the Communist party, and the illegal status accorded the party (1929-1934). All of this was compounded by the activities of the Soviet diplomats in the country.

Other Comintern agents appeared during the 1930's, but their presence did not produce major changes in the Communist party until the purges of the 1940's. Dimitri Manuilsky arrived again in 1940 with Victorio Codovilla and others. Largely through their efforts, the principal leaders of the Communist party were purged, many militants left the party, and a rival Communist party came into being. In all probability, Moscow continued to direct the Communist party during World War II through the Soviet Embassay, reestablished in 1942.

The principal role of the various agents sent by the Comintern was to direct and guide the Communist party. Their efforts resulted in bringing the party more securely under the control of the Comintern and Soviet leaders. But the Comintern agents did not improve the position of the local Communists. The greatest setback to the Communist movement, the abortive insurrection of the Third Period, was caused primarily by these Comintern agents. The Communist party gain in strength during the administration of Lázaro Cárdenas was the result of a variety of factors *within* Mexico (the Popular Front environment, the ideological orientation of the government, and so forth) and was not caused by the agents of the Comintern as such. However, the attitude of the Communist party was determined by the change in the Comintern line.

In the second place, the Mexican Communists and the "friends of the Soviet Union" followed the policies and tactics of the Soviet and Comintern leaders almost without question. Those Communists who vacillated or refused were purged from the party.

The Communists and their allies supported the government against internal rebellions. Although at one time this tactic was rebuked by the Comintern, the criticism was not very sincere. In reality, they were criticizing themselves for their failure to turn the Aguirre-Escobar revolt of the spring of 1929 into a "civil war" against the Portes Gil government. With the initiation of the Popular Front era, the international Communist organization once again encouraged the local Communists to support the government against internal revolts.

The tactic of supporting the government was correct in an ideological sense. The Communists had always viewed the Mexican Revolution of 1910 as a "democratic bourgeois revolution" which had overthrown the feudal regime. It was therefore necessary to prevent the overthrow of the bourgeois government prematurely. According to the Communists, the bourgeois revolution had to develop to a point where it could be replaced by the dictatorship of the proletariat or the government of the workers and peasants.

From 1919-1935, the Mexican Communists followed the Comintern policy of a hard militant attitude toward non-Communist elements. They supported the various policies of the United Front (from below), Bolshevization, and the Third Period. In accordance with the Moscow conferences and the Latin American congresses, they formed a Workers' and Peasants' Bloc. Their own trade union, the CSUM, vigorously opposed the non-Communist labor organizations. They attacked prominent government and labor figures, including President Cárdenas and Lombardo Toledano. And, as we have seen, they were active participants in an unsuccessful insurrection planned by Comintern agents. The Mexican Communists were internationalists: they called for the defense of the Soviet Union, a world revolution, and a revolution against the government. All of their slogans and tactics were fully in accord with the position of the Comintern.

Once the Communists overcame their initial difficulty in making the transition from the Third Period to the Popular Front era, they became strong supporters of the government in the "struggle against the Fascist danger." Although the militant attitude of the Third Period was dropped during the Popular Front era, the goal of the Communists, phrased somewhat differently, was still the same. Hernán Laborde expressed it to the Seventh Congress of the Comintern as "Soviet Power and Socialism."

The Mexican Communists (and others in agreement with the new "line" proclaimed during the Seventh Congress of the Comintern) did everything possible to realize a Popular Front in the country. Another theme of the Comintern congress, trade union unity, was successfully implemented in the creation of the CTM which included both Communist and non-Communist elements. The Mexican Communists and other supporters of Comintern policies also contributed to the formation of a continent-wide labor organization, the CTAL. Through their principal spokesmen and periodicals, labor groups joined the Communist party in the espousal of various slogans which reflected the orientation of the Comintern during the Popular Front era: the Fascist danger, the call for a Popular Front, expressions of friendship for the people of the United States and Franklin D. Roosevelt, and support for Republican Spain. The Mexican Communists even went so far as to recruit volunteers to fight in the Spanish Civil War.

As the Comintern came under the control of Stalin, the Mexican Communists and their allies continued to support the policies of the Comintern evidenced by their extreme virulence toward the presence of Leon Trotsky in the country. Both the Communist periodicals and those under the control of Lombardo Toledano were unrelenting in their attacks on the former Bolshevik leader.

Although the Communist party denied that Siqueiros and others who led the first assault on Trotsky's home were party members, the party was not exonerated. They were also involved in the second assault which resulted in the assassination of Trotsky. When they volunteered to participate in the assassination of Stalin's enemy, the Mexican Communists were brought completely under the control of Moscow. Those who remained in the party after the purges of the 1940's were unswerving in their support of Stalin's policies. There was no doubt that they would follow any new "line" or tactic which was handed down by the Comintern.

When the Nazi-Soviet Pact was signed almost one year before Trotsky's death, Comintern supporters fell into line and advocated the explanation of the conflict as an imperialist war, the neutrality of Mexico, extreme anti-Americanism, and supported Soviet territorial gains. The Communist party, the CTM, the CTAL, Lombardo Toledano (and the periodicals under his direction) issued similar slogans in support of the tactics of the Nazi-Soviet Pact. Within the country the Communists reflected the increased militancy of the period by escalating their attacks on the government and calling for the transformation of the Mexican Revolution into a "Socialist revolution."

But when the Soviet Union entered the war and it became a "people's war," these same groups completely reversed themselves in accordance with the Comintern directives. Dionisio Encina and Lombardo Toledano agreed that the "imperialist" phase of the war had come to an end. Now all nations were called upon to participate in the war effort with the Allies. Anti-Americanism became pro-Americanism, and no sacrifice was considered to be too great to bring the war to a victorious conclusion. Soviet interests were fully supported: various groups called for a second front in Europe and the resumption of diplomatic relations with the Soviet Union. There was no longer any clear distinction between the Communist party and other supporters of the Soviet Union (e.g., the CTM, the CTAL, Lombardo Toledano and his periodicals). All of these groups were now nationalists who called for national unity and the maintenance of the status quo.

The Mexican Communists, particularly after the purges of the Third Period and the Nazi-Soviet Pact, opposed the policies of the government and called for a "Socialist" revolution. During the Popular Front era, however, the "people's war" was of a national character and the Communists played down the theme of opposing the government. As indicated by these complete reversals in tactics, the Soviet supporters in the country provided an example of a cardinal principle of international Communism handed down by Lenin many years ago: When a doctrinaire creed comes into contact with social reality, the Communist movement must be capable of great flexibility in the continuous effort to achieve its ends.

A third conclusion is that the evolution of "Communism in Mexico" went through many stages and encompassed several elements. For all practical purposes, the Communist party began with the establishment of two Communist parties shortly after the Russian Revolution of 1917. One party, that of Gale and his associates, certainly was formed without the aid of the Comintern or its agents. (This was probably true of the party of José Allen and M. N. Roy as well). Michael Borodin, the Comintern agent, arrived in the country and found two Communist parties already in operation.

It is evident, however, that the Communist Party of Mexico fell under the control of the Comintern in succeeding years. Still later (in 1942), the Party of Workers and Peasants of Mexico (POCM) came into being and competed with the Communist Party of Mexico as a direct result of a Communist-directed purge of the regular party.

The Communist Party of Mexico was not a workers' party and the

Secretary General of the party, Dionisio Encina, admitted as much. It was made up of the petty bourgeoisie: artists, middle class intellectuals, lawyers, and students. The majority of the working class was usually attracted to one of the principal labor organizations—the CROM, the CTM, or to the official government party.

Except for a few years in the 1920's the Communist movement did not include the peasants. Ursulo Galván brought the Communists their greatest success with the peasants, but when he was purged from the Communist party and resigned from the Workers' and Peasants' Bloc, the majority of the peasants were never again to turn to the Communists. In later years, the government was able to win their allegiance through the official government party.

It is true that the Communists were successful with the peasants for a limited period in the state of Yucatán and the Southeast of the country through the efforts of Felipe Carrillo Puerto. But in this case, policy was determined by local conditions. Carrillo Puerto was a peasant leader who happened to be in the Communist party for a few years. It is very doubtful that he was under the influence of the Comintern or its agents. When Carrillo Puerto traveled to a town in Yucatán, "Communist influence" was with him through his speeches and slogans. But when he left the town, the Indians returned to their usual activities without preoccupying themselves with the tenets of Communism.

Labor proved to be one of the most fertile grounds for the Communist movement through World War II. Although the workers did not adhere to the party in any appreciable number, the labor movement was heavily infiltrated by Communists. The peak of this success was the Communist influence in the CTM, in the latter part of the 1930's prior to he signing of the Nazi-Soviet Pact. Several Communists were important officials in the CTM, and many of the trade unons affiliated with the organization were Communist-controlled. As we have seen, the CTM was the most important organization in the labor sector of the official government party. Its officials were very close to President Cárdenas. Furthermore, the Communists and their sympathizers, with Mexico represented through the CTM, gained control of the continent-wide CTAL.

Víctor Alba, a prominent specialist in Latin American affairs, depreciates the impact of Marxism on the labor movement: "Marxism never exercised an influence on the Mexican labor movement. There was in it, on the other hand, a certain influence of anarcho-syndicalism . . . and of a non-Marxist humanitarian socialism." [1] This interpretation is generally valid of the labor movement although the writer would qualify it with reference to the CTM when it was under the leadership of Lombardo Toledano. Communist influence in the CTM comprised an important part of the Communist movement; the growth of this influence was facilitated by the line taken during the Popular Front era and the relative acceptance of the Communists. It was not a phenomenon which was brought about by the activities of the Comintern. The importance of the CTM, in relation to the Communist movement, was aptly expressed by a well-known Mexican author: "In truth the Communist and Marxist elements organized the CTM and, sometimes with its immediate collaboration and other times indirect, gave concrete expression to the movement in international ideas which Communism needs for its growth and influence. . . . The Marxist struggle can be considered as a constant impulse toward proletarian unity with sights on Communism." [2]

Lombardo Toledano's strong support of the policies of the Comintern and the Soviet Union was a decisive factor toward making the Communists more palatable to certain non-Communist groups within the country—students, middle class intellectuals, and some labor officials. He spoke as the Secretary General of the CTM, the strongest labor organization of the country, and as the President of the CTAL, the strongest labor organization of Latin America. The ideological orientation of this powerful labor figure, a development independent of the Comintern, strengthened the Communist movement of Mexico. In one of his many denials that he had ever been a Communist, Lombardo Toledano presented his views of the local Communists:

"The danger of Communism at this hour? I have said it a thousand times and everyone knows it—in Mexico, in Latin America, in Europe, in the United States. I have never been nor am now a member of the Communist Party. I have never made commitments of any kind to the Communist International. If I had ever been a member of the Communist Party, or were now, I would announce it with pride and boastfully.

"But I am not. I have many times disagreed with the position taken by the Party's leaders. That, however, does not mean that I do not consider the Communists sincere revolutionaries, despite some things they have done which from my point of view were mistakes. It does not mean that I do believe the Communists of Mexico, whom I have known and dealt with in the past, to be patriots who love their Fatherland." [3]

The Communist movement reached its peak in strength during the administration of Lázaro Cárdenas and began to wane with the signing of the Nazi-Soviet Pact in August of 1939. The process was accelerated when Leon Tortsky was assassinated one year later. The Communists were able to recoup some of their losses with the initiation of the "people's war," but they never regained the strength they enjoyed earlier.

When Lázaro Cárdenas was President of the country, the Communist party had more members than at any other time before or during World War II. Communists were very strong in the CTM (itself a powerful force in the official government party), in other labor and agricultural organizations, and in student organizations. Furthermore, as we have seen, the Communists were very influential in the Secretariat of Education; their doctrine was preached throughout the country under the guise of "Socialist education." Added to these factors was the influence of Communism with a substantial number of the articulate middle class intellectuals, who, in reality, comprise the public opinion.

It is difficult to determine with any precision how the Communist movement would have developed during the administration of President Cárdenas without the Popular Front environment. The Communists might have gained strength regardless of who was President. It is plausible that the Communists would have eventually supported the policies of the President regarding land distribution and nationalization of some basic industries and thereby strengthen their own position, regardless of the Popular Front era. In the writer's view, the Communists consciously identified themselves with the policies of the government and benefited as a result. In addition, the ideological orientation of the government, as exemplified through the Secretariat of Education, proved to be advantageous to the Communist movement. The Communist movement would have been strengthened during the Cárdenas administration, although possibly to a lesser degree, in the absence of the Popular Front environment.

There is a currently popular theory that those countries of Latin America which have strong and dynamic liberal movements, or native social revolutionary movements, under the guidance of democratic left wing political parties, can offer the strongest resistance to the influence of Communism.[4] During the Cárdenas administration several basic industries were nationalized, and more land was distributed to the peasants than during all the previous administrations combined. Labor was represented in the official government party and the workers received more benefits than in previous years. The government made great strides in alleviating illiteracy and generally improved the condition of the mass of the people. The social promises of the Revolution were pushed forward by the government and the official party.

In light of these social reforms, the growth of Communism during the Cárdenas administration indicates that the above-cited theory is in need of qualification: a left-of-center democratic government does not necessarily offer the best resistance to Communism. Furthermore, the non-Communist revolutionary movement may be led by a democratic left wing party and weakend by Communist elements within the official circles which affects the party's ability to struggle against the spread of Communism. In the case of Mexico, we saw that the Communists were very strong in the CTM, and the labor organization was one of the vital parts of the official government party.

The theory is also in need of qualification in another sense. One must analyze the government's attitude toward the Communist movement within the country in order to determine if such a government offers effective resistance to the growth of Communism. If the left-of-center democratic government is sympathetic to Communism, as exemplified by the Cárdenas administration, then the growth of Communism will not be effectively resisted. On the contrary, the Communist movement will probably increase in strength. However, if the left-of-center democratic government actually fights the Communist movement within the country, then such a government can offer the best means of resisting Communism. Recent reform governments of Rómulo Betancourt and Raúl Leoni in Venezuela were anti-Communist; they actively struggled against the Communists of Venezuela, and, as a result, Communism had been effectively resisted within the country. Thus, the attitude of the left-of-center democratic government toward Communism is an extremely important consideration in the application of the theory.

The theory is still valuable, however, in analyzing the political development of Latin America but it must be used with a note of caution. One cannot make a blanket statement that native social revolutionary movements, under democratic left wing political parties, are the answer to Communism in Latin America. They may be the answer in certain countries, given particular conditions, but this interpretation does not necessarily apply to all countries under any conditions. Mexico, under the Cárdenas administration, again teaches us the lesson that our general theories of political behavior are normally subject to qualification and re-examination.

There is another popular theory, related to the one just discussed, which pertains to Mexico. This one contends that Communism cannot take hold in Mexico because the country had experienced its own revolution prior to the Russian Revolution of 1917.[5] In the writer's view, the question is not whether a country has had its own revolution but how successful the revolution has been. As we have seen in the second chapter, the Mexican Revolution, through 1945, was only partially successful. Chronic social and economic problems continued to exist. There was rampant inflation, particularly in the 1940's. Many thousands of peasants still did not have land; the ejido system left a great deal to be desired. These failures drove a number of middle class intellectuals to the Communist party.

The Communists certainly never accepted the idea that the Mexican Revolution was complete. Throughout the various periods they continued to call for a "social revolution" which would complete the "bourgeois revolution" and overthrow the Capitalist system. This was their slogan as far back as 1924,[6] and they never ceased emphasizing it. The slogan may have been toned down during certain periods and the phrases may have varied to "dictatorship of the proletariat," "government of workers and peasants," and "Socialist revolution to implant a Soviet system," but the meaning was clear and the goal never changed.

It is true that a majority of the workers and peasants supported the Revolution. They felt it was their Revolution and that they had a stake in it. As a result, Communism did not make much of an impression on them. However, as pointed out in this study, the Communist movement was primarily identified with a segment of the middle class; it was not a workers' and peasants' movement. A few middle class intellectuals were disillusioned with the Revolution. It was they who recognized the poverty of the peasants, although the latter seemed to feel their problems would be solved by the land distribution program. It was they who recognized the seriousness of inflation, although the workers seemed to be content with increases in salary. The failures of the Revolution, then, facilitated the development of the Communist movement in regard to this all-important segment of the middle class.

One final point to be considered concerns whether "Communism in Mexico" was a generalized feeling with a Marxist flavor or whether it existed in the form of a real Communist movement. If the latter was the case, was the Communist movement mainly a Soviet and Comintern creation or was it determined primarily by conditions within the country?

Lombardo Toledano believed that Communism was a philosophy for some intellectuals in Mexico. The Comintern and its agents did not leave a lasting impression, and the Communist party had always been small. Communism in Mexico, according to Lombardo Toledano, had been more of an abstraction.[7]

It is true that the subject of Communism was only an intellectual pastime for some people, but the existence of a Communist movement in the forms analyzed throughout this study was real. We have seen that the movement comprised various elements: one or more Communist parties, Communist influence in the CTM, and, consequently, in the official government party, Comunist influence in the Cárdenas administration (the Secretariat of Education in particular) and throughout various parts of the country during President Cárdenas' term of office. The Communist movement also became closely identified with anti-Americanism throughout the period to 1945. Added to these factors was the ideological orientation of Lombardo Toledano and his influence in the labor movement. With the exception of certain developments in the Communist party, all of these factors which affected the Comunist movement were not created by the Comintern or Soviet leaders.

The writer substantially agrees with Lombardo Toledano that the Comintern did not have any lasting effect on the Comunist movement. The Mexican Communist movement, perhaps like that in other countries of Latin America, was largely a product of local social conditions.

REFERENCES

CHAPTER I

1. Eduard Bernstein, *Evolutionary Socialism: A Criticism and Affirmation,* (New York: B. W. Huebsch, 1909).

2. For the activities of the Socialist parties during World War I see Merle Fainsod, *International Socialism and the World War,* (Harvard University Press, 1935).

3. V. I. Lenin, *Left-Wing Communism: An Infantile Disorder,* (International Publishers Co., 1934), p. 10.

4. It is interesting that the idea of mass parties took hold in Soviet thinking during the era of the Popular Front in the mid-1930's.

5. Franz Borkenau, *World Communism—A History of the Communist International,* (New York: W. W. Norton, 1939), p. 87.

6. *Ibid.,* p 181. There were several other elements which attended the Congress. These included the Anarcho-Syndicalists such as the Spanish CNT. Furthermore, many of the "delegates" to the first Congress were in fact foreigners resident in Moscow, such as the U. S. delegation.

7. *Manifesto of the Communist International,* (Chicago: Chicago Labor Printing Office, 1919), p. 16. As we shall observe presently, Lenin modified this revolutionary call to arms somewhat by emphasizing the importance of Communist work in "bourgeois" parliaments.

8. Jane Degras, *The Communist International 1919-1943—Documents,* Vol. I, 1919-1922, "Invitation to the First Congress of the Communist International," (Oxford University Press, 1956), p. 2.

9. V. I. Lenin, *The Foundation of the Communist International,* (New York: International Publishers, 1919), p. 23.

10. *The Communist International,* May 1, 1919, p. 44.

11. *Ibid.,* p. 46.   12. *Ibid.,* p. 33.

13. Jane Degras, "Manifesto of the Communist International to the Proletariat of the Entire World," p. 38.

14. *Manifesto of the Communist International,* p. 19. The Communists distinguished Socialists of the "right," Socialists of the "left," and even Socialists of the "center." Their criticism of these groups was equally severe.

15. O. Piatnitsky, *The Twenty-One Conditions of Admission Into the Communist International,* (New York: Workers Library Publishers, 1934), p. 14.

16. V. I. Lenin, *Left-Wing Communism: An Infantile Disorder,* p. 42.

17. *Ibid.,* p. 47.   18. *Ibid.,* p. 36.   19. *Ibid.,* p. 38.

20. *Ibid,* pp. 36-38.

21. *The 2nd Congress of the Communist International,* (Washington: Government Printing Office, 1920), p. 115.

22. Jane Degras, "Theses on the National and Colonial Question," p. 139.

23. *The 2nd Congress of the Communist International,* p. 25.

24. A complete list of the Twenty-One Conditions is given by Jane Degras, pp. 168-172.

25. The Amsterdam International was the trade union organization loosely associated with the Second International before World War I. The Red Trade Union International (Profintern) was created during the Second Congress as a trade union subsidiary of the Communist International. Losovski, a Russian, was made president.

26. Jane Degres, "Extracts from the Manifesto of the Second World Congress of the Communist International," p. 177.

27. *Ibid.,* "Extracts from the Theses on the World Situation and the Tasks of the Comintern," p. 230.

28. *Theses and Resolutions Adopted at the Third World Congress of the Communist International,* (New York: Contemporary Publishers Ass'n, 1921), p. 191.

29. Based on a discussion by Hugh Seton-Watson, *From Lenin to Khrushchev,* (New York: Praeger, 1960), p. 100.

30. *Theses and Resolutions Adopted at the Third World Congress of the Communist International,* p. 99.

31. *International Press Correspondence* (Inprecorr), Nov. 1, 1921, pp. 29-30.

32. Jane Degras, "The Third Congress of the Communist International," p. 225.

33. *Ibid.,* "Extracts from the Directives for Communist Action in the Trade Unions Adopted by the Fourth Comintern Congress," pp. 415-416.

34. *Ibid.,* "Fourth Congress of the Communist International," p. 378.

35. *Towards a Communist Programme* (London: Communist Party of Great Britain, 1922), p. 12.

36. Michael T. Florinsky, *World Revolution and the U.S.S.R.* (New York: Macmillan, 1933), pp. 107-110.

37. *Ibid.,* pp. 116-117.

38. Jane Degras, Vol. II, 1923-28, "Extracts from the Theses on Tactics Adopted by the Fifth Comintern Congress," pp. 153-154.

39. *Inprecorr,* Jan. 22, 1925, p. 64.

40. Jane Degras, Vol. II, "Extracts from the Theses on Tactics Adopted by the Fifth Comintern Congress," p. 150.

41. See Michael T. Florinsky, Chapter IV, "'Socialism in a Single Country."

42. *Inprecorr,* May 30, 1925, p. 605.

43. Michael T. Florinsky, p. 130.

44. *Inprecorr,* Nov. 23, 1928, p. 1567.

45. Tension developed between the Soviet Union and Great Britain during the period 1924-1927, although developments did not lead to the point of war as the Comintern periodicals indicated. This involved a letter supposedly written by Zinoviev, the head of the Comintern, to a representative of the British Communist Party giving instructions for the conduct of subversive work in England. The letter was a forgery, but it did influence the British election in which the Conservatives returned to power. After the British government raided the Soviet Trade Delegation in London, citing as justification evidence of subversive activity, it broke relations with the Soviet Union in 1927. They were not resumed until 1930. See George F. Kennan, *Russia and the West Under Lenin and Stalin,* (Little, Brown 1961), pp. 234-238.

46. *Inprecorr,* Aug. 13, 1928, p. 864.

47. Jane Degras, Vol. II, "Extracts from the Theses of the Sixth Comintern

Congress on the International Situation and the Tasks of the Communist International," p. 459.

48. *Inprecorr,* Nov. 23, 1928, p. 1517.

49. *The Communist,* April, 1930, p. 309.

50. The Comintern leaders were not always consistent in their use of slogans. The "United Front from below" was used in the early 1920's. During that time, there was a tendency toward the "Right" as a reaction to the failure to the "imminent world revolution."

51. *Inprecorr,* Oct. 7, 1932, p. 943.

52. *Ibid.,* Oct. 20, 1932, p. 1008.

53. *Ibid.,* Jan. 30, 1934, p. 107.

54. George F. Kennan, *Soviet Foreign Policy, 1917-1941,* (New York: Van Nostrand, 1960), p. 77.

55. *Ibid.,* pp. 80-85.

56. Georgi Dimitrov, *The United Front—The Struggle Against Fascism and War,* (London: Lawrence & Wishart, 1938), p. 19.

57. Robert V. Daniels, *A Documentary History of Communism,* "Resolutions of the Seventh World Congress of the Communist International," (New York: Random House, 1960), p. 114.

58. *Ibid.,* p. 116.

59. *Inprecorr,* Aug. 8, 1935, p. 890.

60. *Ibid.,* Aug. 24, 1935, p. 1019.

61. Georgi Dimitrov, p. 75.

62. *Inprecorr,* Aug. 20, 1935, p. 970.

63. *Ibid.,* p. 976.   64. Franz Borkenau, p. 386.

65. The Communists joined other parties of the left in the formation of the Popular Front, which won a convincing victory at the general election in the spring of 1936. Although the Communists did not appear in the ministerial list, they strongly supported the left-of-center government of Leon Blum.

66. *Inprecorr,* Jan. 9, 1937, p. 22.   67. *Ibid.,* p. 466.

68. *Ibid.,* Aug. 8, 1935, p. 889.   69. *Ibid.,* Aug. 24, 1935, p. 1022.

70. *Ibid.,* Nov. 13, 1937, p. 1180.

71. George F. Kennan, *Russia and the West Under Lenin and Stalin,* p. 314.

72. Robert V. Daniels, pp. 123-124.

73. Jane Degras, *Soviet Documents on Foreign Policy,* Vol. III, 1933-1941, (London: Oxford University Press, 1953), p. 406.

74. *World News and Views,* Oct. 7, 1939, pp. 1011-1012.

75. *Ibid.,* Nov. 11, 1939, pp. 1081-1082.

76. *Ibid.,* Dec. 16, 1939, p. 1144.

77. *Ibid.,* Jan. 20, 1940, pp. 33-34.

78. *Ibid.,* Sept. 6, 1941, p. 563.

79. Martin Ebon, *World Communism Today,* (New York: McGraw-Hill, 1948), pp. 23-24.

80. *World News and Views,* July 18, 1942, p. 305.

81. Robert V. Daniels, p. 130.

CHAPTER II

1. Quotations from Communist sources have been utilized in this chapter in

reference to the above-cited themes. A chronological description of the Mexican Communist movement, as such, has been presented in the following chapters.

2. Moises Saénz and Herbert I. Priestly, *Some Mexican Problems*, (Chicago: University of Chicago Press, 1926), p. 90. In discussing anti-Americanism or using the word "American," the reference here is to the United States as distinguished from other American countries of Latin America.

3. *El Machete*, Primera Quincena de Mayo de 1924, p. 8.

4. Francisco I. Madero, *La Sucesión Presidencial*, (México: San Pedro, Coahuila, 1908), p. 211.

5. Frank Tannenbaum, *Mexico: The Struggle for Peace and Bread*, (New York: Knopf, 1954), p. 248.

6. Howard F. Cline, *The United States and Mexico*, (Cambridge, Massachusetts: Harvard University Press, 1953), p. 133.

7. *Archivo Histórico Diplomático Mexicano*, Num. 39, "Un Siglo De Relaciones Internacionales De México: Publicaciones de la Secretaría de Relaciones Exteriores, 1935), p. 301.

8. *The Liberator*, June, 1919, p. 21.

9. *Archivo Histórico Diplomático Mexicano*, pp. 284-285.

10. *Gale's*, Sept. 1920, pp. 5-6.

11. *World News and Views*, Jan. 21, 1939, p. 57.

12. *The Communist International*, July , 1938, p. 664.

13. Ricardo Flores Magón, *Semilla Libertaria*, (México, D. F., Ediciones del Grupo Cultural "Ricardo Flores Magón," 1923), pp. 69-70.

14. Interview with José C. Valadés.

15. Bertram D. Wolfe, *Portrait of Mexico*, (New York: Covici, Friede, 1937), p. 177.

16. Frank Tannenbaum, *Peace by Revolution*, (New York: Columbia University Press, 1933), p. 47.

17. *El Machete*, Junio 29 de 1929, p. 4.

18. J. Lloyd Mecham, *Church and State in Latin America*, (Chapel Hill: The University of North Carolina Press, 1934), p. 462.

19. *El Machete*, Julio 28 de 1936 p. 2.   20. *Ibid.,* Marzo 9 de 1929, p. 2.

21. Frank Tannenbaum, *Mexico: The Struggle for Peace and Bread*, p. 133.

22. *El Machete*, Marzo 9 de 1929, p. 2.

23. *Ibid.*, Julio 28 de 1928, p. 2.

24. William Cameron Townsend, *Lázaro Cárdenas—Mexican Democrat*, (Ann Arbor, Michigan: George Wahr Publishing Co., 1952), p. 89.

25. William W. Pierson and Federico G. Gil, *Governments of Latin America*, (New York: McGraw-Hill, 1957), pp. 331-332, and S. Walter Washington, "Mexican Resistance to Communism," *Foreign Affairs*, April 1958, p. 509.

26. Frank Tannenbaum, *Mexico: The Struggle for Peace and Bread*, p. 126.

27. Víctor Alba, *Las Ideas Sociales Contemporáneas en México*, (México, D. F., Fondo de Cultura Económica, 1960), p. 105.

28. Ricardo Flores Magón, A. De P. Araujo and William C. Owen, *Land and Liberty—Mexico's Battle for Economic Freedom and Its Relation to Labor's World-Wide Struggle*, (Los Angeles: Mexico Liberal Party, 1913), p. 46.

29. Marjorie Ruth Clark, *Organized Labor in Mexico*, (Chapel Hill: University of North Carolina Press, 1934), p. 9.

REFERENCES

30. Alfonso López Aparicio, *El Movimiento Obrero en México*, (México: Editorial Jus, 1952), p. 245.

21. *The Red International of Labor Unions*, Dec. 1928, p. 128.

32. *El Trabajador Latino Americano*, Feb. de 1929, Marzo 15 y 31 de 1929, p. 5.

33. Confederación Sindical Latino Americano, *Bajo la Bandera de la C.S.L.A.*, Resoluciones y Documentos del Congreso Constituyente de la C.S.L.A.., (Montevideo, 1929), p. 209.

34. *Inprecorr*, Nov. 17, 1933, p. 1113.

35. Víctor Alba, p. 104.

36. *Futuro*, Mayo de 1934, p. 48. 37. *Ibid.*, p. 76.

38. Dionisio Encina, *Fuera El Imperialismo y Sus Agentes!*, (México, D. F., Editorial Popular, 1940), p. 123.

39. *El Machete*, Enero 23 de 1937, p. 4.

40. Vicente Lombardo Toledano, *What Does the C.T.A.L. Mean?*, (New York: Workers Library Publishers, 1944), p. 20. By 1944, a majority of the Executive Committee of the CTAL were Communists.

41. Frank Tannenbaum, *Mexico: The Struggle for Peace and Bread*, p. 87.

42. *El Trabajador Latino Americano*, Feb. de 1929, Marzo 15 y 31 de 1929, p. 4.

43. Frank Tannenbaum, *Peace By Revolution*, p. 79.

44. Martin C. Needler, "Putting Latin American Politics in Perspective," *Inter-American Economic Affairs*, Autumn 1962, p. 43.

45. *Ibid.*, p. 49. 46. *El Machete*, Primera Quincena de Mayo de 1924, p. 8.

47. *Imprecorr*, Aug. 14, 1930, p. 742. 48. *The Communist*, Oct. 1928, p. 648.

49. Hannah Arendt, "Authority in the Twentieth Century," *The Review of Politics*, Oct. 1956, p. 403.

50. S. Walter Washington, p. 505.

51. *El Trabajador Latino Americano*, Nos. 34 y 35, Agosto y Septiembre, 1930, p. 4.

52. *Mexico-Review of Commercial Conditions*, (London: Published for the Department of Overseas Trade by His Majesty's Stationery Office, 1945), pp. 10-11.

53. Sanford A. Mosk, *Industrial Revolution in Mexico*, (Berkeley and Los Angeles: University of California Press, 1950), p. 287. The inflationary spiral continued through the administration of Miguel Aleman and did not come to and end until 1953. The end of the Korean War decreased the demand for raw materials, and prices dropped. During that period, the tourist business fell by approximately one-half. In 1954, the government devalued the currency.

54. Frank Tannenbaum, *Mexico: The Struggle for Peace and Bread*, p. 182.

55. Ricardo Flores Magón, *Semilla Libertaria*, p. 104.

56. *The Communist*, Feb. 1931, p. 124.

57. Frank Tannenbaum, *The Mexican Agrarian Revolution*, (Washington, D. C.: Brookings Institution, 1930), p. 162.

58. Rodrigo Garcia Treviño believes that the *Plan de Texcoco*, published by Andres Molina Enriquez three months prior to Zapata's *Plan de Ayala*, had a great influence on "Zapatismo." See Víctor Alba, p. 301.

59. Baltasar Dromundo, *Emiliano Zapata*, (México, Imprenta Mundial, 1934), "Plan de Ayala," p. 66-67.

60. *El Machete*, Abril 14 de 1928, p. 1.

61. *The Communist,* Jan., 1936, p. 72.

62. Isidro Fabela, *Documentos Históricos de la Revolución Mexicana,* (México, D. F., Fondo de Cultura Económica, 1960), p. 520.

63. *El Machete,* Marzo 23 de 1929, p. 1.

64. Robert Hammond Murray, *Mexico Before the World—Public Documents and Addresses of Plutarco Elías Calles,* (New York: Academy Press, 1927), p. 8.

65. *El Machete,* Marzo 23 de 1929, p. 1. 66. *Ibid.,* p. 1.

67. William Cameron Townsend, p. 88. 68. Nathan L. Whetten, p. 128.

69. *La Voz de México,* Enero 4 de 1939, p. 11.

70. Partido de la Revolución Mexicana, *Avila Camacho y Su Ideología,* (México, D. F., La Impresora, 1940), p. 28.

71. *World News and Views,* Dec. 14, 1940, p. 722. This criticism had nothing to do with the shelving of the Popular Front when the Nazi-Soviet Pact was signed in August of 1939. The Communists supported the candidacy of Avila Camacho after the signing of the Nazi-Soviet Pact. Their criticism of his land policy was influenced by conditions within Mexico, not by any change in the orientation of the Comintern.

72. For the operation of the National Bank of Ejido Credit see Nathan L. Whetten, pp. 191-202.

73. Howard F. Cline, *Mexico: Revolution to Evolution, 1940-1960,* (London: Oxford University Press, 1962), p. 221.

74. *La Voz de México,* Nov. 14 de 1938, p. 1.

75. S. Walter Washington, p. 504.

76. Hernán Laborde, *El Enemigo Es Almazán,* (México, D. F., Editorial Popular, 1939), p. 4.

77. Martin C. Needler, *Latin American Politics in Perspective,* (New York: Van Nostrand, 1963), p. 51. It is significant that very few workers and peasants were attracted to the Communist movement.

78. Interview with José C. Valadés.

CHAPTER III

1. Two authors who believe that Roy was sent by the Comintern are Ricardo Treviño, *El Espionaje Comunista y La Evolución Docrtinaria del Movimiento Obrero en México,* (México, 1952), p. 20, and Rodrigo García Treviño, *La Ingerencia Rusa en México (y Sudamérica),* (México, Editorial América, 1959), p. 29.

2. There are at least two versions of why Roy was forced to leave the United States. One is that he was indicted on a gun-running charge and fled to Mexico to have the Germans provide him with money to provoke a revolt in India. When he got the money, he refused to have anything more to do with the Germans. See Carleton Beals, *Glass Houses—Ten Years of Free-Lancing,* (New York: Lippincott, 1938), pp. 43-44. Another version is that the United States government put a great deal of pressure on Irish and Indian pacifists because of American involvement in World War I. As a result, Roy went to Mexico. The latter version was told to the writer by Bertram D. Wolfe.

3. Interview with Bertram D. Wolfe.

4. A more detailed list of the groups and individuals that attended the Congress is given by Rosendo Salazar y José G. Escobedo, *Las Pugnas de la*

Gleba, (México, D. F., Editorial Avante), pp. 63-64.

5. *Gale's,* March, 1920, pp. 7 and 26. 6. Rosendo Salazar y José G. Escobedo, p. 64.

7. *Gale's,* Feb. 1920, p. 7. 8. *Ibid.,* March 1920, p. 26.

9. It seems that Roy had a substantial amount of money at his disposal and was able to find enough support to have Gale removed from the Mexican Socialist Party. Gale made reference to the fact that Roy paid the expenses of the National Socialist Congress. See *Gale's,* March, 1920, p. 7.

10. *Ibid.,* p. 26.

11. *Gale's* stated that the party was formed in December, 1919—*Ibid,* p. 26. José C. Valadés believes it was formed in January, 1920—Interview with José C. Valadés.

12. One version is that Roy had left Mexico before the party was formed. See Robert J. Alexander, *Communism in Latin America,* (New Brunswick, New Jersey, Rutgers University Press, 1957), p. 320, and Víctor Alba, *Historia del Comunismo en América Latina,* (México, D. F., Ediciones Occidentales, 1954), p. 23. However, *Gale's* referred to the "fake 'Mexican Communist Party' organized by Roy and some of his tools." See *Gale's,* March, 1920, p. 20. Roy left Mexico in the summer of 1920, after the Communist Party of the Mexican Proletariat was formed, to attend the Second Congress of the Comintern in Moscow. In all probability, therefore, he attended the meeting with José Allen and others to form the party.

13. *Constitución del Partido Comunista Revolucionario Mexicano,* (México, D. F., 1921), pp. 11-13.

14. José C. Valadés, *Revolución Social o Motín Político,* (México, D. F., Biblioteca del Partido Comunista, 1922), p. 3.

15. *The Liberator,* May, 1920, p. 6. 16. *Gale's,* June-July, 1920, pp. 5-6.

17. *Ibid.,* Feb. 1920, p. 1. 18. *The Liberator,* Jan. 1920, p. 25-28.

19. *Gale's,* Feb. 1920, p. 1. 20. *Ibid.,* May, 1920, p. 29.

21. Elizabeth Dilling, *The Red Network,* (Chicago, 1934), p. 172.

22. *Gale's,* March, 1920, p. 26.

23. *Ibid.,* p. 26. 24. *Ibid.,* p. 26.

25. *Ibid.,* March, 1921, p. 2.

26. Miguel Aroche Parra, *Unidad Anti-Imperialista! Unidad Proletaria!,* (México, D. F., 1962), pp. 12-13.

27. The expulsions were reported extensively by American newspapers. See the *New York Times* and the *Christian Science Monitor* of Sept. 3, 1920.

28. *The Liberator,* Sept. 1921, p. 25.

29. The story of how Borodin hoped to finance his operation in Mexico reminds one of a mystery thriller. He was supposed to have brought Tsarist jewels with him from Russia. Somewhere along the way he lost possession of the jewels to an official of the Haitian government. In the end, Roy paid his expenses and the jewels were never found. See Carleton Beals, pp. 44-46.

30. From the evidence the writer has obtained, namely, that the Communist party of José Allen and his group was formed in December, 1919 or January, 1920, it sems quite possible that two Communist parties existed before Borodin arrived. This possibility casts doubt on the theory that Borodin convinced Roy to form a Communist party—see Carleton Beals, p. 50. It is plausible that Borodin recommended that the Comintern recognize one of these parties and

that he gave assistance to the party during his stay in the country.

31. The credentials committee of the Second Congress of the Comintern gave the right of vote to "two Communists from Mexico." See *The 2nd Congress of the Communist International,* p. 39. The reference was to Roy and Frank Seaman.

32. Interview with Bertram D. Wolfe.

33. José C. Valadés told the writer that Katayama stayed in his house for six months. He rarely left the premises because of fear of the police and he did not accomplish very much while in the country. In addition, Katayama accused Fraina of stealing jewels, which came from Russia, and selling them in Mexico— Interview with José C. Valadés. However, it is doubtful that Katayama's accusation was accurate. Fraina already had money, in the form of paper currency, when he arrived. See Theodore Draper, *The Roots of American Communism,* (New York: Viking Press, 1957), p. 294.

34. Interview with Bertram D. Wolfe.

35. *The Liberator,* Oct. 1920, p. 23. The quotation is taken from an article by Carleton Beals and Robert Haberman. The authors referred to the "Confederación Comunista Obrera," formed in 1920. However, this was the Federación Comunista del Proletariado Mexicano (Communist Federation of the Mexican Proletariat).

36. Jane Degras, Vol. I, 1919-1922, "Invitation to the First Congress of the Communist International," p. 3.

37. Prior to the Great Red Radical Convention, which formed the CGT, there was another assembly called the "First Red Radical Convention." During the first convention, the Comintern agent, Michael Borodin, and the non-Comintern "agent," Robert Haberman, disagreed over tactics. This lead to a split in which Haberman and his followers presented a manifesto which publicly denounced the work of Russian espionage. See Ricardo Treviño, p. 24.

38. Marjorie Ruth Clark, p. 83. 39. See pp. 22-23.

40. *Inprecorr,* June 18, 1925, p. 698.

41. *Ibid.,* Oct. 29, 1925, p. 1165.

42. Partido Comunista de México, *Resolución Sobre La Situación Actual Y Las Tareas Del Partido,* (México, 1927), p. 11.

43. Jane Degras, Vol II, 1923-1928, "Extracts From the Theses of the Fifth ECCI Plenum on the Peasant Question," pp. 204-205.

44. *Inprecorr,* Feb. 11, 1925, p. 188.

45. *The Workers Monthly,* Feb. 1925, p. 160.

46. *The Communist,* July-Aug. 1927, p. 263.

47. *Strategy of the Communists—A Letter from the Communist International to the Mexican Communist Party,* (Chicago: Workers Party of America, Aug. 21, 1923), p. 4.

48. *Inprecorr,* June 18, 1925, p. 698.   49. *The Liberator,* April, 1924, pp. 21-22.

50. *Inprecorr,* Aug. 5, 1924, p. 579.   51. Cited by *Gale's,* Oct. 1920, p. 3.

52. *The Liberator,* Jan. 1920, p. 25.

53. Anastasio Manzanilla Domingues (Hugo Sol), *El Comunismo en México y el Archivo de Carrillo Puerto,* (México, 1921), pp. 67-68.

54. John W. F. Dulles, *Yesterday in Mexico* (Austin: University of Texas Press, 1961), p. 139.

55. *The Liberator,* April, 1924, p. 21.

56. Emiliano Zapata was another revolutionary who was influenced by the Russian Revolution. Shortly before his death, he declared that the salvation of Mexico lay in the Soviet system.

57. Diplomatic relations between the Soviet Union and Mexico were not resumed until 1942.

58. Carleton Beals, "Red Star South," *Current History*, Dec. 1938, p. 28.

59. Emiliano Portes Gil, *Quince Años de Politica Mexicana*, (México, D. F., Ediciones Potas, 1941), p. 373.

60. *Ibid.*, pp. 374-376. Portes Gil believed that Dr. Makar's secretary, Boliniski, was behind the Soviet movement in Mexico.

61. *Ibid.*, pp. 376-377.

62. Rosendo Salazar, *Historia de las Luchas Proletarias de México*—1930-1936, (México, 1956), p. 9. The complete text of the note is given on pp. 9-10.

63. *Inprecorr*, March 6, 1930, p. 203.

64. The Communist party issued a few periodicals of limited duration which preceded *El Machete*—*El Soviet, Boletín Comunista, El Obrero Comunista*— however, none of these had the wide circulation or lasted as long as *El Machete* (1924-1938).

65. *The Liberator*, Dec. 1923, p. 14.

66. Bertram D. Wolfe, "The Strange Case of Diego Divera," *The New Leader*, Oct. 11, 1954, p. 12.

67. *The Workers Monthly*, June, 1925, p. 374.

68. *The Liberator*, July, 1920, pp. 6-8. President Carranza chose Ignacio Bonillas as his successor. The revolutionary generals, as well as the Communists, were vehemently opposed.

69. *Ibid.*, p. 8.

70. *Strategy of the Communists—A Letter from the Communist International to the Mexican Communist Party*, p. 8.

71. *The Liberator*, Nov. 1923, p. 20.

72. *La Voz de México*, Enero 2 de 1939, p. 11.

73. Partido Communista de México, *Resolución Sobre La Situación Actual Y las Tareas Del Partido*, p. 9.

74. *The Liberator*, Jan. 1924, p. 12.

75. *Strategy of the Communists—A Letter from the Communist International to the Mexican Communist Party*, p. 10.

76. Rosendo Salazar, *Historia de las Luchas Proletarias de México*—1923-1929, (México, Editorial Avante), p. 100.

77. *The Liberator*, Jan. 1924, p. 13.   78. *Inprecorr*, Feb. 3, 1927, p. 224.

79. *The Workers Monthly*, July 1926, p. 427.

80. *Inprecorr*, June 18, 1925, p. 698.

81. *Ibid.*, Dec. 9, 1926, p. 1487.   82. *Daily Worker*, Oct. 8, 1927, p. 1.

83. *El Machete*, Enero 8 al 15 de 1925, p. 3.

84. *The Workers Monthly*, April, 1925, p. 251.

85. Partido Comunista de México, *Resolución Sobre La Situación Actual Y Las Tareas Del Partido*, p. 9.

86. The Communist party had been trying to gain recognition from the Comintern since its foundation.

87. *Strategy of the Communists—A Letter from the Communist International to the Mexican Communist Party*, pp. 12-13. Perhaps this could be explained

as a 1-2 sequence. However, the manner in which it was presented in the letter ruled out any certainty.

88. Partido Comunista de México, *Resolución Sobre La Situación Acutal Y Las Tareas Del Partido*, p. 11.

89. *El Machete*, Segunda Quincena de Julio de 1924, p. 4.

90. *Strategy of the Communists—A Letter from the Communist International to the Mexican Communist Party*, p. 14.

91. *The Liberator*, April 1924, p. 23.

92. Bertram D. Wolfe went to Mexico in 1922. Like many foreigners who were in Mexico in the early 1920's, he was a pacifist who opposed the participation of the United States in World War I. This brought him into the Communist Party of Mexico and a subsequent position on the Executive Committee. He was deported by the Mexican Government in 1925. Interview with Bertram D. Wolfe.

93. *Inprecorr*, June 18, 1925, p. 697. The Communists received subsidies from the Calles government and were given one seat in the Senate, in the person of Luis G. Monzón.

94. *Ibid.*, p. 698.

95. Communist support of Mexican governments against revolts was not strictly in accord with the Comintern position. During the Third Congress of the Comintern in 1921, Communists were cautioned against premature revolutionary attempts by their own forces—See pp. 98-99. However, at no time did the Comintern leaders suggest that Communists should support the bourgeois governments in the face of a revolt by non-Communist forces. This was a particular tactic which the Mexican Communists followed, according to their interpretation of developments in the country.

96. General Francisco Mujica, one of the principal revolutionary military leaders, and one of the main authors of the 1917 Constitution, spent approximately a year in the Communist party.

CHAPTER IV

1. *El Trabajador Latino Americano*, Septiembre 15 de 1928, p. 5.

2. *Resoluciones de la Conferencia Sindical Latino Americano*, (Montevideo, April, 1928), p. 10.

3. *Ibid.*, p. 16.   4. *Ibid.*, p. 14.

5. *El Trabajador Latino Americano*, Oct. 30 de 1928, pp. 12 and 27.

6. *Resoluciones de la Conferencia Sindical Latino Americano*, p. 19.

7. A. Losovsky, *El Movimiento Sindical Latino Americano (Sus virtudes y sus defectos)*, (Montevideo: Ediciones Comité Pro Confederación Sindical Latino Americano, 1929), pp. 7-11.

8. *Ibid.*, pp. 13-14.   9. *Ibid.*, pp. 20-21   10. See pp. 16-17.

11. *Inprecorr*, Nov 23, 1928, pp. 1576-1577. The ECCI was the Executive Committee of the Communist International.

12. *Ibid.*, Oct. 17, 1928, p. 1300.

13. *Ibid.*, p. 1300.   14. *Ibid.*, pp. 1303-1304.

15. *Ibid.*, Dec. 12, 1928, p. 1675.

16. *Ibid.*, Oct. 17, 1928, p. 1304. In theory, the Workers' and Peasants'

Bloc did not differ significantly from the tactics which were used toward the end of the previous period. It appeared to be an atteempt to reach the masses through a more broadly based "United Front from below."

17. During the Congress, it was decided to form a Latin American Bureau— *Ibid.*, May 10, 1929, p. 490. It was first established in Buenos Aires, but there was no fixed location. The Bureau later appeared in Montevideo and then in Guatemala. The first director was the Russian, "Luis" Guralsky. Other individuals appeared from Moscow and parts of Latin America using false names.

18. *Ibid.*, Aug. 13, 1928, p. 871.   19. *Ibid.*, p. 37.

20. *Ibid.*, May 10, 1929, p. 1204.

21. Confederación Sindical Latino Americana, p. 301.

22. *Ibid.*, pp. 7-8.   23. *Ibid.*, p. 218.   24. *Ibid.*, p. 200.

25. *Ibid.*, p. 206.   26. *Ibid.*, pp. 200, 206.   27. *Ibid.*, p. 222.

28. *Ibid.*, p. 226.   29. *Ibid.*, p. 217.   30. *Ibid.*, p. 71.

31. *Ibid.*, p. 244.   32. *Ibid.*, p. 296.   33. *Ibid.*, p. 212.

34. Secretariado Sudamericano de la Internacional Comunista, "El Movimiento Revolucionario Latino Americana," *La Correspondencia Sudamericana,* Versions de la Primera Conferencia Latino Americana, (Buenos Aires, Junio de 1929), p. 3.

35. *The Communist*, Aug. 1929, p. 430.

36. Secretariado Sudamericano de la Internacional Comunista, pp 102-103. An interesting observation has been made that the Communist tactic of infiltrating the Workers' and Peasants' Bloc, during the Third Period, was pronounced again by Dimitrov at the Seventh Congress of the Comintern, to be used in the Popular Front. See Rodrigo García Treviño, p. 93.

37. *The Communist*, Aug. 1929, p. 432.   38. *Ibid.*, pp. 432-433.

39. Secretariado Sudamericano de la Internacional Comunista, p. 95.

40. *Ibid.*, pp. 182-183.

CHAPTER V

1. *El Machete*, Mayo 26 de 1928, p. 1.   2. *Ibid.*, Diciembre 8 de 1928, p. 2.

3. *El Trabajador Latino Americano*, Feb. 28 de 1929, Marzo 15 y 31 de 1929, p. 3.

4. *The Red International of Labor Unions*, Aug. 1929, pp. 296-297.

5. Confederación Sindical Latino Americano, pp. 32 and 34.

6. *Inprecorr*, July 5, 1929, p. 705.

7. *El Trabajdor Latino Americano*, Febrero 28 de 1929, Marzo 15 y 31 de 1929, pp. 4-5.

8. Interview with Vicente Lombardo Toledano. He died at the age of 74 in December, 1968.

9. *Ibid.*

10. *Inprecorr*, Jan 3, 1929, p. 15. Actually Portes Gil was the one who broke with Morones.

11. Majorie Ruth Clark, p. 265.

12. Interview with Rodrigo García Treviño. García Trevino was an official in the CROM and also in the CTM.

13. Interview with Vicente Lombardo Toledano. However, in a pamphlet which he wrote several years earlier as an official of the CROM, the Marxist-

Leninist orientation was clearly in evidence. See *La Libertad Sindical en México*, (México, D. F., 1926).

14. The CROM, particularly during its early years, was also ideologically oriented towards Marxism-Leninism. However, with time, this became ideological lip service, and the CROM was under incessant attack by the Communists.

15. Rosendo Salazar, *Historia de las Luchas Proletarias de México*—1930-1936, p. 91. It might be pointed out that the CGOCM, as the Communist-controlled CSUM during the Third Period, was "a-political" in a sense. Both organizations opposed any cooperation with the government. The CGOCM commended "as a tactic of struggle the employment of the arms of revolutionary syndicalism, . . ." See *Futuro*, Mayo de 1934, p. 79.

16. *Ibid.*, p. 11. 17. *Ibid.*, p. 92.

18. *Futuro*, Diciembre de 1934, p. 121.

19. *Inprecorr*, Sept. 18, 1930, p. 904.

20. *The Communist*, May, 1933, p. 473.

21. *El Machete*, Febrero 2 de 1929, p. 3.

22. Julio Caudros Caldas, *El Comunismo Criollo*, (Puebla, Pue., México, 1930), pp. 61-67.

23. *El Machete*, Junio 29 de 1929, p. 1.

24. The League itself split during the first part of 1930. A small group remained with the Communists in the CSUM and another group joined the National Revolutionary Party. However, most of the members followed Galván, who continued as president of the independent League. He died very suddenly in 1930, and the League added his name to its title (and became known as the National Peasants League "Ursulo Galván") in order to distinguish it from other peasant organizations. By 1932, it came under government control and patronage (Marjorie Ruth Clark, pp. 157-158).

25. *The Communist*, Sept. 1928, pp. 555-556.

26. *Inprecorr*, March 29, 1929, p. 317.

27. *The Communist*, May, 1929, p. 230.

28. *El Machete*, Octubre 6 de 1928, p. 1.

29. In January of 1929 the Cuban Communist leader, Julio Antonio Mella, was assassinated in Mexico. One interpretation of his death is that the Comintern agent known by the names of Sormenti, Contreras, and Vidale, who was directing the Communist Party of Mexico from 1927-1932, cooperated with a paid assassin of the Cuban dictator, Gerardo Machado y Morales, to have the Cuban Communist killed. For some reason, the Comintern leaders believed their interests were being compromised by the activities of Mella in Mexico.

30. The activities of Manuilsky were described in an article written by Diego Rivera, "Siqueiros Según Diego," *Resaca*, (México, D. F., Asociación Por La Cultura, Enero de 1955), pp. 25-58. The article originally appeared in the magazine *Octubre*, October 1, 1935.

31. It has been pointed out that Diego Rivera (and others purged from the party) "had merely been caught in a world-wide 'purge' emanating from the factional politics of the Soviet Union." See Bertram D. Wolfe, "The Strange Case of Diego Rivera," p. 14.

32. Bernado Claraval, *Cuando Fuí Comunista*, (México, D. F., Ediciones Polis, 1944), pp. 113-114.

33. *El Machete,* Julio 13 de 1929, p. 2.
34. Confederación Sindical Latino Americano, p. 279.
35. *Inprecorr,* May 22, 1930, p. 439.
36. *The Communist,* May, 1930, pp. 449-450.   37. *Ibid.,* pp. 454-455.
38. *Inprecorr,* Feb. 13, 1930, p. 118.   39. *Ibid.,* Feb. 9, 1933, p. 159.
40 *El Machete,* Julio de 1929, p. 1.   41. *The Communist,* May, 1933, p. 478.
42. *Ibid.,* p. 472.   43. *Ibid.,* May, 1930, p. 445.   44. *Ibid.,* May, 1933, p. 479.
45. *Inprecorr,* Nov. 3, 1934, pp. 1491-1492.
46. *The Communist,* May, 1929, p. 228.   47. *Ibid.,* Feb. 1931, p. 123.
48. *El Machete, Agosto* 17 de 1935, p. 4.

CHAPTER VI

1. pp. 19-21.   2. *El Machete,* Agosto 17 de 1935, p. 3.
3. *Inprecorr,* July 13, 1935, pp. 755-756.
4. *Ibid.,* Dec. 2, 1935, p. 1617.
5. *The Communist,* Jan. 1936, pp. 74-75.
6. Partido Communista de México, *La Neuva Politica del Partido Communista de México,* (México, D. F., Ediciones Frente Cultural, Marzo de 1936), p. 6. The pamphlet is a reproduction of a letter written by the Mexican delegation, attending the Seventh Congress of the Comintern, to the Central Committee of the party.
7. *The Communist,* Jan. 1936,, p. 76.
8. *Ibid.,* p. 78.   9. *Ibid.,* p. 79.
10. *Inprecorr,* Dec. 2, 1935, p. 1617.
11. *The Communist,* Jan. 1936, p. 83.
12. Partido Comunista de México, *La Nueva Política del Partido Comunista de México,* p. 6.
13. *Ibid.,* p. 14.   14. *Ibid.,* p. 19.   15. *Ibid.,* p. 20.
16. *Ibid.,* pp. 18-19.
17. *El Machete,* Enero 30 de 1937, p. 4.
18. *Inprecorr,* Feb. 13, 1937, p. 192.
19. Hernán Laborde, *Unidad a Toda Costa,* (México, Yuc., Editorial "Hul-Kin," 1937), p. 27.
20. *Inprecorr,* Dec. 24, 1937, p. 1387.
21. *The Communist,* Dec. 1937, p. 1116.
22. *Inprecorr,* Jan. 8, 1938, p. 16.
23. Ricardo Treviño, p. 39.
24. *World News and Views,* Sept. 3, 1938, p. 979.
25. *La Voz de México,* Octubre 16 de 1938, p. 1. Consonant with the Popular Front era, the name of the Communist periodical was changed from *El Machete* to *La Voz de México.*
26. *Ibid.,* Enero 2 de 1939, pp. 1 and 11.
27. Robert E. Scott, *Mexican Government in Transition.* (Urbana: University of Illinois, 1959), p. 130.
28. Cited by Ricardo Treviño, p. 182.
29. *World News and Views,* Aug. 27, 1938, p. 963.
30. *Ibid.,* Nov. 27, 1937, pp. 1257-1258.
31. Interview with Rodrigo García Treviño. García Treviño also told the

writer that the CTM, under Lombardo Toledano's leadership, wanted to stop the strike of the petroleum workers, which was proving effective. However, the workers refused to stop the strike and it continued. The same point was made by Rodolfo Piña Soria in his article "Viaje Por Suscripción Popular," *Acción Social,* Marzo 15 de 1943.

32. Quoted by Victor Alba, *Las Ideas Sociales Contemporáneas en México,* p. 395.

33. *Ibid.,* p. 395.

34. *World News and Views,* July 23, 1938, p. 860.

35. *La Voz de México,* Enero 30 de 1939, p. 1.

36. *Inprecorr,* Aug. 15, 1936, p. 1000.   37. *The Communist,* Dec. 1937, p. 1113.

38. *El Machete,* Junio 26 de 1937, suplemento.

39. *World News and Views,* Sept. 3, 1938, p. 979.

40. *Ibid.,* March 11, 1939, p. 204.   41. *New York Times,* Sept. 23, 1946, p. 7.

42. *Inprecorr,* Nov. 27, 1937, p. 1238.

43. *World News and Views,* April 13, 1940, p. 230.

44. *World News and Views,* March 11, 1939, p. 205.

45. Miguel Aroche Parra, pp. 28-29.

46. Nathaniel and Sylvia Weyl, *The Reconquest of Mexico—The Years of Lázaro Cárdenas,* (London: Oxford University Press, 1939), p. 315.

47. Bernardo Claraval, pp. 175-177.

48. Nathaniel and Sylvia Weyl, p. 316.

49. Luis G. Monzón, *Detalles de la Educación Socialista Implantables en México,* (México, D. F., Secretaría de Educación Pública-SEP, Comisión Editora Popular, Talleres Gráficos de la Nación, 1936), p. 19. The Stamp of SEP which appears in the publication signifies the Secretariat of Education. The "Comisión Editora Popular" is a branch of the Secretariat in charge of books. The "Talleres Gráficos de la Nación" is the government printing office.

50. *Ibid.,* p. 48.   51. *Ibid.,* p. 381.   52. *Ibid.,* p. 458.

53. *Ibid.,* p. 52.   54. *Ibid.,* p. 170.   55. *Ibid.,* p. 428.

56. *Ibid.,* pp. 244-246.   57. *Ibid.,* p. 382.   58. *Ibid.,* pp. 244-246.

59. *Ibid.,* p. 459.

60. *The Communist,* Jan. 1936, p. 80.

61. *El Trabajador Latino Americano,* Nos. 60-61, Octubre-Noviembre, 1935, p. 18.

62. Interview with Fidel Velázquez. Fidel Velázquez is a Senator in the Mexican Congress and the present Secretary General of the CTM.

63. Interview with Vicente Lombardo Toledano.   64. *Ibid.*

65. The Red International of Trade Unions was dissolved in 1934. Losovsky, however, remained very influential in high Comintern circles.

66. The latter was reprinted by *Acción Social,* Número 14, Marzo 15 de 1941, p. 16.

67. The organization supported the position of the Comintern, but this does not necessarily mean that it was an instrument of the international Communist organization. Although infiltrated with Communists, the CTM was not officially connected with the Comintern. Interview with Rodrigo García Treviño.

68. *CTM 1936-1941,* (1936) (México, D. F., Talleres Tipográficos Modelo, S. A.), p. 12.

69. *Ibid.,* p. 37.   70. *Ibid.,* p. 150.

71. *Inprecorr*, Feb. 13, 1937, p. 192.

72. *CTM 1936-1941*, (1937), p. 260.

73. L. O. Pendergast, "Growing Pains of Mexican Labor," *The Nation*, June 12, 1937, p. 672-673.

74. The discussion of the maneuvers within the CTM is based on a letter the writer received from Rodrigo García Treviño. The letter goes on to state that several trade unions within the CTM wanted the anti-Communist leaders to leave the organization and form a new labor group. Some of the anti-Communist leaders believed they would be able to take one half of the CTM membership with them. However, they were persuaded not to do so by Piña Soria, who feared the effects of such a move on the CTM and the Mexican labor movement.

75. *CTM 1936-1941*, (1937), pp. 258-267.

76. *Inprcorr*, Oct. 16, 1937, p. 995.

77. The report has been published in pamphlet form—Hernán Laborde, *Unidad a Toda Costa*.

78. *Ibid.*, p. 20. 79. *Ibid.*, p. 7.

80. Miguel Aroche Parra, p. 37.

81. *Acción Social*, Número 14, Marzo 15 de 1941, p. 14.

82. The information concerning the founding of *El Popular* was included in the letter from Rodrigo García Treviño.

83. *CTM 1936-1941*, (1938), p. 481.

84. *The Communist*, Nov. 1938, p. 1013.

85. *El Popular*, Junio 10 de 1938, p. 2.

86. *CTM 1936-1941*, (1940), p. 885.

87. *Ibid.*, (1938), p. 468.

88. *El Machete*, Enero 23 de 1937, p. 1.

89. Alfonso López Aparicio, p. 223.

90. *CTAL 1938-1948—Resoluciones de sus Asambleas* (México, 1948), pp. 6-7.

91. *Ibid.*, p. 21. 92. Robert J. Alexander, p. 335.

93. *La Voz de México*, Septiembre 28 de 1938, p. 11.

94. There is an article in *Ultimas Noticias*, April 13, 1939, describing the activities of Gómez Lorenzo in the recruitment of Mexican nationals.

95. *La Voz De México*, Enero 4 de 1939, p. 3.

96. Many of the Spanish refugees who arrived in Mexico, probably a majority, were non-Communist.

97. Hernán Laborde, *El Enemigo Es Almazán*, p. 5.

98. Rodrigo García Treviño, pp. 214-216. García Treviño also describes how Ramírez changed his roles (and names) during his activities with the Communist Party of Mexico in accordance with the changing "lines" of the Comintern. He was purged with Lamborde and his group in 1940 and readmitted to the party in 1954. Here was a case of a Comintern agent, active in the Communist party, who became a victim of a purge.

99. *The Communist*, Dec. 1937, p. 1111.

100. *World News and Views*, May 13, 1939, p. 539.

CHAPTER VII

1. Diego Rivera was alternately expelled and readmitted to the Communist party during his lifetime For a time he was a Trotskyite, and Leon Trotsky lived

in his home. Shortly before Trotsky's death, the old Bolshevik leader and the Mexican painter had a falling out and they were critical of each other. Rivera was readmitted to the Communist party in 1957, shortly before his death.

2. Interview with Fidel Velázquez.

3. Interview with Vicente Lombardo Toledano.

4. Interview with Rodrigo García Treviño.

5. *El Machete,* Enero 30 de 1937, p. 4.

6. *The Communist,* Dec. 1937, p. 1111.

7. *La Voz de México,* Sept. 28, 1938, p. 11.

8. *World News and Views,* Vol. 18, No. 36, July 23, 1938, p. 861. Although the theme of the danger of Fascism was played down during the period of the Nazi-Soviet Pact, the Mexican Communists continued to identify Trotsky with Fascism.

9. *Futuro,* Enero de 1937, p. 10.   10. *CTM 1936-1941,* (1938), p. 271.

11. Confederación de Trabajadores de México, *CTM, 1936-1937—Informe del Comité Nacional,* (México, D. F., 1937), pp. 97-99.

12. *Labor Condemns Trotskyism,* (New York: International Publishers, 1938), pp. 21-22.

13. *Clave—Tribuna Marxista,* Num. 2, Noviembre de 1938, p. 39.

14. *Ibid.,* Num. 2, Segunda Epoca, Octubre de 1939, p. 21.

15. *Ibid.,* p. 24.

16. *Ibid.,* Num. 2, Noviembre de 1938, p. 1. The writer questions whether the Communist Party of Mexico was ever a "party of the proletarian vanguard."

17. León Trotsky, *Qué Significa La Lucha Contra El "Trotskyism"?,* (México, D. F., Publicado por la Sección Mexicana de la IV Internacional), p. 12. No date was given on the pamphlet, but since it was critical of the First Congress of the CTM, it was probably written between 1938 and 1940.

18. *Clave—Tribuna Marxista,* Num. 3, Diciembre de 1938, p. 2.

19. *Ibid.,* Num. 1, Segunda Epoca, Septiembre de 1939, p. 5.

20. *Ibid.,* Num. 2, Segunda Epoca, Octubre de 1939, p. 4.

21. *Ibid.,* Num. 6, Segunda Epoca, Febrero de 1940, p. 138.

22. León Trotsky, p. 10.   23. *Ibid.,* p. 11.

24. General Leandro A. Sánchez Salazar y Julian Gorkin, *Así Asesinaron A Trotsky,* (Santiago de Chile: Editorial Del Pacífico S. A., 1950), pp. 51, 60, 64. Siqueiros was also aided in his plans by another Mexican Communist, Antonio Pujol—See pp. 120, 215.

25. *Ibid.,* p. 57.   26. *Ibid.,* pp. 61, 183.   27. *Ibid.,* pp. 103-105.

28. *Ibid.,* pp. 42-43.

29. *Acción Social,* Año 3, Número 6, Julio 15 de 1940, p. 5.

30. *El Popular,* Junio 5 de 1940, p. 5.

31. *Ibid.,* Junio 27 de 1940, p. 5.

32. The authors of *Así Asesinaron A. Trotski* are convinced that Jacques Mornard was an agent of the GPU. See pp. 247-250.

33. *CTM 1936-1941,* (1940), p. 1021.

34. *Acción Social,* Año 3, Número 8, Septiembre 15 de 1940, p. 2.

35. Ricardo Treviño, pp. 43-44.

36. *World News and Views,* Dec. 14, 1940, p. 721.

37. See pp. 23-24.

38. *La Voz de México,* Agosto 27 de 1939, pp. 4-5.

39. Hernán Laborde, *El Enemigo Es Almazán, p. 7.*

40. Vicente Lombardo Toledano, *Nuestra Lucha Por La Libertad,* (México, D. F., Universidad Obrera de México, 1941), pp. 22-23.

41. *Futuro,* Septiembre de 1939, p. 16.   42. Dionisio Encina, pp. 14-15.

43. *Ibid.,* p. 15.   44. *La Voz de México,* Enero de 1941, p. 1.

45. *The Communist,* May, 1941, p. 443.

46. *El Popular,* Junio 5 de 1940, Primera Sección, p. 4.

47. *CTAL 1938-1948—Resoluciones de sus Asambleas,* p. 25.

48. Dionisio Encina, p. 54.

49. *The Communist,* May, 1941, pp. 443-444.

50. *El Popular,* Julio 5 de 1940, Segunda Sección, p. 5.

51. *CTM 1936-1941,* (1940) p. 918.

52. Partido Comunista de México, *Primer Congreso Extraordinario,* (México, D. F., Editorial Popular, 1940), p. 7.

53. *The Communist,* May, 1941, p. 448.

54. *La Voz de México,* Noviembre 24 de 1940, p. 1.

55. *Futuro,* Febrero de 1940, p. 18.   56. Dionisio Encina, p. 34.

57. *La Voz de México,* Abril 17 de 1941, p. 6.

58. *Futuro,* Enero de 1940, p. 13.

59. Hernán Laborde, *El Enemigo Es Almazán,* p. 8.

60. *El Popular,* Septiembre 20 de 1939, p. 1.

61. Dionisio Encina, p. 30.   62. *Ibid.,* p. 31.   63. *Ibid.,* p. 31.

64. *Ibid.,* p. 32.   65. *New York Times,* April 14, 1940, p. 31.

66. *La Voz de México,* Febrero 18 de 1940, p. 3.

67. *Ibid.,* Marzo 31 de 1940, p. 1.

68. *World News and Views,* March 16, 1940, p. 172.

69. Miguel Aroche Parra, p. 38.

70. Partido Comunista de México, *Primer Congreso Extraordinario,* p. 24.

71. Interview with Rodrigo García Treviño. This argument is also referred to by Víctor Alba, *Historia del Comunismo en América Latina,* p. 97.

72. Eudocio Ravines, *La Gran Estafa, (La Penetración del Kremlin en Iberoamérica),* (México, D. F., Libros y Revistas, S. A., 1952), p. 438. It might be pointed out that there are those who do not have much faith in the authenticity of Ravines' accounts.

73. Arturo Ramírez (Rudi Brusilovski) was not included in this group. He remained in the country and subsequently rejoined the Communist Party of Mexico.

74. Miguel Aroche Parra, p. 40.

75. Interview with Fidel Velázquez.

76. Vicente Lombardo Toledano, *Teoría y Práctica del Movimiento Sindical Mexicano,* (México, Editorial Del Magisterio, 1961), pp. 81-82. Fidel Velázquez officially became Secretary General of the CTM in 1941.

77. Dionisio Encina, p. 122.   78. *Ibid.,* pp. 149-150.

79. Partido Comunista de México, *Primer Congreso Extraordinario,* pp. 8-9.

80. *World News and Views,* April 30, 1940, p. 244.

81. *Ibid.,* Nov. 23, 1940, p. 647.

82. Partido Comunista de México, *Primer Congreso Extraordinario,* p. 26.

83. Dionisio Encina, p. 95.   84. See pp. 148-150.

85. *La Voz de México,* Agosto 4 de 1941, p. 7.

86. *Futuro,* Agosto de 1941, p. 2.

87. *CTM 1936-1941,* (1941), p. 1141.

88. *CTAL 1938-1948—Resoluciones de sus Asambleas,* p. 42.

89. *La Voz de México,* Julio 27 de 1941, p. 3.

90. *World News and Views,* Oct. 3, 1942, p. 397. Mexico declared war on the Axis in May of 1942.

91. *Ibid.,* March 3, 1945, p. 70.

92. *Segundo Congreso General de la Confederación de Trabajadores de la América Latina,* (Cali, Colombia, Diciembre, 1941), p. 17.

93. *CTAL 1938-1948—Resoluciones de sus Asambleas,* p. 78.

94. Confederación de Trabajadores de América Latina (CTAL), *Reunión de Montevideo* (Febrero-Marzo, 1944), p. 7.

95. Vicente Lombardo Toledano, *The United States and Mexico, Two Nations— One Ideal,* (New York: Council for Pan-American Democracy, 1942), pp. 8-9, p. 21.

96. *World News and Views,* Oct. 3, 1942, p. 397.

97. Vicente Lombardo Toledano, *El Proletariado De La América Latina Ante Los Problemas Del Continente Y Del Mundo* (México, D. F. 1941), no page given.

98. *La Voz de México,* Agosto 16 de 1942, p. 3.

99. *Ibid.,* Noviembre 15 de 1942, p. 1.

100. *World News and Views,* Oct. 3, 1942, p. 397.

101. *Futuro,* Septiembre de 1943, p. 2.

102. CTAL 1938-1948—*Resoluciones de sus Asambleas,* p. 43. The United States government also supported the recognition of the Soviet Union by Latin American governments during World War II.

103. *La Voz de México,* Agosto 23 de 1942, p. 8.

104. See pp. 25-26.

105. *La Voz de México,* Mayo de 1943, p. 1.

106. *Futuro,* Julio de 1942, p. 16.

107. A complete list of the Executive Committee is given in *Segundo Congreso General de la Confederación de Trabajadores de la América Latina,* p. 149.

108. The fourth commission, Directive Commission of Social Matters, was under Fidel Velázquez—*Ibid.,* p. 27.

109. Actually the Communists retained control of the CTAL until its dissolution in the early 1960's.

110. Louis Saillant, *The WFTU in the Service of the Workers of all Countries,* (London: WFTU Publications Ltd., 1960) pp. 15-31. Louis Saillant, an ex-Socialist-Communist fellow traveler, was Secretary General of the WFTU. He followed the Communist line so completely that in 1949 the American CIO and the British TUC led the walkout from the WFTU of virtually all non-Communist groups. These joined with the American AFL and other groups which had not been in the WFTU to form the International Confederation of Free Trade Unions in 1950.

111. *La Voz de México,* Septiembre 15 de 1943, p. 8.

112. Vicente Lombardo Toledano, *Prolegomenos para una Nueva América,* (México, D. F. 1942), no page given.

CHAPTER VIII

1. Víctor Alba, *Las Ideas Sociales Contemporáneas en México*, p. 425.

2. Rosendo Salazar, *Lideres y Sindicatos*, (México, D. F., Ediciones T. C. Modelo, S. C. L., 1953), p. 114.

3. Vicente Lombardo Toledano, *5th Column in Mexico*, (New York: Council for Pan-American Democracy, 1941), p. 14.

4. Some of the authors in accord with this view are Robert J. Alexander, *Communism in Latin America*, p. 12, and William W. Pierson and Federico G. Gil, *Governments of Latin America*, pp. 330-331.

5. Two authors who believe that Communism failed in Mexico because of the Mexican Revolution are Robert J. Alexander, *Communism in Latin America*, pp. 319, 348 and Howard F. Cline, *Mexico: Revolution to Evolution, 1940-1960*, pp. 178-179.

6. *El Machete*, Primera Quincena de Mayo de 1924, p. 8.

7. Interview with Vicente Lombardo Toledano.

Appendix I

COMMUNIST AND NON-COMMUNIST POLITICAL PARTIES*

Mexican Socialist Party—1878. The party split, and a small group continued as the Socialist Party.

Mexican Liberal Party—1911. The party declined after the death of the Flores Magón brothers and the abatement of Anarchist influence.

Socialist Labor Party—1917. The party existed for approximately one year.

Mexican Labor Party—1919. The party declined after the death of General Obregon in 1928 and went out of existence in the middle 1930's.

Communist Party of Mexico—September, 1919. The party of Linn A. E. Gale and his associates went out of existence one or two years after the death of President Carranza in 1920.

Communist Party of the Mexican Proletariat—December, 1919 or January, 1920. The party of José Allen and his associates was recognized by the Comintern and became known as the Communist Party of Mexico. It is still in existence (1972).

National Revolutionary Party (P.N.R.)—1928. This was the official government party which was formed by President Calles. The name was changed to the Party of the Mexican Revolution (P.R.M.) in 1938. The party was renamed the Institutional Revolutionary Party (P.R.I.) in 1946.

Party of the Workers and Peasants of Mexico (P.O.C.M.)—1942. The party was formed by Herman Laborde and his associates after they were expelled from the Communist Party of Mexico. It eventually merged with the Popular Socialist Party (P.P.S.) of Lombardo Toledano.

*Only those parties which have been mentioned in the study are listed.

Appendix II

COMMUNIST AND NON-COMMUNIST LABOR ORGANIZATIONS*

Great Circle of Workers of Mexico—1870-1880.

House of the World's Workers—1912. The organizations went out of existence in a few years, and many of its members joined other labor groups.

Confederation of Labor of the Mexican Region—1916. This organization also gave way to the larger, more permanent labor groups after a few years.

Mexican Confederation of Labor (C.R.O.M.)—1918.

Communist Federation of the Mexican Proletariat—1920-1921. The group was incorporated into the C.G.T.

General Confederation of Workers (C.G.T.)—1921.

Unitary Trade Union Confederation of Mexico (C.S.U.M.)—1928. The Communist-controlled organization went out of existence when the C.T.M. was formed in 1936.

Latin American Trade Union Confederation (C.S.L.A.)—1929. The Communist-controlled organization went out of existence when the C.T.A.L. was formed in 1938.

General Confederation of Workers and Peasants of Mexico (C.G.O.C.M.)—1933. The C.G.O.C.M. was dissolved with the formation of the C.T.M. in 1936.

Mexican Confederation of Workers (C.T.M.)—1936. The C.T.M. is still in existence (1972).

Latin American Federation of Labor (C.T.A.L.)—1938. The C.T.A.L. was dissolved in 1962.

*Only those organizations which have been mentioned in the study are listed.

APPENDIX III

SECRETARIES GENERAL OF THE MEXICAN COMMUNIST PARTY

José Allen—December, 1919 or 1920-1921.

Manuel Díaz Ramírez—1921-1924.

Rafael Carrillo—1924-1928.

Herman Laborde—1928-1940.

Dionisio Encina—1940-1960.

APPENDIX IV

CONGRESSES OF THE MEXICAN COMMUNIST PARTY THROUGH WORLD WAR II

First Congress—December, 1921.
Second Congress—September, 1923.
Third Congress—April, 1925.
Fourth Congress—July, 1927.
Fifth Congress—April, 1928.
Sixth Congress—January, 1937.

Seventh Congress—January-February, 1939.

First Extraordinary Congress— March, 1940.

Eighth Congress—May, 1941.

Ninth Congress—July-August, 1942.